What *Did* Jesus Do?

What *Did* Jesus Do?

Gospel Profiles of Jesus' Personal Conduct

F. Scott Spencer

TRINITY PRESS INTERNATIONAL
A Continuum imprint
HARRISBURG • LONDON • NEW YORK

Trinity Press International, P.O. Box 1321, Harrisburg, PA 17105

Trinity Press International is a member of the Continuum International Publishing Group.

Cover image: *Christ and the Samaritan Woman.* Nicolas Colombel (1644–1717). Residenzgalerie, Salzburg, Austria. Copyright Erich Lessing/Art Resource, NY

Cover design: Wesley Hoke

Library of Congress Cataloging-in-Publication Data

Spencer, F. Scott (Franklin Scott)
  What did Jesus do? : gospel profiles of Jesus' personal conduct / F. Scott Spencer.
      p. cm.
Includes bibliographical references and index.
  ISBN 1-56338-392-6
  1. Jesus, Christ—Biography—Sources, Biblical. I. Title.
  BT299.3 .S67 2003
  232.9'04—dc21
                                        2003005026

Printed in the United States of America

03 04 05 06 07 08   10 9 8 7 6 5 4 3 2 1

To Janet Marie, Lauren Michael, and Meredith Leigh
(again)

Contents

Preface

On the following day, when they came from Bethany, he was hungry. Seeing in the distance a fig tree in leaf, he went to see whether perhaps he would find anything on it. When he came to it, he found nothing but leaves, for it was not the season for figs. He said to it, "May no one ever eat fruit from you again." And his disciples heard it.

Then they came to Jerusalem. And he entered the temple and began to drive out those who were selling and those who were buying in the temple, and he overturned the tables of the money changers and the seats of those who sold doves; and he would not allow anyone to carry anything through the temple. . . .

In the morning as they passed by, they saw the fig tree withered away to its roots. Then Peter remembered and said to him, "Rabbi, look! The fig tree that you cursed has withered." (Mark 11:12–21)

Presuming that what Jesus would do today has some correlation with what he actually did then—in first-century Roman Palestine as reported in the New Testament—how in the world might a contemporary Christian go about replicating and applying these bizarre incidents of tree-cursing and temple-disrupting? If our favorite grocery store happens not to stock a particular fruit we are craving—because it's out of season!—do we proceed, with Jesus' blessing, to curse the fruit bin, the produce manager, and everything else in sight? And if the preacher goes on too much about money one Sunday or if we are just generally miffed at various church personnel and programs, do we bust in during a worship service and start upending pews, pulpits, altars—anything not nailed down—and bouncing ushers from the premises?

No Christians I know, however literalistic they might claim to be, would endorse such an aberrant application of Jesus' activity in the modern world, any more than they would advocate physical amputation as the proper response to Jesus' challenge, "If your right hand causes you to sin, cut it off"(Matt 5:30). As we recognize elements of metaphor and hyperbole in Jesus' teaching, we acknowledge that some of his actions may be overly dramatic or deliberately extreme for effect (though we may hotly disagree about which actions fit this bill). Not everything Jesus did provides a clear model for human behavior.

But, on the other hand, most Christians I know assume that much or most of what Jesus did has exemplary value for contemporary behavior and that if Jesus walked the streets of modern America today, he would do pretty much the same things the gospels claim he originally did (perhaps in jeans and T-shirt rather than cloak and tunic—in any case, the sandals stay). But here's the rub: I am doubtful that even a majority of American Christians (I cannot speak for the rest of the Christian world) know enough about the *content* of Jesus' actions in the gospels to justify this assumption of relevance. By all accounts, biblical literacy is in sharp decline, even among the devout and fervent. Accordingly, our view of what Jesus would do today is only tenuously tied to what Jesus *did* do in the gospel narratives.

How then can we properly use the life of Jesus as an ethical model? How can we prudently sort out the strange and unique actions of Jesus from his more acceptable and imitable behavior? Are gestures like his "tree-witching" and "temple tantrum"[1] truly eccentric or in fact symptomatic of other arcane rituals, and do they have any redeeming ethical value that sensitive environmentalists (who protect trees) and liturgists (who respect holy sites)—or for that matter, most ordinary, decent folk—wouldn't object to?

Alas, despite all these "how" questions, this book is not a comprehensive "how to" manual on using the gospels to address contemporary moral problems.[2] My aim is much more basic and modest—something more like a preliminary "what" resource. In brief, this text attempts to collate and discuss gospel information about Jesus' personal conduct in a lively and accessible format conducive to subsequent ethical reflection. It springs from the bedrock assumption that we cannot begin to grapple with "What *would* Jesus do?" until we have more than a vague inkling of "What *did* Jesus do?"

Commentaries and monographs on individual gospels provide a wealth of data about particular features of Jesus' professional career but often fail both to correlate this material with other gospel presentations and to concentrate on more personal dimensions of Jesus' life—his family, friends, health, occupation, finances, and reputation—in other words, the stuff of which much of our ethical lives consist. This book focuses on precisely these topics, drawing on pertinent incidents from all four canonical gospels. I try to walk a tightrope between synthesis and description, unity and diversity, endeavoring to bring some coherence to the accounts of Jesus' conduct but all the while respecting the integrity of each gospel's narrative and resisting tendencies to impose a superficial harmony on the four presentations.

My appreciation and interpretation of the gospels' portraits of Jesus is indebted to more scholars than I could possibly mention and, in fact, given the more popular nature of this project, I have not cluttered the body of the text with scholars' names, lengthy citations, or the spectrum of academic arguments currently in vogue. But I have tried to compensate for this less technical style with ample use of endnotes, supplying more detailed explication of gospel passages and pointing the interested reader to supporting primary and secondary literature.

Given the suggestive rather than definitive nature of this book, I will be happy if it simply encourages readers to probe the gospels for themselves, to ground their Christian moral reasoning and decision making more firmly in the gospels' testimony, and to "examine the scriptures every day to see whether these things are so," as the Berean audience responded to Paul's message (Acts 17:10–11). I further hope that this study will spur a spate of fresh investigations of other practical dimensions of Jesus' ethics (e.g., *What Did Jesus Teach His Followers to Do?*; *How Did Jesus Treat Others?* [social ethics], *Women* in particular [feminist ethics], *Nature* [environmental ethics], and *the State?* [political ethics]), as well as the ethics of other scriptural figures (e.g., *What Did the Hebrew Prophets Do?*; *What Did the Apostle Paul Do?*) under the broad rubric of "Biblical Resources for Ethical Reflection."

Special thanks go to Henry Carrigan—visionary, polymath, and editor extraordinaire (not to mention an incredibly nice guy)—for soliciting and shepherding this project every step of the way. After I wandered with the idea in the publishing wilderness (not quite forty years), Henry graciously brought it to fruition, if not in the promised land, at least in the TPI catalog—and that's good enough for me.

Finally, I dedicate this volume to my wife and daughters, who continually astonish me with their intelligence, imagination, and consummate abilities. Apart from putting up with my silliness and sloppiness (I really don't know why I can't keep food off my shirt), their enthusiastic support of my scholarly pursuits and my recent transition to the Baptist Theological Seminary at Richmond (which brought many changes for them) means more to me than they will ever know. Janet, Lauren, and Meredith: "What Would *I* Do" without you?

NOTES

1. I picked up this tongue-in-cheek description of Jesus' temple cleansing from public lectures and panel discussions offered by Prof. Paula Fredriksen. She meant no disrespect by such a witticism, and neither do I. But "temple tantrum" does provocatively capture the strangeness and volatility of Jesus' action, which cannot be denied. It should also be noted that Fredriksen treats this incident quite seriously and provides numerous insights into its meaning in her published works: *From Jesus to Christ: The Origins of the New Testament Images of Christ* (2nd ed; New Haven: Yale University Press, 2000), 111–14; *Jesus of Nazareth, King of the Jews: A Jewish Life and the Emergence of Christianity* (New York: Knopf, 1999), 207–14, 225–34.

2. In fact, the whole notion of a "how to" manual applying biblical passages and principles to contemporary ethical problems is itself highly problematic (not to mention naïve), as Fowl and Jones have perceived:

> [T]here are some significant problems with the methods and presumptions upon which much current work on the use of Scripture in ethics rests. In fact, casting the issue in terms of "use" (as in the use of Scripture in Christian ethics) suggests that Scripture is something out there waiting to be "used." All that is needed is the proper method which will (1) excavate the meaning of the Bible, (2) apply that meaning to this or that situation, and (3) identify how the meaning found in the Bible ought to be understood in relation to other possible sources of guidance.
>
> We think this approach is problematic. (Stephen E. Fowl and L. Gregory Jones, *Reading in Communion: Scripture & Ethics in Christian Life* [Grand Rapids, Mich.: Eerdmans, 1991], 4)

Eschewing a formulaic approach, their book sketches a dynamic process of integrating biblical study and ethical reflection rooted in communities of faith. See also the promising recent studies by Daniel J. Harrington and James Keenan, *Jesus and Virtue Ethics: Building Bridges Between New Testament Studies and Moral Theology* (Lanham, Md.: Sheed & Ward, 2002); and Charles H. Cosgrove, *Appealing to Scripture in Moral Debate: Five Hermeneutical Rules* (Grand Rapids, Mich.: Eerdmans, 2002).

First Questions First

As a little girl she'd made a rule for herself: if she petted or fed one animal in the presence of others, she must pet and feed them all. It was what Jesus would have done if he had lived intimately with animals.

What *would* Jesus do?—that's what I ask myself. I try, and I try, but my good intentions break down when I'm with other people.[1]

Oh, dear me, it *is* complicated. No surprise that people are always trying to simplify life. What's that question our evangelical brethren are always asking? "What Would Jesus Do?" What, indeed?[2]

These citations, not from religious or devotional literature, but from critically acclaimed novels by two of America's leading writers, illustrate two curious features of contemporary American society. First, the question: "What Would Jesus Do?"—often represented by the acronym "WWJD" brandished on T-shirts, key chains, lanyards, bracelets, bumpers, and license plates—constitutes a key motto, an organizing principle, for Christian faith and practice, chiefly but not exclusively among the influential bloc of "evangelical brethren" in this country. The question has become part of our popular culture and thus fair game for the nation's novelists, politicians, journalists, and comedians, as well as for the faithful.

Second, the task of applying this simple formula to current moral dilemmas is not that simple; indeed, "it *is* complicated," extremely so, not least because of the innumerable contemporary issues Jesus never faced. The little girl portrayed above sorts out easily enough how Jesus would have treated a barnyard of animals if he had grown up on a farm like hers, which the girl knows full well he didn't. But current environmental, ecological, and biomedical quandaries are a good bit more complex than equal opportunity petting and feeding of God's furry creatures. What would Jesus do about global warming, stem-cell research, and cloning? What, indeed? Such issues were not just ignored in first-century Galilee: they were inconceivable. But surely not to God or to God's Son, the Alpha and Omega. Time is no barrier to the Eternal Mind—or is it? Fundamentally, there is a tension between Jesus' uniqueness and universality from both ends of the liberal-historical (left) and conservative-theological (right) spectrum. Both conservatives and liberals stress Jesus' singularity: the former, as the uniquely incarnate Son of the Eternal God; the latter, as the peculiarly individual Jesus of ancient Nazareth. If Jesus is either so far above us spiritually and metaphysically or so far behind us culturally and historically, how can he effectively serve as a model for everyday, twenty-first century conduct? Traditionally, however, this gap (chasm?) between Jesus and us, while appreciable, has not been insurmountable. Conservatives insist that the pre-existent divine Son of God took on real humanity in the person of Jesus—"the Word became flesh" (John 1:14)—and thus demonstrated what it means to be authentically human in the image of God. Thus, when Jesus said, "follow me," he intended more than just "tag along and worship me"; he meant: "Do what I say, do what I do, act like me." Or, as the apostle Paul develops the point: "Be imitators of me, as I am of Christ"(1 Cor 11:1). It must be assumed that we can never fully match Jesus' perfect standard in this life, but that should not keep us from trying.

On the liberal side, while punctuating the strange, conditioned identity of the historical Jesus within the milieu of eastern Mediterranean antiquity—millennia of years and miles from modern America—most scholars who care to bother with this figure do so from some pressing conviction that if Jesus is not exactly a man for all seasons, he still has much to offer our time. And so, as many critics have pointed out, the portraits of the historical Jesus that continue to flood the market often bear an uncanny resemblance to Martin Luther King, Jr., Mahatma Gandhi, Mother Teresa, or some other major twentieth-century social reformer, political activist, or spiritual guru, who themselves, to some degree or another, drew strength and motivation from Jesus' example. Despite repeated warnings against "the peril of modernizing Jesus,"[3] contemporary scholars persist in translating this ancient Galilean's life and teaching into a very modern image and idiom. In their own way, liberals as well as conservatives are dying to know what Jesus would do with the mess we find ourselves in today. How would he tackle the thicket of daunting ethical challenges we face at this moment in our history?

In grappling with the whole "What Would Jesus Do?" enterprise, I acknowledge its popularity, complexity, and importance. I write as an interested, hybrid "believer," with both conservative religious roots and liberal academic values. But I have a nagging concern. In a rush to reach the worthy goal of living as Jesus' disciples in the modern world, we believers often fail to anchor our moral reflection sufficiently in the gospel reports of what Jesus himself actually did. We seize on a convenient capsule or popular sketch of Jesus' activities that we can easily (cheaply) apply to our own behavior. Relevance trumps evidence. We ask the wrong question first: "What *would* Jesus do?" is meaningless without prior understanding of "What *did* Jesus do?" in the gospel narratives.

Of course, it might be objected that ancient literary evidence has little to do with the issue because of the prospect of immediate communication with the living Jesus. If we have "ears to hear" what Jesus says through his Spirit, we simply ask him what he would do about a current problem or decision, and he tells us. Here prayer trumps study. However, while I do not presume to limit the scope of genuine spiritual experience, I confess to only modest personal success in this area (I am not aware that Jesus has ever "spoken" to me as such, except in some vague, impressionistic sense) and to a certain skepticism that much of what is attributed to Jesus these days is more wishful thinking (we hear what we want to hear) than reliable testimony. But I may be wrong about that and simply too spiritually tone deaf to know it. Be that as it may, even the most mystically minded believers have traditionally advocated biblical study as a necessary spur and aid to contemplative prayer, and logic dictates that if the risen Jesus is the same person (albeit in a transformed body) that traversed Galilee two thousand years ago, what he might do and say today would be consistent with what he showed and told then. And so, any way we come at the matter, we are back to the foundational question: What *did* Jesus do?

This book makes no attempt to answer the question fully. It is not a comprehensive treatment of either gospel literature, the figure of Jesus, or Christian ethics—which would represent a near-Herculean task these days, given the avalanche of available information and bibliography, not to mention the even deeper mound of ancient artifacts (textual and material) awaiting excavation. But this study does aim to offer a fresh perspective on the gospels, Jesus, and ethics in order to elucidate further the complicated mystery of "What did Jesus do?" I begin with a brief sketch of three distinctive emphases governing this investigation, followed by a fuller discussion of each point.

1. GOSPELS. Unlike most recent scholarly examinations of Jesus' life, which favor the first three (synoptic) gospels and bracket out the fourth gospel as a later, independent development, this study, while sensitive to historical trajectories and diverse perspectives among the gospels, includes John as a full dialogue partner. The goal is to catch a wide-angled vision of Jesus' behavior in the gospels, without privileging earlier images as more "authentic" or later portraits as more "spiritual."

2. JESUS. Distinct from many studies of Jesus' ethics that concentrate on his sayings or pronouncements as an authoritative code of conduct, this one focuses chiefly on Jesus' deeds or actions as an integral component of his identity and vocation. While not ignoring Jesus' teaching, this work is more interested in discovering how Jesus personally lived out and lived up to his own moral instruction.

3. ETHICS. The social and political implications of Jesus' message and mission as a boundary-breaking prophet have been heavily explored in a number of recent studies. While appreciating Jesus' staunch commitment to social justice, the present project concentrates on the neglected area of Jesus' personal conduct— how he treats himself and those closest to him. A chapter each is devoted to Jesus' actions with respect to his family, his friends, his body, his possessions, his work, and his reputation.

Evidence: Gospel Quartet

Virtually all the information we have about the ancient figure of Jesus comes from "gospel" literature: that is, from the religious-biographical narratives that proclaim the "good news" (*euangelion*) of Jesus as Israel's—and indeed, as the world's—Lord and Messiah. As much as the gospel writers or evangelists regarded Jesus as the chief protagonist of human history, Rome took little notice at the time. A few Roman historians confirm in passing that someone called Christ was crucified in Judea under the auspices of Pontius Pilate, but that's all they have to say on the subject.[4] Studies of Greek, Roman, Jewish, and other eastern Mediterranean literary and material remains uncover a wealth of data about Jesus' cultural environment but not about Jesus' specific, personal behavior. Archaeology, for example, has in recent years recovered remnants of a first-century fishing boat from the Sea of Galilee commonly called the "Jesus Boat." However, while this craft may be typical of the one Jesus and his disciples might have used, there is no way of proving that Jesus ever sat or sailed on these planks (no JESUS WAS HERE etched in the wood). Similarly, archaeology may offer a sketch of typical synagogue architecture and worship in ancient Galilee, but it has not unearthed— and likely never will—a bench in the Nazareth synagogue where a boy named Jesus sat and inscribed his name during a boring Sabbath address or a "bulletin" from a worship service citing "Jesus, son of Joseph" as the Scripture reader for the day.[5] If we want to know anything about Jesus' particular Sabbath or synagogue habits—or any other activities—we must investigate the gospels.[6]

But while this conclusion may seem to settle matters, it in fact raises two critical questions: "Which gospels do we focus on?" and "How do we interpret the gospels we've selected?"

In the first few centuries following Jesus' death, the early Christians produced various—more than four—written accounts of Jesus' career, some concentrating on his childhood (infancy gospels), others on his teaching (sayings gospels), as well as broader accounts of his adult ministry, passion, and resurrection. Currently we have evidence of about thirty such "gospels."[7] There may have been many more that didn't survive. Whatever the complete tally, by the end of the fourth century the four gospels—Matthew, Mark, Luke, and John—had securely won the day among the majority of church officials as the divinely inspired and duly authorized accounts of Jesus' life and death. In short, they became part of the Christian canon.

But why these four and not others? The argument of a leading church father, Irenaeus of Lyon, that the number four is self-evident because "there are four directions of the world in which we live, and there are four principal winds . . . four living creatures [in Revelation] . . . and there were four principal covenants made with humanity, through Noah, Abraham, Moses, and Christ,"[8] seems forced and flimsy. Why not five gospels because God gave us five fingers on each hand, five points to a star, five books of the Law—and while we're playing the game—five principal covenants, if we add the important Davidic pact to Irenaeus's list? Less fanciful reasons for the ascendancy of the four gospels include their comparatively early dating (in the last third of the first century), their traditional claims to apostolic authorship, and their wide circulation and affirmation among the "established" churches.

But however committed Irenaeus and company were to the fourfold gospel, should Christians today be so limited, given our awareness of other ancient gospels? Shouldn't we want to consider all the early testimony of Jesus' conduct before formulating judgments concerning "What Would Jesus Do?" in modern society? But is all this testimony equally reliable or relevant? These huge theological and historical issues cannot be fully tackled here, but some discussion is required to justify the focus of this study.

Few scholars would place the so-called infancy gospels on a par with the four canonical gospels. They are entertaining, to be sure, but obviously represent later attempts to fill in the gaps of Jesus' "hidden" childhood years with fanciful tales of "superboy" exploits. In *The Infancy Gospel of Thomas*, for example, the five-year-old Jesus magically transforms twelve clay sparrows he has sculpted on the Sabbath into live, "chirping" birds in order to cover up his improper Sabbath "work." He also puts a death hex on a boisterous child who happens to bump his shoulder while running through the village and resuscitates another little tyke who had fallen off the roof while playing with Jesus.[9] In the last case, Jesus demonstrates that he wasn't responsible for his playmate's tragic accident, but overall he appears as a strange and volatile lad to hang around with. Although Matthew and company also present a wonder-working Jesus, they do so in a much more reserved manner: his miracles comprise but one part of a multifaceted mission of ushering in God's kingdom, with special emphasis on helping those in dire need, not on serving Jesus' own interests or zapping meddlesome opponents.

On the whole, Jesus' miraculous activity does not fit well with a modern "What Would Jesus Do?" agenda. We might like to perform (or receive) a miracle to solve every personal problem or ethical dilemma, but normally our options are more mundane. While certain Christians today (often labeled "charismatics") stress that the faithful are destined to do "even greater things" in Jesus' name than Jesus himself did,[10] most believers regard Jesus' supernatural power as something that sets him apart from most, if not all, human beings. We may depend on Jesus' gracious exercise of power for our ultimate salvation but not as a pattern for personal emulation in everyday matters. In any case, however awkward Jesus' traditional miracles may be for modern ethical reflection, the impetuous feats of Wunderkind Jesus in the infancy gospels are off the charts. If Jesus cursed a kid to death for bumping his shoulder, what would he do today if a careless motorist banged his fender? This is hardly a promising model for dealing with road rage.

Setting aside the infancy gospels, we confront a more formidable canonical challenge in two sayings collections: 1) the Q gospel, as it is typically dubbed, and 2) the *Gospel of Thomas,* distinct from the "infancy" gospel of the same name.

To the uninitiated, mention of a Q gospel sounds like some covert code or the work of some secret agent in a James Bond or Star Trek adventure.[11] Actually, the label is of German derivation and has nothing to do with the Gestapo or any other intelligence operation; in fact, it comes from the quite ordinary word *Quelle,* meaning "source." Source for what? Q designates a putative source for the material—mostly sayings of Jesus—uniquely shared by Matthew and Luke. The proposal is at once logical and therefore possible, but also hypothetical and therefore not provable. The logic comes from the multiple overlapping samples of Jesus' teaching (e.g., the beatitudes and the Lord's Prayer) found only in Matthew and Luke, without parallel in Mark or John. It is thus a reasonable presumption that the first and third evangelists had access to some common sayings tradition. But we cannot be certain that this material ever existed in written form as an independent "gospel," still less that it reflects the history of some discrete early Christian community. There is no manuscript copy, early or late, complete or fragmentary, of the Q gospel under glass at the British Museum or anywhere else. It is a hypothetical document, pure and simple, which doesn't automatically discredit it but does limit its value for our purposes. We are concerned chiefly with sketching a composite gospel profile of Jesus' activities as a foundation for contemporary ethical practice, not plotting a chronological history of gospel traditions. By focusing on the canonical Matthew and Luke in their final forms, we will be taking into account the Q material irrespective of speculative theories concerning its development. As a first order of business, grappling with the Jesus evidence we have takes precedence over reconstructing what might have been. Moreover, this study targets the actions of Jesus (see below) more than his sayings, whatever form they might have taken inside or outside the gospels.

Likewise, the *Gospel of Thomas* (*Gos. Thom.*) comprises an early collection of 114 "secret sayings" of Jesus, purportedly revealed to Didymos Judas Thomas ("doubting Thomas" the apostle? Jesus' twin brother?), with no narrative structure or accounts of Jesus' deeds. Unlike Q, however, much of *Gos. Thom.* reflects distinctive pronouncements of Jesus, overlapping only sporadically with the four New Testament gospels (about a third of *Gos. Thom.* sayings parallel Q). What is the relationship, then, between this "fifth" gospel and the traditional quartet? Some scholars contend that the *Gos. Thom.* sayings reflect an early, independent strand of Jesus' teaching, potentially as "authentic" or "authoritative" for Christian origins as the New Testament material. Others, however, stress that while a first-century Greek original is possible, the earliest hard evidence we have is a second-century Coptic (ancient Egyptian) translation found at Nag Hammadi in 1945. This datum, together with the esoteric, "gnostic" cast of many *Gos. Thom.* sayings, suggest a later development, a century or so removed from the first layers of Jesus tradition disclosed in the canonical gospels.[12]

However we assess these thorny chronological and theological issues (and they are complicated), we must acknowledge that for the vast majority of Christians, early and modern, the Coptic *Gospel of Thomas,* if

known at all, constitutes a maverick and in some cases aberrant assort-
ment of Jesus' teachings, adding nothing of value to the New Testament
evidence. The majority can be wrong, of course. Religious reform is typically sparked by a reassessment of established traditions and openness to
new perspectives. But at the present I do not see *Gos. Thom.* (or Q) ignit-
ing a fresh Reformation. I do not see most believers poring over modern
Gos. Thom. translations for spiritual or ethical guidance, nor do I envision *Gos. Thom.* texts inspiring rousing sermons in most Christian pulpits. But, then again, I am no prophet and could be mistaken.
Nevertheless, whatever happens in the future, we seem to have enough
on our plates right now dealing with the four gospels most Christians
agree on. The problem, I'm convinced, is not so much that we need new
material as it is that we haven't sufficiently studied or taken seriously the
gospels we've had and affirmed for two millennia.

So, for better or worse, we will keep the spotlight trained on the four
New Testament narratives of Jesus' life. But selection is just the beginning: How should we interpret these accounts? While some scholars have
rushed to open the canon and add new gospels, other interpreters have
effectively reduced the canon and privileged one or more of the four
gospels over the others. One trend, launched by Tatian's *Diatessaron* in
the second century, merged the four distinct gospels into one continuous, blended account.[13] This harmonizing phenomenon has persisted in
popular Bible studies among the faithful. There remains a powerful pull
in Sunday schools and study groups to collapse the multiple versions of
Jesus' life into one. The traditional Christmas nativity scene is a banner
example, with shepherds, wise men, angels, animals, and the lot all packed
into the stable around the manger, irrespective of the unique portraits
that Matthew and Luke provide.[14]

Apart from flattening the four gospels into one, a second tendency in
the history of interpretation has been the practice of favoritism. Originally, the communities in which and for which the individual gospels
were composed likely regarded their gospel as superior, if not exclusive.
Later, as knowledge of multiple gospels spread and the "final four"
became more popular, one or more gospels might still carry greater
weight among certain groups for various reasons. Or, conversely, one or
more might be slighted, even denigrated, in some way. The controversial

second-century bishop Marcion didn't really want any of the four gospels in his canon (they were all too Jewish and "earthy" for his tastes). He found all the "gospel" he needed in Paul's writings (that is, in ten of the thirteen letters attributed to the apostle; the three Pastoral missives— 1 and 2 Timothy and Titus—didn't cut the mustard). Marcion conceded some value, however, in Luke's gospel, but only in a truncated form (minus the birth stories), consistent with his esoteric brand of Paulinism.[15] While on the whole the Christian church has repudiated Marcion's minimalist, anti-Judaic agenda, the propensity to elevate one gospel over the others persists. Part of this stems from a natural desire to differentiate and exalt individual components within a group. Among the myriads of Beatles fans who idolize the entire band, most would still admit to a particular favorite among the famous foursome.

And so it is with the gospels. My mother, for example, will tell you flat out that her favorite gospel is John. And she is not alone. Many believers prefer Jesus' extraordinary, straightforward "I am" statements in the fourth gospel—along with the unmistakable presentation of Jesus' divine authority and promise of eternal salvation (encapsulated in that most celebrated of all Bible verses, John 3:16)[16]—over the more subtle, "human" sketches of Jesus in Matthew, Mark, and Luke. For years, the multitude of respondents who "came forward" at Billy Graham's evangelistic crusades were given individual copies of the Gospel of John to help them grow in their faith. Now neither Graham nor any of his associates (nor my mother) would suggest for a second that John was the "best" or the "only" gospel worth reading: they wouldn't dream of altering the canon. But it is interesting that they were willing to publish and distribute a single gospel under separate cover, which at least implicitly gave this work a special status.[17]

On the more liberal, critical end of the spectrum, different priorities among the gospels often come into play. Here, John has typically been rated last and least of the four—the last to be written and the least historically reliable, reflecting a more "spiritualized" or "mythologized" portrait of Jesus.[18] The three Synoptic Gospels—so-called because they share a more common "vision" of Jesus' life with each other than with John— fare much better in this scheme, but even here, distinctions are made. The prevailing theory, building on the premise of "Markan priority," posits that Mark was written first and served as the foundation for

Matthew and Luke's expanded accounts. Overall, a certain bias favors the most primitive layers of the Jesus tradition, which can supposedly be uncovered through a variety of "scientific" means. The "real" Jesus becomes the earliest Jesus we can find, unadorned (uncorrupted) by later theological imagination.

Over against these tendencies either to amalgamate the four gospels into one or to accentuate certain gospels or strata of gospel tradition above others on either historical or devotional grounds, the present study aims to grapple with both the common and the distinctive literary portraits of Jesus in all four gospels. While appreciating the parallel or overlapping episodes among the gospels, we can also find variations within these similar accounts. Rarely does one gospel's report perfectly match another's; they are not carbon copies, but rather distinctive presentations of similar events. To ignore these differences or to roll them into one conglomerated mosaic dilutes the singular contribution of each evangelist. Superficial harmonization impoverishes rather than enriches our understanding of Jesus' life. Furthermore, we must consider not merely the fact, but also the extent, of common material. Does a story appear in one, two, three, or all of the gospels? Does it represent a single (unique), double (as with the Q sayings in Matthew and Luke), triple (synoptic), or quadruple (unanimous) tradition?

But why bother with such questions if, as my students regularly remind me, one report of a particular saying or action of Jesus in the New Testament is sufficient to take seriously. If it's there, we have to deal with it. I agree—I don't want to exclude any pertinent data—but I further contend that frequency matters; repetition reflects emphasis. If multiple evangelists regarded an incident important enough to include in their gospels, that may give that incident stronger weight in influencing contemporary ethical conduct among those who want to pattern their lives after Jesus. Put another way, if all four gospels highlight a certain activity of Jesus, it should be much harder to dismiss that activity as an idiosyncratic, one-off experience of limited relevance to Christian faith and practice. Yes, all the gospel evidence is important, but some of it is earmarked for special attention by virtue of its multiple attestation.[19]

As a further check against imposing an artificial unity upon the gospels, we must also acknowledge that differences among the four narratives may reflect not simply alternative or more elaborate accounts, but perhaps points of tension, debate, even disagreement over Jesus' conduct. Concerning Jesus' treatment of his immediate family, for example, we will discover (in chapter 2) a range of responses from dismissive to support- ive, running along a rough trajectory from Mark (harshest responses), to Matthew and Luke (somewhat softer), to John (most tender). This pat- tern may also betray an editorial process from the earliest (Mark) to the latest (John) gospel, according to the dominant scheme pointed out above.

But while appreciating the phenomenon of conflicting reports about Jesus and the possibility of tracking these developments chronologically, we must be cautious about privileging one of these stages—usually the earliest—as more "authentic," more representative of the "real" Jesus. My reservations are twofold: one theoretical, the other practical. First, the process of detecting the earliest layers of the Jesus tradition is far from an exact science. For the most part, scholars in search of the historical Jesus depend upon analytical and imaginative reconstructions of literary data, not precise electronic and microscopic measurements (except, to some extent, in archaeology), and they hotly contest which methods or criteria to use. Moreover, while most Jesus "questers" continue to give priority to Mark's gospel, a growing number of scholars are giving greater con- sideration to Matthew[20] and even to John[21] as repositories of primitive testimony.

Secondly, as we have already stressed, the practical reality for most Christians through the ages is that the "real" Jesus is the Jesus revealed in the four New Testament gospels. Jesus "lives" through these authoritative books that are accepted, venerated, and interpreted in communities of faith.[22] While I have been radically challenged and richly illuminated by the spate of historical Jesus studies in the past two decades, I seriously doubt whether any speculative reconfiguration of Jesus' life is capable of winning the day over two thousand years of New Testament tradition. Among those who care most today about Christian discipleship, follow- ing Jesus somehow entails emulating Jesus' actions as found—uniquely or repeatedly—in Matthew, Mark, Luke, and/or John. Of course, this is easier said than done; in fact, I think that "doing what Jesus did" proves to be a good bit more difficult than most believers recognize because of the complexity of the gospels' portraits of Jesus, rife with narrative gaps and tensions, and the cultural distance between Jesus' world and ours.

The main purpose of this book is to uncover the gospel evidence of Jesus' ethical conduct, tensions and all, in the context of first-century, eastern Mediterranean society. But my guess (and my own bias) is that most Christians are willing to live and struggle with whatever the four gospels offer—in all of their multiplicity and strangeness—rather than jettison them for some bowdlerized abridgement or modernized alternative.

In short, the four New Testament gospels, in their final forms, comprise our primary field of inquiry. In part they are like a "gospel quartet" (while my musical tastes have expanded over the years, I cut my teeth on four-part gospel tunes sung by popular groups like the Blackwood Brothers, the Statesmen, and the Imperials), in which four distinct voices offer complementary renditions of the good news about Jesus. This image suffers, however, from a potential over-emphasis on harmony: the New Testament gospels do not always blend as tightly as finely tuned gospel or barbershop quartets. At times, they may even sound discordant. Shifting models, fans of American collegiate basketball might appreciate comparing the gospels to "The Final Four." Starting with a field of sixty-five teams, the championship tournament whittles down to a climactic competition among the final four survivors. This analogy reminds us that Matthew, Mark, Luke, and John represent the canonical "winners" among a larger pool of gospel accounts, and that they are four full-fledged, distinct entities, each vigorously wrestling in its own way with the significance of Jesus' life, death, and resurrection. But here we can easily overdo the competitive element. The unabashed goal of the NCAA tournament is to crown one ultimate champion from out of the final four (the battle cry is "We're #1"—not "We're in the top 4"). With respect to the gospels, however, this study resists the tendency to rank one over the others. Whatever model we employ, all four New Testament evangelists merit a fair hearing—in all their marvelous unity and diversity.

Jesus: Action Figure

Both inside and outside the community of faith, among both the devout and merely curious, perceptions of Jesus' ethics characteristically zoom in upon Jesus' classic admonitions, such as:

Love your neighbor as yourself.
Love your enemies and pray for those who persecute you.
Do unto others as you would have them do unto you.
Be merciful, just as your Father is merciful.
(Matt 22:39//Mark 12:31//Luke 10:27–28; Matt 5:44; 7:12;
Luke 6:31, 36)

Priority is given to the teachings of Jesus, particularly those in imperative mode, which seem to encapsulate his ethical ideals. Like the foundational Ten Commandments in the Old Testament, with their pointed
focus, terse style, and absolute "thou shalt not" tone, Jesus' pithy commandments command special attention. Accordingly, gospel segments
that feature Jesus' "laying down the law"—as in the so-called "Sermon
on the Mount" in Matthew 5–7—take on extraordinary importance.
People who otherwise know little about Jesus and the gospels will likely
be acquainted with some of Jesus' instruction in this famous "sermon"
(it's really more of a lecture), even if they can't identify it as such. Apho-
risms (like "The first will be last" and "The one who saves his life will
lose it") and parables (like "The Good Samaritan" and "The Prodigal
Son") are also widely known samples of Jesus' teaching, but they offer
more ambiguous ethical guidance because of their slippery paradoxical
and multivalent meanings. We tend to prefer clear, simple, straightforward calls to action.

Nevertheless, while Jesus' commands or marching orders to his followers undoubtedly constitute a vital component of his "moral vision,"[23] the
picture is skewed if these mandates are given exclusive or predominant
authority. In particular, I enter a special plea on behalf of Jesus' deeds or
actions as living illustrations of Jesus' teaching. One cannot properly be
considered apart from the other (separating Jesus' words and deeds is
indeed a "dreary dichotomy," as Crossan and Reed aver).[24] But for the
sake of redressing an imbalance in most discussions of Jesus' ethics, this
study focuses on Jesus' enacted or embodied ethics as a potential model
for our own conduct. Such an action-oriented approach is wholly consistent with (1) the process of interpretation required for applying biblical
laws, (2) the principle of integrity embedded in Jesus' message, and (3)
the mystery of incarnation, foundational to Christian theology.

Laws like "Remember the Sabbath day to keep it holy" or "Honor your father and mother" in the middle of the Decalogue represent important ideals or mottoes that must be interpreted or unpacked in terms of specific moral actions. What precisely does it mean to sanctify the Sabbath? To rest, certainly, but to rest from what? All labor or just certain tasks? In short, what exactly may we do and not do on this hallowed day in order to keep the fourth commandment? Similarly, how does the attitude of honoring one's parents translate into action? It certainly includes respectful speech and obedience, but to what extent and for how long? Are dutiful children expected to do everything their parents say, even what appears to be ethically questionable? When do children become morally responsible for their own actions? It's not enough simply to affirm scriptural laws as abstract principles—they must be applied in the concrete grit of daily living.

Interestingly, Jesus frequently enters into heated discussion with the legal scholars of his day over the practical meaning of God's commandments—including the two regarding the Sabbath and filial obligations. But he does more than just muse about the issues as an armchair philosopher. He lives them; he works them out in the crucible of experience. As a Galilean Jew, he does certain things on the seventh day of the week (see chapter 6), and as a son of Mary and Joseph, he treats his parents in certain ways (see chapter 2). In the gospel narratives, such conduct— often controversial—functions both as a spark for Jesus' teaching (he defends his action) and as a clue to its meaning (he models his message).

The vital nexus between word and deed, teaching and action, is hammered in no uncertain terms by Jesus himself in his insistence upon integrity—or, negatively put, his crusade against hypocrisy. Both Jesus' closest companions and his staunchest competitors[25] receive stern warnings against the duplicitous trap of saying one thing and doing another. At the end of his hortatory "sermon" to his disciples in both Matthew and Luke, Jesus stresses the need not merely to hear, but to heed his teaching; not only to proclaim his message, but to put it into practice.

> You will know them by their fruits. . . . Not everyone who says to me, "Lord, Lord," will enter the kingdom of heaven, but only the one who does the will of my Father in heaven. . . . Everyone then

who hears these words of mine and acts on them will be like a wise man who built his house on rock. (Matt 7: 16–24)

Why do you call me, "Lord, Lord," and do not do what I tell you? I will show you what someone is like who comes to me, hears my words, and acts on them. That one is like a man building a house, who dug deeply and laid the foundation on rock. (Luke 6:46–48)

Similarly, Jesus regularly rips into the leading biblical tutors of his time (scribes and Pharisees) with a resounding, "Woe to you, hypocrites," for "not practicing what they teach."[26] While the content of their instruction is praiseworthy, the conduct of their lives misleads and causes their students to stumble.

Under the principle of reciprocal judgment affirmed by Jesus in Matthew ("For with the judgment you make you will be judged, and the measure you give will be the measure you get," 7:2), he effectively invites his audience, whether friendly or hostile, to evaluate his character as he evaluates others: based on his actions. After washing his disciples' feet in the fourth gospel, Jesus enjoins: "I have set you an example, that you also should do as I have done to you" (not as I have told you) (13:15). How and to what extent does Jesus live out and live up to his own ethical standards throughout his career? That's the key question at the heart of this study. The popular preoccupation with "What Would Jesus Do?" is on the right track, I think.[27] Notice the question is not, "What Would Jesus Say to Do?" although respect for his teachings is no doubt implied. Ultimately, "actions speak louder than words" is more than empty cliché— it's bedrock for Jesus' ethics, the rock on which Christian character is built.

The seminal Christian doctrine of incarnation, rooted in the Johannine prologue ("the Word made flesh") and other New Testament texts and elaborated in later ecclesiastical creeds, stipulates that in some mystical-yet-substantial fashion Jesus of Nazareth represents a perfect commingling of divine and human natures. In brief, God became man in Jesus Christ. The significance of this conviction is usually understood in

terms of Jesus' revelation of God: if you want to know what God is all
about, how God thinks, speaks, acts, and "looks," look at Jesus. Jesus is
God incarnate. But the flip side of the incarnation coin is equally important, especially for Christian ethics. As the God-man, Jesus also reveals the
perfect character of humanity molded in the image of God. If you want
to know how human beings should think, speak, act, and "look" as God's
agents, look at Jesus. The action element is paramount in this perspective.
Jesus is not some disembodied voice floating through the airwaves or
abstract metaphysical idea irradiating the cosmos. He is a living, breath-
ing human being who models human goodness in tangible, bodily form.
He enacts the will of God on earth for our instruction and emulation.

Ethics: Getting Personal

About a century ago, debate waxed hot and heavy within American
Christianity over the so-called "social gospel," which advocated that
Jesus' saving mission chiefly targeted the prevailing societal ills of his
day—poverty, prejudice, intolerance, infirmity, and the like—and that
he charged his followers to "do likewise" in promoting God's kingdom of
peace and justice on earth. In this program, the Christian "good news"
has profound social and political implications. Opponents objected that
such an agenda diluted the spiritual force of the gospel and deflected its
focus away from Jesus' clarion call to repent of one's sins against God and
receive God's gift of eternal life. In this scheme, individual conversion
and heavenly destiny take priority over social reform and earthly duty.

   While certain polarizing voices may still be heard emphasizing the
personal/spiritual thrust of Jesus' message and ministry over against
social/material concerns, most contemporary believers acknowledge
some blend (not necessarily equal) of both dimensions. It has become
particularly difficult in recent years to ignore or impugn the social
impact of Jesus' gospel.[28] Despite the widely divergent portraits of Jesus
that have emerged over the past two decades—for example, Jesus as
eschatological or apocalyptic prophet of restoration,[29] proponent of an
inclusive "politics of compassion,"[30] agent of free, "unbrokered" healing
and "commensality,"[31] nonviolent social revolutionary,[32] or subversive

prophetic sage[33]—they share a firm conviction that Jesus had something significant to say and do about the precarious condition of corporate Israel, the people of God (not isolated individuals), under foreign rule.

I applaud this renewed appreciation of Jesus' social gospel, with its obvious ethical emphasis rooted firmly in Israel's Scriptures on acting justly and mercifully toward others, including strangers and aliens as well as neighbors and compatriots. However, alongside this vital social component, a key personal dimension to Jesus' life and work has not received adequate attention in recent studies. My concern is not with Jesus' private devotional life (Jesus as "mystic"), or his commitment to individual conversion (Jesus as "evangelist"), or his probing of his own and others' emotional states (Jesus as "psychoanalyst"), although each of these "personal" matters is intriguing and worth pursuing.[34] Rather, I am interested in the personal side of Jesus' moral conduct as a complement to his social action. This interest flows from Jesus' own classic ethical formulations, grounded in the Holiness Code of Leviticus and indeed in the entire corpus of "law and prophets," immortalized in the Golden Rule, and dramatized in the parable of the Good Samaritan: "In everything do to others as you would have them do to you. You shall love your neighbor as yourself."

While cultural historians have cautioned that notions of personality in Mediterranean antiquity were much more "dyadic," collectivist, or group oriented and less individualistic, introspective, and self-absorbed than modern Western perceptions,[35] ancient persons were still self-conscious to some degree and differentiated from others in some fashion. Despite the frequent comparisons to sheep and other livestock, human beings, then as now, did not always follow the herd. Although deeply embedded in clan, tribe, and nation, each individual Israelite was still self-determining and responsible for his or her own actions, as the prophets Jeremiah and Ezekiel make especially clear (Jer 31:27–34//Ezek 18:1–32). And so Jesus avers that, however outreaching and community-centered one's behavior should be ("love your neighbor"), understanding what it means to treat others with love and mercy begins at home with proper treatment of oneself and one's "own" ("as yourself"). Again applying Jesus' own rhetoric to himself, we seek to discover how Jesus' self love reflected in his personal conduct meshes with his ethical instructions and social interactions.

Six areas of Jesus' life are explored in the following chapters. The first two focus on Jesus' dealings with his immediate family and most intimate friends: that is, those within his closest communal network privy to his most personal responses. If political platforms (every campaign these days has something to say about "family values"), televisions programs (the longest running American sit-com in the past decade has been *Friends*), and telephone companies (each tries to outdo the other with a special "family and friends" plan) are any gauge of contemporary American culture, then such issues rank high on our ethical agenda.

The third study (chapter 4) targets Jesus' treatment of his own physical body in matters pertaining to dirt, diet, sex, and pain (all points of hyper-interest today). As with kinship and friendship ties, body matters, though deeply private and personal, spill over into the social arena. The apostle Paul's use of the human body—with its several "members" linked together under one "head" as a dynamic metaphor for the church, the body of Christ[36]—exemplifies a common cultural-symbolic link between the individual physical body and the corporate body politic.

The next two areas of inquiry, dealing with Jesus' relationship to money and work, delve into his means of personal survival or what we might call his "standard of living." Labor and economics are notorious hotbeds for fraud, exploitation, and other questionable ethical practices, not least in our own capitalist society. In his day, Jesus leveled some of his most scathing criticism against the powerful and well-to-do for abusing the weak and the poor. We want to see how he measured up to his own standards of honesty, generosity, and fairness in his financial and vocational habits.

The sixth topic examines what some scholars regard as the most cherished "possession" of all in eastern Mediterranean culture: one's honor or good name. More than money, more than property, more than material goods, one's reputation defined the core of personal identity. Of course, such a conception of personal identity is integrally tied to matters of social standing because, by definition, one's "honor rating" is calibrated by public opinion. Jesus' interest in "Who do people say that I am?" represents more than passing curiosity.[37] In some vital sense, his character and mission are determined by what others think of him and how they react to him. Within this honor-sensitive worldview, ethical considerations especially come into play in relation to acts of self-promotion and self-protection. What is Jesus willing to do and not do to advance his position and defend his reputation? While in our own day money no doubt talks louder than anything (including honor: if you're rich, who cares what others think?), we still pay close attention to the polls, and we still rely heavily on friends and "patrons" to further our careers. Despite the "shameless" effrontery of certain public figures, honor is far from dead in our society.

NOTES

1. Joyce Carol Oates, *We Were the Mulvaneys* (New York: Plume, 1997), 77.

2. Richard Russo, *Empire Falls* (New York: Knopf, 2001), 172.

3. I owe this apt phrase to the important study of Henry J. Cadbury, *The Peril of Modernizing Jesus* (New York: Macmillan, 1937). Despite its age, this work remains relevant to our time. If anything, the tendency to "update" Jesus has accelerated in recent decades, stimulated in part by the spate of modern, "contemporary language" versions of the Bible.

4. See, for example, the comments of Tacitus—"Christus, from whom the name [Christians] had its origin, suffered the extreme penalty during the reign of Tiberius at the hands of one of our procurators, Pontius Pilate" (*Annals* 15.44.6–9), cited in C. K. Barrett, *The New Testament Background: Selected Documents* (London: SPCK/New York: Harper & Row, 1956), 15–16; and the first-century Jewish historian, Josephus, writing for a Roman audience, "About this time lived Jesus, a wise man, a teacher of those who delight in accepting the truth (or, the unusual). . . . He was the so-called Christ. On the accusation of our leading men Pilate condemned him to the cross" (*Antiquities* 18.116–119), cited in Graham N. Stanton, *The Gospels and Jesus* (Oxford: Oxford University Press, 1989), 143.

5. For an interesting pioneering attempt to correlate what we know about Jesus from both "stones and text," "ground and gospel," see the collaborative study by well-known biblical scholar John Dominic Crossan and archaeologist Jonathan L. Reed, *Excavating Jesus: Beneath the Stones, Behind the Texts* (New York: HarperSanFrancisco, 2001). The "Jesus Boat" is discussed on pp. xvi–xvii, 4, 85–87.

6. The longest and most dramatic account of Jesus' reading and interpreting Scripture on the Sabbath in the Nazareth synagogue is found in Luke 4:16–30.

7. See Helmut Koester, *Ancient Christian Gospels: Their History and Development* (Harrisburg, Pa.: Trinity Press International, 1990); Mark Allan Powell, *Fortress Introduction to the Gospels* (Minneapolis, Minn.: Fortress, 1998), 139–43; Stanton, *Gospels,* 125–35.

8. Irenaeus, *Adv. Haer.* III.11.8, cited in Stanton, *Gospels,* 134.

9. See *Infancy Gospel of Thomas* 2, 4, and 9; Robert J. Miller, ed., *The Complete Gospels: Annotated Scholars Version* (Sonoma, Calif.: Polebridge/San Francisco: HarperSanFrancisco, 1994), 371–79.

10. The idea of accomplishing "greater things" is drawn from John 14:12–14.

11. "Q" is the moniker of the British intelligence agent in charge of 007's secret gadgets in numerous James Bond movies, and "Q" also designates a whimsical, godlike, super-wise being in several episodes of *Star Trek: The Next Generation*. Given the massive popularity of these cinematic adventures, I'm guessing most people today would think of "Q" in these terms. A further alphabetical quirk may be seen in the use of "M" to label Matthew's special material, which just happens to coincide with another Bond agent ("M" is actually Bond's boss, ably portrayed by Dame Judi Dench in recent films).

12. See Bart D. Ehrman, *The New Testament and Other Early Christian Writings: A Reader* (Oxford: Oxford University, 1998), 116–23.

13. *Diatessaron* "is a musical term, meaning 'harmony of four'; it indicates clearly what this edition was. It was a continuous gospel narrative, produced by unstitching the units of the four individual gospels and restitching them together in what was taken to be their chronological order. The gospel of John provided the framework into which material from the gospels of Matthew, Mark, and Luke was fitted" (F. F. Bruce, *The Canon of Scripture* [Downers Grove, Ill.: InterVarsity, 1988], 127).

14. Another classic case of harmonizing is the composite profile of the "Rich Young Ruler" whom Jesus challenges to sell everything he owns and give the proceeds to the poor. The Synoptic Gospels agree the man was rich, but only Matthew labels him "young" and only Luke indicates he was a "ruler" (Matt 19:16–30//Mark 10:17–31//Luke 18:18–30).

15. See the brief but helpful discussion of these canonical issues in Raymond E. Brown, *An Introduction to the New Testament* (Anchor Bible Reference Library; New York: Doubleday, 1997), 12–15.

16. For the uninitiated, John 3:16 has long been the foundational verse of Scripture memorized in evangelical Sunday schools across the nation. Like most good churchgoing kids of my generation, I learned it in the King James Version: "For God so loved the world that he gave his only begotten Son, that whosoever believeth in him should not perish but have everlasting life." It is deemed so familiar in our culture that believers need only brandish the "John 3:16" reference on banners and T-shirts—most often at football games, for some strange reason (I also think some popular wrestler uses this as his "logo").

17. A similar reductive tendency is manifest in the publication of popular "pocket New Testaments"—sometimes with Psalms and/or Proverbs tacked on the end, but otherwise lacking the Old Testament.

18. See the clear discussion, incorporating both autobiographical and scholarly material, in the works of Marcus J. Borg: *Jesus, A New Vision: Spirit, Culture, and the Life of Discipleship* (San Francisco: Harper & Row, 1987), 1–21; and

Meeting Jesus for the First Time: The Historical Jesus and the Heart of Contemporary Faith (San Francisco: HarperSanFrancisco, 1994), 1–19.

19. This is different from the criterion often used in historical Jesus studies, which stresses that a tradition that evinces multiple independent attestation is most likely to go back to Jesus himself. In this approach, if it is assumed that Luke and Matthew, for example, derived certain material from Mark, that still counts as only one source. A canonical approach, like that adopted in this study, appreciates repetition (whatever the original source) as a means of emphasis. See the helpful discussion in Bart D. Ehrman, *The New Testament: A Historical Introduction to the Early Christian Writings* (2nd ed.; Oxford: Oxford University Press, 2000), 202–4.

20. The so-called "Griesbach hypothesis" (named after a nineteenth-century gospel scholar) contends that Matthew was written first (hence its appropriate priority in the canon) and used subsequently first by Luke, then by Mark. Although a minority opinion among contemporary scholars, it still has its staunch defenders. See, e.g., William R. Farmer, *The Synoptic Problem* (New York: Macmillan, 1964), and his *The Gospel of Jesus: The Pastoral Relevance of the Synoptic Problem* (Louisville, Ky.: Westminster/John Knox, 1994); B. Orchard and H. Riley, *The Order of the Synoptics: Why Three Synoptic Gospels?* (Macon, Ga.: Mercer, 1987); David B. Peabody, ed., *One Gospel from Two: Mark's Use of Matthew and Luke* (Harrisburg, Pa.: Trinity Press International, 2002); David Laird Dungan, *A History of the Synoptic Problem: The Canon, the Text, the Composition, and the Interpretation of the Gospels* (Anchor Bible Reference Library; New York: Doubleday, 1999). Note the helpful survey of various source hypotheses for the gospels in Christopher M. Tuckett, "Jesus and the Gospels," in *The New Interpreter's Bible,* vol. 8 (Nashville, Tenn.: Abingdon, 1995), 71–86.

21. In recent years various historical and literary biographies of Jesus by prominent scholars have given much more emphasis to the Gospel of John. On the historical side, see Paula Fredriksen, *Jesus of Nazareth,* and Bruce Chilton, *Rabbi Jesus: An Intimate Biography* (New York: Doubleday, 2000). For a fresh literary biography of Jesus using the framework of the fourth gospel, see Jack Miles, *Christ: A Crisis in the Life of God* (New York: Knopf, 2001), a sequel to his Pulitzer Prize-winning biography of God in the Hebrew Bible. See also the helpful discussion by Robin Griffith-Jones, "The Un-Gospel of John," in *Bible Review* 18 (2002): 14–21, 46–47.

22. A point vigorously stressed by Luke Timothy Johnson in two recent works: *The Real Jesus: The Misguided Quest for the Historical Jesus and the Truth of the Traditional Gospels* (New York: HarperCollins, 1996); *Living Jesus: Learning the Heart of the Gospel* (New York: HarperCollins, 1999).

23. I borrow this phrase from the title of Richard B. Hays's book, *The Moral Vision of the New Testament: Community, Cross, and New Creation: A Contemporary Introduction to New Testament Ethics* (New York: HarperCollins, 1996).

24. The full comment comes from Crossan and Reed, *Excavating Jesus,* 124 (emphasis added):

> [S]cholars sometimes debate whether the words or deeds, the sayings or actions of Jesus should receive primary or even exclusive emphasis. This unit [Matt 10:7–15//Mark 6:7–13//Luke 10:4–12//*Gospel of Thomas* 14] cuts across that often *dreary dichotomy,* because it contains words about deeds, sayings about action, and, as such, it emphasizes their mutual dependence and reciprocal importance.

25. The felicitous labeling of the people Jesus encounters as "companions and competitors" comes from *Companions and Competitors,* the third volume of John P. Meier's massive study of the historical Jesus, *A Marginal Jew: Rethinking the Historical Jesus* (New York: Doubleday, 2001).

26. For example, see the extended diatribe in Matthew 23.

27. Although it's certainly not the only track. Leander E. Keck offers an important caution: "[A] 'Christ-like' life . . . is not formed by asking, What would Jesus do?, for the moral life in view here does not result from astute second guessing; it comes from asking, rather, What is the appropriate thing to do and be in light of the kind of person Jesus was?" (*Who Is Jesus?: History in the Perfect Tense* [Minneapolis, Minn.: Fortress, 2001), 175. Still, it seems to me that "the kind of person Jesus was," by Jesus' own admission, was revealed in large measure through his deeds. Being and doing are inextricably entwined in Jesus' anthropology.

28. See, e.g., Bruce J. Malina, *The Social Gospel of Jesus: The Kingdom of God in Mediterranean Perspective* (Minneapolis, Minn.: Fortress, 2001).

29. See E. P. Sanders, *Jesus and Judaism* (London: SCM, 1985), and his *The Historical Figure of Jesus* (London: Penguin, 1993); Paula Fredriksen, *From Jesus to Christ,* 65–130; Dale C. Allison, *Jesus of Nazareth: Millenarian Prophet* (Minneapolis, Minn.: Fortress, 1988); Bart D. Ehrman, *Jesus: Apocalyptic Prophet of the New Millenium* (Oxford: Oxford University Press, 1999); Craig C. Hill, *In God's Time: The Bible and the Future* (Grand Rapids, Mich.: Eerdmans, 2002), 130–69.

30. Borg, *Jesus: A New Vision,* 125–49, and his *Conflict, Holiness, and Politics in the Teachings of Jesus* (New York: Mellen, 1984; repr. Harrisburg, Pa.: Trinity Press International, 1998).

31. Crossan, *The Historical Jesus: The Life of a Mediterranean Jewish Peasant* (New York: HarperSanFrancisco, 1991), and his *Jesus: A Revolutionary Biography* (New York: HarperSanFrancisco, 1994), 54–101.

32. Richard A. Horsley, *Jesus and the Spiral of Violence: Popular Jewish Resistance in Roman Palestine* (New York: Harper & Row, 1987).

33. Ben W. Witherington, III, *Jesus the Sage: The Pilgrimage of Wisdom* (Minneapolis, Minn.: Fortress, 1994).

34. On Jesus' spirituality or personal religious experience, see James D. G. Dunn, *Jesus and the Spirit* (Philadelphia: Westminster, 1975); Borg, *Jesus: A New Vision,* 23–75; John J. Pilch, "The Transfiguration of Jesus: An Experience of Alternate Reality," in *Modeling Early Christianity: Social-Scientific Studies of the New Testament in its Context* (ed. Philip F. Esler; London: Routledge, 1995), 47–64. On the matter of individual religious conversion, see Beverly Roberts Gaventa, *From Darkness to Light: Aspects of Conversion in the New Testament* (Overtures to Biblical Theology; Philadelphia, Pa.: Fortress, 1986); Ronald D. Witherup, *Conversion in the New Testament* (Collegeville, Minn.: Liturgical Press, 1994); Scot McKnight, *Turning to Jesus: The Sociology of Conversion in the Gospels* (Louisville, Ky.: Westminster/John Knox, 2002). For psychological probes of Jesus, see John W. Miller, *Jesus at Thirty: A Psychological and Historical Portrait* (Minneapolis, Minn.: Fortress, 1997); Donald Capps, *Jesus: A Psychological Biography* (St. Louis, Mo.: Chalice, 2000).

35. See Bruce J. Malina, *The New Testament World: Insights from Cultural Anthropology* (3rd ed; Louisville, Ky.: Westminster/John Knox, 2001), 58–80; Bruce J. Malina and Jerome H. Neyrey, "First-Century Personality: Dyadic, Not Individualistic," in *The Social World of Luke-Acts: Models for Interpretation* (ed. Jerome H. Neyrey; Peabody, Mass.: Hendrickson, 1991), 67–96.

36. Rom 12:1–8; 1 Cor 12:12–31; Eph1:22–23; 4:1–16.

37. Malina, *New Testament World,* 27–57; Malina and Neyrey, "Honor and Shame in Luke-Acts: Pivotal Values in the Ancient Mediterranean World," in *The Social World of Luke-Acts,* 25–66.

2

Family Ties

For the last several years, heated debate has swirled within American politics around the thorny issue of "family values." An increasingly vocal and powerful bloc of concerned citizens has decried the perceived breakdown of traditional family structures and moral commitments necessary for a productive and healthy society. Not only in the so-called Bible Belt stretching across the southern states, but throughout the country, the Bible is frequently invoked as the tried-and-true arbiter of proper family conduct. After all, nothing is more fundamental to the moral fabric of our society than the Ten Commandments, and three of these pointedly address domestic activity and protect the sanctity of the home: honor father and mother; do not commit adultery; and do not covet anyone or anything in others' households.[1] Building on this Hebraic legal foundation, a Christian perspective adds the authoritative teaching and example of Jesus disclosed in the gospel narratives. In word and deed, Jesus sets the standard for wholesome family life.

Although not an American, the venerable Mother Teresa of Calcutta spoke for many Christians in this country while also signaling the global relevance of the family values crisis:

> I think the world today is upside down, and is suffering so much, because there is so very little love in the homes and in family life. We have no time for our children, we have no time for each other, there is no time to enjoy each other. *If we could only bring back into our lives the life that Jesus, Mary, and Joseph lived in Nazareth,*

*if we could make our homes another Nazareth, I think peace and joy
would reign in the world* [emphasis added].[2]

While applauding the concern and appreciating the sentiment of
these poignant words, we must honestly face the fact that, upon close
examination, the Jesus of Nazareth portrayed in the gospels confronts us
with a much more complex and at times ambiguous family figure than is
often assumed. For starters, the son Jesus does not always enjoy a smooth
relationship, to put it mildly, with his mother and other kinfolk. The
Nazareth clan is more than a little perplexed about some of Jesus' behavior, and at times Jesus seems to care little about easing their minds.
Beyond that, the adult Jesus does not exactly settle down to a "normal"
family life: until the day of his violent death he remains single, never
courting, marrying, or siring children, as far as we know. Not quite the
pristine family portrait Norman Rockwell or Hallmark might design.
Ancient Nazareth of Galilee is a long way from contemporary New
York or Nashville or Nazareth, Pennsylvania, U.S.A. This chapter offers a
fresh and sometimes surprising glimpse into the gospels' family album.

Extending Kin

As a devout Jew, Jesus knew and respected the Mosaic law, not least the
bedrock stipulations of the Decalogue. Two incidents underscore his
affirmation of the commandment to honor one's parents. First, in a
debate with legal experts reported in Matthew and Mark, Jesus understands this mandate to include the duty of offspring to support both
father and mother financially in their advancing years and staunchly
resists any attempt to wiggle out of this responsibility, even by diverting
family funds to the temple treasury. Robbing parents to pay God effectively "voids" the divine word (Mark 7:9–12//Matt 15:3–6). Secondly, in
response to a wealthy visitor's query about obtaining eternal life presented in the Synoptic Gospels, Jesus begins by stressing the importance
of keeping the commandments, explicitly citing "honor your father and
mother" as a key example.[3] The man claims to have indeed been a faithful adherent to the law from childhood ("since my youth"), whereupon
Jesus proceeds to announce the next radical step he must take—giving

all his possessions to the poor. While ultimately Jesus demands more than honoring parents and more than the wealthy seeker is willing to give, he demands no less and never disputes or disparages the man's devotion to the law. This incident also reinforces the persisting duty of children to their parents beyond the chronological bounds of childhood ("since my youth," presumably continuing into adult life). The dignity of elders, including their right to command the honor and obedience of offspring throughout their lifetimes, comprised a core kinship value in the ancient Mediterranean world.[4]

So far, so good; nothing out of the ordinary here. Jesus publicly endorses the fifth commandment. But how does he live up to this rhetoric in his personal dealings with his own parents? As it happens, two additional gospel scenes depict decidedly strained relations between Jesus and his family. The first culminates in Jesus' radical neutralizing of the primacy of biological kinship ties; the second discloses his shameful "scandalizing" of hometown relatives by his audacious actions.

A House Divided

"The beginning of the good news of Jesus Christ" in Mark's gospel (1:1) does not commence with Jesus' birth or childhood, but rather with his adult baptism at the hands of John and attendant "adoption" by the heavenly voice and anointing with the Holy Spirit (1:9–11). Accordingly, we learn nothing about Jesus' upbringing or family origins except that he "came from Nazareth of Galilee" (1:9). After his baptism, Jesus embarks on an itinerant mission of teaching and healing throughout the region of Galilee. His closest companions are not his blood relatives but rather a motley crew of fishermen, a tax collector, and others—a dozen disciples in all—whom Jesus summons to follow and assist him (1:16–20; 2:13–14; 3:13–19). Seemingly independent of his own family, Jesus likewise calls his followers to leave their homes and businesses; Mark poignantly notes that James and John "immediately[5] . . . left their father Zebedee in the boat with the hired men" to join Jesus' movement (1:19–20).

While for the most part Jesus and his disciples remain on the road, they periodically sojourn in Simon and Andrew's house in the seaside city of Capernaum. This residence functions as a kind of base of operations for Jesus' mission.[6] When Mark reports that Jesus "went home" in the early stages of his Galilean ministry, the destination is this Capernaum headquarters, not his Nazareth home (1:29; 2:1; 3:19). It is ironic, then, that Mark's Jesus first encounters his natural family during one of these retreats to his adopted home in Capernaum. The situation is surprisingly tense. Jesus has not invited his relatives for a special family reunion. They have left Nazareth on their own initiative and come, unbidden, seeking Jesus. And they do not come in a welcoming, warm-hearted spirit. They come to "seize" or "lay hold of" Jesus, presumably to haul him back home to Nazareth where he belongs.[7]

Why such rough treatment? The family's intervention is triggered by disturbing rumors going around about Jesus. Word has it that he is behaving very strangely, very un-Nazareth-like, maybe even "losing his mind" (3:21). The term suggesting mental instability (*existēmi*) is often used in a transitive sense of "amazing" others, causing them to adjust their view of reality in light of some extraordinary phenomena. Thus far, Jesus has been doing some pretty incredible things, indeed provoking "amazement" throughout Galilee (1:27; 2:12). Such a dynamic reputation cuts two ways, however. On the one hand, needy persons hoping to benefit from Jesus' special power throng to him in adoration; on the other hand, though, serious questions arise concerning the source and ultimate effects of Jesus' abnormal energy. Is he dangerous, disoriented, deranged? He certainly seems detached from his humble Nazareth roots. What might he do next? Where might he go? How can he be controlled? This one who astounds and bewilders others might himself be addle-brained and befuddled, a threat to society.[8]

In any case, he clearly poses a threat to his own family's stability. Ancient eastern Mediterranean family values did not conform to the modern American dream. Sons were not encouraged to leave their one-horse towns, get ahead in the world, make a name for themselves, and "do their parents proud" in the global marketplace. Good sons knew their place, however lowly, and stayed there. Honor came from filling one's inherited role in the family, not from forsaking it or rising above it.[9] Whatever aid Jesus might be offering other families, he was shaming his own kin by his eccentric behavior outside the family circle. Whether he had lost his mind or not, he had definitely lost his way from his relatives' perspective, and they were aiming to bring him back.

Following Mark's technique of splicing one story into another,[10] a distinct but related conflict episode is sandwiched between the beginning of the scene focusing on Jesus' family and its conclusion. In this new incident, expert scholars (scribes) from Jerusalem further fuel suspicion concerning Jesus' sanity by attributing his ability to work wonders, especially his exorcising demons, to some perverted devilish dementia (3:22). In the face of this serious challenge to his honor and integrity, Jesus fires back with a vindicating point of logic: "If I myself am so demon driven, how could I or why would I drive demons out of others?" (3:23). He then adds an effective clarifying metaphor: "If a house is divided against itself, that house will not be able to stand" (3:25). It's hard to argue against such logic, and in fact the scribes don't even try. Point, game, and match to Jesus. But in the process, has he not ironically succeeded where the scribes failed—in undermining his own position? For is not his vivid picture of a "house divided" an apt portrayal of what is happening in his own household? His own family members are divided against him and seeking to divert his mission. How then can Jesus hope to build a stable kingdom when those closest to him are sabotaging his efforts?

As if anticipating such an objection, the narrative returns to Jesus' family crisis and finally offers Jesus' own views on the situation. As his family, now identified as his mother and siblings,[11] continue to press their claim upon him "outside" the Capernaum residence, Jesus proceeds to define what he means by family ties and commitments: "Who are my mother and my brothers? . . . Here are my mother and my brothers [referring to his followers inside the house]. Whoever does the will of God is my brother and sister and mother" (3:33–35). Jesus is not advocating some kind of self-sufficient, maverick existence apart from the nurturing bonds of kinship. He is still very much pro-family. But the family he envisages stretches beyond lines of blood and genealogy to encompass all who adhere to God's will. The biological family unit is superceded by what social scientists describe as a "fictive" or "pseudo" kinship network.[12] In Jesus' terms, the native household of his birth and rearing in Nazareth has been replaced by the spiritual community of faith and discipleship, the people of God. He is not rejecting his natural family—they are welcome to join his movement of doing God's will—but he is "relativizing" the primacy of their claims upon his life. It is lamentable and tragic if they remain divided against Jesus and his mission, but it is not fatal. The household of God will "stand" firm on the faithful foundation of Jesus and his followers, dedicated to fulfilling God's purpose.

Mark's account of Jesus' domestic trials may offer special encouragement to readers, then and now, who suffer some type of familial ridicule—and even rejection in extreme cases—for their commitment to Christ and the Christian faith.[13] Not all believers, however, take comfort in Mark's report that Jesus' relatives attempted to "restrain" him for alleged insanity. Such information could prove embarrassing to the Christian cause. Matthew and Luke, for example, conveniently omit this scene from their narratives. A later New Testament writing conveys a strict requirement that a Christian bishop "must manage his own household well, keeping his children submissive and respectful in every way—for if someone does not know how to manage his own household, how can he take care of God's church?" (1 Tim 3:4–5). One wonders what this author might have thought of Mark's frank testimony to "unmanageable" strife in the family of Jesus. On these terms, could Jesus himself have qualified as bishop?[14]

A Homecoming Disaster

Jesus eventually does return home to Nazareth in Mark's gospel, but he does so on his own terms and timetable after further ministry around the Sea of Galilee. Still, he has obviously not completely abandoned his native kinfolk and even appears to be reaching out to them. But they are not in a receptive mood. This is not a happy homecoming; there is no tickertape parade. Nonetheless, Jesus makes hometown headlines with his remarkable words and mighty deeds in the neighborhood synagogue; in fact, he downright "astounds" many (6:1–2). But remember, amazement is not necessarily a positive reaction. It can reflect a judgmental "Whoa!"—"Can you believe he said and did that! Who does he think he is?"—as much as an enthusiastic "Wow!"—"Have you ever heard and seen anything so wonderful? Who is this guy?" The hometown buzz about Jesus' visit likely includes both responses, but in Mark's account the former, negative opinion predominates.

What is Nazareth's problem with Jesus? Far from being a favorite son, as we might imagine, Jesus comes across as a fickle son who has betrayed his heritage and village: "'Where did this man get all this? What is this wisdom that has been given to him? What deeds of power are being done by his hands! Is not this the carpenter, the son of Mary and brother of James and Joses and Judas and Simon, and are not his sisters here with us?' And they took offense at him" (6:2–3). While Hollywood and Madison Avenue might love the story of the small-town carpenter who becomes a renowned sage and miracle worker, ancient Nazareth is not so pleased. Jesus' "hands" are made for working with wood,[15] not for working wonders, and his identity is that of son and brother within a humble local family, not some sort of roving, independent philosopher or prophet. In the eyes of his relatives and neighbors, Jesus is acting "above his raising," beyond his ascribed station in life. This is not the path to becoming a hometown hero or celebrity in Nazareth; quite the contrary, the charismatic Jesus has become a shameful "scandal"[16] within his own native neighborhood—someone who no longer "fits in," who does not conform to traditional community norms.

Realizing his alien status in his home village, Mark's Jesus justifies his experience by appealing to the pattern of rejected prophets in Israel's history: "Prophets are not without honor, except in their hometown, and among their own kin, and in their own house" (6:4). This was certainly true of Elijah, Elisha, Amos, Jeremiah, and other prophets in the Jewish Scriptures. By definition, prophets were nonconformists who rankled the status quo in God's name; they valued the honor ascribed by God at the expense of conventional grants of social favor. However, while a certain amount of public resistance validates Jesus' role as a true prophet of God, does this rejection have to extend to his own family? After all, Samuel's mother fully supported his vocation, and Isaiah's wife and children were partners in his prophetic mission. Matthew again softens Mark's emphasis on Jesus' family struggles by eliminating the reference to prophets' dishonor "among their own kin," but Matthew cannot deny altogether the trouble that prophets like Jesus have "in their own house" (13:57). If Jesus had run for office, he would not have even carried his home district.

Lest we think that Jesus accepts his persona non grata status in Nazareth with calm equanimity or, worse, smug superiority, Mark recounts that Jesus is "amazed at their unbelief," which in turn throttles his ability to perform good deeds beyond aiding a few sick folk (6:5–6). This, however, is more frustration than Matthew can handle when it comes to Jesus. For Matthew, like many Christians since, Jesus must appear less vulnerable, more in control of the situation. So he tidies up Mark's account by simply reporting the unbelief in Nazareth without commenting on Jesus' reaction to it and by stressing that Jesus chose not to, rather than could not, work many wonders there.[17] This dispassionate, deliberative Jesus may seem more noble, more Lord-like, more religiously "orthodox," but Mark's candid admission of how Jesus is distressed and debilitated by his family's opposition must not be glossed over or explained away. It stands as a critical piece of canonical testimony concerning Jesus' personal conduct.

Missing Son

Matthew and Luke both notably expand Mark's gospel to include accounts of Jesus' birth and infancy in their opening two chapters. It is from these materials that Christians derive the famous Christmas stories and nativity scenes. Luke's account goes further than Matthew's in depicting Jesus' developing relationship with his parents, extending even into adolescence. The Lukan Jesus is reared in a traditional Jewish home, circumcised on the eighth day, and consecrated by his parents in the temple as a God-given firstborn son. Everything unfolds precisely "according to the law of Moses,"[18] with the implication that this child will grow up to be a law-abiding, God-fearing, and parent-honoring young man.

However, the elderly Simeon, who presides over the baby's dedication, charts a future of dramatic ups and downs for Jesus, sure both to impress and distress his mother and father. He directs a particularly ominous prophecy toward Mary: because of the trouble destined to surround Jesus, Simeon warns her, "a sword will pierce your own soul too" (2:34–35). While Simeon provides only a bare outline of Jesus' family trials, two scenes early on in Luke begin to fill in the gaps. The very next scene, offering the canonical gospels' sole glimpse into Jesus' youth,[19] discloses the anguish of Jesus' parents over their missing son, whom they finally find in the Jerusalem temple. The second episode, featuring Jesus' inaugural public act of ministry, exposes the anger of Jesus' hometown neighbors and relatives over his conduct in the Nazareth synagogue, a substantial revision of Mark's account.

Parental Anguish in Jerusalem

One of the most popular movies of the 1990s, although a comedy, trades on every parent's worst nightmare. *Home Alone* features the resourceful antics of a young boy inadvertently left at home by himself while his family heads overseas on vacation. While the child proves to be quite the trooper—even in the face of menacing, albeit bungling, burglars—the parents become apoplectic when they realize their son is missing. Any parent who has shopped with a young child in a crowded mall knows the feeling well.

The basic scenario recalls the incident involving the twelve-year-old Jesus at the end of Luke 2.[20] While this story is often conceived as a wonderful tale about Jesus as a precocious child phenomenon, dazzling the scholars and all who hear him in the temple, this is far from the way Jesus' parents see the situation. When they finally locate him after a three-day search, their first response is not—"We didn't realize how talented you were; everyone is raving about you in the temple; you've done us proud!"—but rather, "Child, why have you treated us like this? Look, your father and I have been searching for you in great anxiety" (2:48). The term expressing their level of anxiety is a strong one, used elsewhere in Luke-Acts for the torments of fiery punishment and sorrows of a final farewell.[21] In effect, Jesus' parents are asking their son: "Why have you just put us through three days of hell, worrying whether we would ever see you again?"

Now it might be thought that Mary and Joseph are overreacting here, as parents sometimes do under stress, or overcompensating for their own feelings of fear and guilt. Are they blaming the victim here to mitigate their own fault? Shouldn't they have kept a better eye on Jesus? Such questions, however plausible to modern perceptions, have no place within the logic of Luke's story. In no sense are Jesus' parents portrayed as neglecting or abandoning their son. Returning home from the Passover festival in Jerusalem, they "assume" that Jesus is among the caravan of trusted "relatives and friends"—a perfectly proper inference

within a conventional, Mediterranean extended-family structure. Mary
and Joseph do not leave or lose Jesus; rather Jesus deliberately "stayed
behind in Jerusalem." Instead of dutifully remaining "in the group of
travelers . . . among their relatives and friends"—that is, within his natural kinship network—Jesus reorients himself "in the temple . . . among
the teachers" (2:43–46).

Upon discovering the missing Jesus, Mary takes the lead in voicing
parental frustration—a predictable move given both her prominence in
Luke's infancy stories and a Mediterranean mother's primary bond with
her male children, especially the firstborn.[22] She plays out the typical
part of the "anxious mother" (*anxia mater*).[23] The related role of "ambitious mother," anxious for her son's success in the public arena, is not
featured here.[24] She does not regard Jesus' exceptional performance in
the temple as a cause for family pride. Quite the contrary, her opening
challenge—"Child, why have you done this to us?"—interprets Jesus'
actions as a direct affront to parental honor and authority. The query is
cast in formulaic terms reminiscent of indignant reactions to incredulous
behavior in well-known biblical narratives, frequently involving some
breach of traditional family values. For example, at the end of all three
Genesis stories in which Abraham or Isaac deny their wives and abandon
them to foreign harems, the kings reproach the gutless husbands, ex-
claiming, "What have you done to me?," when they finally learn the
truth.[25] The fullest retort is directed by Abimelech to Abraham. With
modest paraphrasing of Abimelech's words, we can capture the poignancy
of Mary's disappointment in Jesus: "Child, what on earth have you done
to us? How have we failed you that you have brought such shame on our
family? You have done something to me a young son should never do to
his mother. What were you thinking when you left us the way you
did!"[26]

While Mary does all the talking, she makes a point of Joseph's sharing
her distress: "Look, your father and I have been searching for you" (2:48).
This paternal emphasis is important for two reasons: (1) what it suggests
further about the family crisis triggered by Jesus, and (2) how it sets the
stage for Jesus' response. First, in a patriarchal society, a father's anxiety
over his absent son would have reached beyond basic concern for the
son's welfare to include the father's own sense of social shame stemming
from his inability to control a member of his household.[27] A missing son

was implicitly a wayward son; a displaced son meant a disgraced father. Secondly, Jesus' reply to his distraught parents, far from constituting an apology, amounts to a defense of his unbroken submission, as he sees it, to necessary and proper paternal authority: "Why were you searching for me? Did you not know that I must be in/about my Father's . . ." (2:49). Whether we fill in the ellipsis with "house" or "business" or "interests" or some combination of these ideas,[28] Jesus clearly affirms that he is right where he should be, physically and socially, in relation to his father. Of course, it is equally clear to readers of Luke that the father Jesus has in mind is not Joseph, but God. Jesus' ascribed status as "Son of the Most High God" has been firmly established by divinely appointed angels and Spirit-anointed prophets (1:32, 35, 76). Now Jesus himself, at twelve years of age, first expresses his own self-understanding as Son of God. And in so doing, rather than setting his parents at ease, Jesus only compounds their confusion ("they did not understand what he said to them," 2:50) and cements his stronger tie, his higher loyalty, to another family, the very household of God.

This reconfiguration of family values—driving a wedge between earthly and heavenly, natural and fictive, exclusive and inclusive households—becomes a major theme in Luke's gospel, confirmed by several of Jesus' sayings. In addition to statements embracing all who keep God's word as true kinfolk (8:19–21; 11:27–28), as we found in Mark, Luke's Jesus lays down the shocking mandate to "hate father and mother"— even to the point of leaving a dead father to bury himself!—as a condition for discipleship (9:57–62; 14:25).[29] Also, no sooner does the rich ruler affirm his faithfulness to the commandment regarding honoring father and mother "since my youth," than Jesus sends him away and commends to Peter the superior benefits of leaving "house or wife or brothers or parents or children for the sake of the kingdom of God"[30]— precisely what Jesus himself had done in his youth.

Although this home-leaving, parent-forsaking trend is prominent in Luke, it is not absolute. In fact, the story of the twelve-year-old Jesus ends with a curious tension and surprising twist: after perplexing his parents with strange talk of devotion to another "father," the young Jesus proceeds to go back home to Nazareth "with them" and be "obedient to them" (2:51). The prodigal son returns home.[31] Having made his point about higher and wider family loyalties, Jesus reinforces humbler and narrower ties with his natural kin. The households of God and Joseph can be mutually supportive. Nonetheless, the young Jesus has established a clear hierarchy between the two family networks, should push come to shove. While his willing return home "softens," as one commentator puts it,[32] his callous treatment of his parents in the temple, it does not nullify it. Jesus retains his independence: he chooses to return home (his parents do not forcibly drag him back) just as he had chosen to leave. At no point does he apologize for any distress he might have caused or neutralize his top-priority commitment to his heavenly Father's business.[33]

We might be tempted to gloss over Luke's tale surrounding the twelve-year-old Jesus, given its unique place within the New Testament and its affinity with later, fanciful legends about Jesus' childhood in the apocryphal "Infancy" gospels.[34] The fact is, we know next to nothing about Jesus' youth. Nevertheless, Luke's story aptly presages the kind of adult Jesus will become and the kind of family values he will espouse—supporting the sacred command to honor one's natural father and mother, yet subordinating this duty to the larger claims of the spiritual household of God.

Familial Anger in Nazareth

From the single snapshot of Jesus' youth at age twelve, Luke fast-forwards his account to Jesus' adulthood at "about thirty years old when he began his work" (3:23). Three examples at the outset of Jesus' public ministry further accentuate his divine sonship and separation from his earthly father. At his baptism, Jesus' favored position as God's beloved son is certified directly by the heavenly Father's own voice. The young Jesus' affiliation with "my Father" in the Jerusalem temple is now answered by the Father's affirmation of "my Son" at the Jordan River (3:21–22). In the genealogy that immediately follows, Jesus' ancestry is traced backward (unlike in Matthew) from his present status as "son of Joseph"—seemingly juxtaposing his earthly heritage with his heavenly adoption. However, Luke interjects a provocative little gloss that Joseph's paternity was merely "supposed," not substantiated (3:23). Still, Joseph's lineage is useful, but not chiefly as a link to David and Abraham (as in Matthew); rather, the line stretches back as far as it can go to "son of Adam, son of God" (3:38). Of course, poor Joseph is thereby rendered irrelevant—you could start with any "Joe" and get back to the first human, and from there to God. Luke stresses Jesus' humanity, to be sure, but in more universal than particular terms. Jesus is "Son of Everyman" more than "son of Joseph," and "Son of God" above all else.

Nonetheless, Jesus cannot quite shake the "son of Joseph" tag. In Luke's expanded and relocated version of Jesus' ministry in Nazareth,[35] the hometown synagogue audience responds to Jesus' "amazing" message (his first public words since addressing his parents in the temple) with an incredulous query: "Is not this Joseph's son?" (4:22). The form of the question suggests cognitive dissonance, cultural disorientation. The idea is not—"There's Joseph's boy for you, a real chip off the old block"—but quite the contrary: "Is that any way for a son of Joseph to talk? Who does he think he is, coming on like an authoritative scribe ('Today this scripture has been fulfilled in your hearing,' 4:21) or charismatic prophet ('The Spirit of the Lord is upon me,' 4:18)? Has he forgotten who he is, where he came from?"

Is not this Joseph's son? No, it really isn't—that's the whole point! What Jesus is saying is perfectly acceptable for God's beloved son and anointed messenger. The problem with local kin (parents included) is that they do not fully apprehend Jesus' true vocation and social location. That Jesus perceives such resistance becomes evident in his reminder of the dishonorable reception that prophets typically experience in their hometowns (no home-field advantage in this game). Like Elijah and Elisha in particular, Jesus implicitly extends his missionary vision beyond local borders to incorporate needy and receptive outsiders. His household constitutes the entire spectrum of God's people—Jew and Gentile, male and female, rich and poor, who heed the prophetic word.[36] For this inclusive vision, the xenophobic folk of Nazareth try to hurl their rebellious native son off the cliff at the edge of town (4:29–30). Clearly, Jesus no longer has a place in his home community.

Peeking ahead into Luke's second volume, the book of Acts, we notice from the outset that Jesus' mother and brothers are numbered among the earliest Christian congregants in Jerusalem (1:14). Obviously, they come to see Jesus in a new light after his crucifixion and resurrection. Later in the same book, one of Jesus' brothers, James, emerges as a principal leader in the Jerusalem church. The letters of Paul confirm this James as one of the "pillar apostles," deriving from his privileged experience of witnessing the risen Jesus.[37] Still, however sympathetic to his mission Jesus' relatives might have become after his death, it is hard to ignore the serious confusion and conflict which simmers within Jesus' family during his lifetime. And it is hard to lay all the blame for this tension on Jesus' recalcitrant parents and siblings. Jesus himself plays a key part,[38] stubbornly affirming his primary tie to the fictive household of all who heed God's word. In Luke's narrative, while he never repudiates his natural kin, he does not bend over backwards to restore family harmony when sparks fly. In this sense, Jesus does "not come to bring peace . . . but rather division"—even within one's own household![39]

Demanding Mother

From the opening words of John's gospel, it is obvious that we have entered a whole new thought-world pertaining to Jesus' origins. Mundane discussions of Jesus' genealogy, conception (even virginal conception), parents, and birthplace give way to cosmic visions of Jesus' eternal preexistence and oneness with God the Father and Creator of the universe. He thus "came down from heaven" (6:33, 38, 41, 50) to take on human flesh and reveal God's glory on earth.

The tradition of Jesus' upbringing by Mary and Joseph in Nazareth is known to the Johannine writer but is largely used as a foil for answering objections concerning Jesus' divine status and heavenly origins. Upon hearing Philip's announcement that "Jesus son of Joseph from Nazareth" fulfills Israel's prophetic hopes, Nathanael sardonically quips, "Can anything good come out of Nazareth?" (1:45). No one looked to tiny, backwater Nazareth for God's anointed leader. However, when Nathanael meets Jesus for himself, he revises his opinion: "Rabbi, you are the Son of God! You are the King of Israel!" (1:49) Through this confession, Joseph's parentage and Nazareth's heritage are effectively neutralized. What matters is Jesus' filial relationship to God and rulership of all Israel. Joseph and Nazareth had nothing to do with making Jesus who he is; indeed, he is God's son and Israel's king in spite of his humble origins. Later in the fourth gospel, certain "Jews" challenge Jesus' claim of heavenly descent because, as they see it: "Is not this Jesus, the son of Joseph, whose father and mother we know?" (6:42). Again, Jesus' lowly earthly background seems to betray his lofty heavenly heritage. But no matter: Jesus wastes no time defending his human pedigree but simply reasserts his heaven-sent status as a transparent truth revealed by God to all who believe (6:43–47).

While Jesus' family ties, especially with Joseph, are downplayed in John, there are two interesting encounters between Jesus and his mother in very different contexts. The first, associated with Jesus' initial miraculous "sign," is set at a wedding feast in Cana of Galilee. The second, coming in Jesus' final "hour," takes place at a political execution on Golgotha outside Jerusalem. The first is a joyous celebration; the second, a sorrowful crucifixion. Both scenes are unique in the gospel tradition and heavily freighted with Johannine language and symbols. But they bear poignant witness in the history of interpretation to a trajectory of improving relations between Jesus and his earthly family, especially his mother Mary. Luke's gospel already showed some signs of rehabilitating Mary's image, with its early emphasis on her obedience to God's word, her Spirit-inspired prophecy, and her willingness to "ponder in her heart" confusing messages about the young Jesus' destiny (Luke 1:26–56; 2:19, 34–35, 51). The fourth gospel makes a further move by demonstrating Mary's continuing faithfulness to the adult Jesus' mission, even unto death.

A Wedding Festival

Jesus' first public act of ministry in John takes place in Cana at a wedding to which he and his disciples had been invited. The proximity of this Galilean village to Nazareth and the presence of Jesus' mother argue that this is a celebration of family and friends. Jesus is no mere casual observer here but part of the close-knit network of bride, groom, and guests. He and his mother are socially invested in the success of the occasion as a point of honor. At the risk of deep shame and embarrassment, everything must be in order, every expectation met.[40] As it happens, a serious shortage of wine threatening to ruin the event forms the backdrop for the exchange between Jesus and Mary.[41]

Jesus' mother crisply informs him of the problem—"They have no wine"—implying Jesus' obligation, as a member of the family, to do something to correct the deficiency. Jesus responds, however, with something less than dutiful compliance: "Woman, what concern is that to you and to me? My hour has not yet come" (2:3–4). To modern ears, this sounds downright rude. The more literal—"What to me and to you, woman?"—too easily translates into a kind of crude, back-street lingo: "What's it to you, lady? This is none of your business." Certainly, this is no way to talk to mom; in fact, this rough paraphrase does not capture Jesus' intent. "Woman" is a perfectly polite form of address in the fourth gospel, suitable even for tender moments as with Jesus' mother at the cross and Mary Magdalene at the tomb (19:26; 20:15).[42] As for the substance of Jesus' reply at the wedding, he definitely puts his mother in her place. She is not to presume on his work or his time: his duty and destiny ("my hour") are set by his heavenly Father.[43] Thus Jesus' words to Mary in John 2 are similar in effect to what we found in Luke 2: he must be about his Father's business, not hers. But unlike in Luke, Jesus' mother in John is not taken by surprise at Jesus' answer nor compelled to mull over the matter in her heart. Without skipping a beat, she orders the servants, "Do whatever he tells you" (2:5). This terse statement achieves two purposes. On the one hand, it discloses Mary's recognition of Jesus' independence and the importance of following his wishes; she is thus a model disciple.[44] On the other hand, Mary's message to the servants provides an opening for Jesus to settle the wine crisis on his own terms— which is precisely what he does! At the end of the day Mary and Jesus both get what they (and the thirsty guests) want and work together to avert a family fiasco.

As a fitting conclusion to these joyous events, John points out that, after the wedding, Jesus "went down to Capernaum with his mother, his brothers, and his disciples; and they remained there a few days" (2:12). Quite the opposite of the Capernaum incident in Mark, which depicted sharp division between Jesus and his followers, on the one side, and his mother and siblings, on the other side, here all parties seem joined together as one big happy family. While for the most part the Johannine Jesus "came unto his own, and his own people did not accept him" (1:12), this pattern of rejection was not pervasive in his immediate family. Later, to be sure, we learn that "not even his brothers believed in him" (7:5), but such doubt never extends to his mother. She remains faithful until the end.

Before proceeding to the farewell scene between Jesus and his mother in John, this is an appropriate place to consider briefly Jesus' involvement with the institution of marriage. A fuller discussion is precluded by the lack of evidence. The gospels consistently assume that Jesus never married. The closest he gets to a wedding is the one he winds up catering in Cana,[45] and while he interacts with a number of individual men and women, he directly deals with a married couple in only one incident throughout the gospels.[46] Although Jesus certainly approves of the Cana nuptials, and elsewhere in his teaching unequivocally affirms the sanctity of marriage and takes a hard line against divorce,[47] he himself never takes a wife as far as we know.[48] And so there is nothing for us to examine regarding Jesus' habits as a husband or father. Of course, this personal choice not to marry demands an explanation. It seems to have something to do with Jesus' sense of urgency about the imminent arrival of the kingdom of God (there is no time for wedding plans and settling down with wife and children),[49] as well as his inclusive vision of the fictive household of God discussed above. Just as disciples might be forced to forsake father and mother for the higher and wider calling of God's royal family, so they might be compelled to leave spouse and children[50]— or to never marry and start a family in the first place. Whatever family might be left behind for the sake of God's kingdom will be recompensed "a hundredfold" both in this life and in the age to come (Matt 19:29–30//Mark 10:29–30//Luke 18:28–30). Besides, remaining unmarried in this life gives the faithful a jump on the soon coming heavenly era in which, like the angels, "they neither marry nor are given in marriage" (Matt 22:23–33//Mark 12:18–27//Luke 20:27–40).

Other factors no doubt play a part in Jesus' decision to remain single, such as his personal views on sexuality and the roles of women. A fuller assessment of his identity as a celibate male awaits our analysis of Jesus' treatment of his own body (chapter 4).

A Touching Farewell

As Jesus' mother was there with her son at the beginning of his ministry, so too at the end of his life. The "hour" of destiny forecast by Jesus has finally arrived, as he "finishes" his work on a Roman cross. Where the Synoptic Gospels stress that Jesus dies alone and forsaken by family and friends (and even by God in Matthew and Mark), John describes the abiding presence of certain women, including Jesus' mother and the

beloved disciple at the base of the cross.[51] Adding further pathos to the
scene, John also discloses a moving final message which Jesus conveys
to his mother and closest disciple standing side-by-side at his feet:
"Woman, here is your son. . . . Here is your mother" (19:27).

In a rush to explore the symbolic significance of this scene, scholars
often trivialize its most obvious, pragmatic dimension, which is quite
touching in its own way. The Johannine writer loves double meanings—
physical/spiritual, earthly/heavenly, human/divine;[52] a full understanding
of the fourth gospel demands careful attention to both levels. In addition
to their symbolic functions (see below), Jesus' mother and the beloved
disciple also represent individual human beings who are particularly
close to Jesus and thus face a terrible loss at his death, both materially
and emotionally. Just as Jesus addressed a tangible, material shortage at
the first family affair involving his mother (however much the new wine
might signify "new life" from the "true vine," it also served to satisfy the
palates and spirits of the wedding guests), so in his final moments, Jesus
responds to another physical and familial loss. By entrusting his cherished mother and disciple to each other's care, Jesus helps them deal with
their immediate anguish over his tortured body and with their precarious
future without his presence and support. The fact that Jesus has other
brothers to watch over Mary is beside the point.[53] As the (eldest?) son of
a widowed mother (the most likely inference from John's total silence
about Mary's husband), Jesus has special responsibility for Mary's welfare; and, in any case, his brothers' abandonment of Jesus (7:5) raises
questions about their loyalty and reliability. Much more than the synoptic tradition, the fourth gospel ultimately presents Jesus as a model of
filial devotion. The messier family portrait of the other gospels has its
own hard-edged, realistic appeal, but one cannot help being moved by
John's tender parting scene between Jesus and his mother.

Jesus' formation of a new family, as it were, at the foot of the cross,
also begs for a broader symbolic explanation. We have here John's
unique illustration of Jesus' fictive household. Jesus' true kin, his true
mother and brother, encompass all who recognize the revelation of God
the Father through his "uplifted" (exalted/crucified) Son—including past
believers in Jesus from the outset of his earthly ministry (like his mother)
and present faithful members of the Johannine community (represented
by the beloved disciple).[54] Together, these followers comprise the one

genuine family of faith—Jesus' "own" who receive him and all related to him as their "own." The beloved disciple's reception of Jesus' mother "into his own home" (*eis ta idia,* 19:27) signifies the loving fellowship of all children "born of God," in contrast to those who spurned Jesus when he first came "unto his own [people]" (*eis ta idia*), born of flesh and blood and human will (1:11–13).[55]

While the gospels offer their own distinctive portraits of Jesus' relations with his biological family, evincing a broad tendency to project a more congenial image as the tradition develops, nonetheless, there is overall agreement that Jesus' principal family values focus on welcoming, nurturing, and guiding all who join him in seeking to do the will of God on earth as it is done in heaven. All who pray and work for the coming of God the Father's kingdom are Jesus' mother and brothers and sisters.[56] Eschatology (the climactic establishment of God's royal and redemptive household) trumps biology. The living water of spiritual rebirth (to use Johannine language)[57] is thicker than the limited blood of natural generation.

Conclusion

In place of a bland, one-dimensional portrait of Jesus' enacted family values, the gospels offer a more textured, multifaceted presentation. Mark candidly exposes the adult Jesus' strained relations with his mother, siblings, and other Nazareth kinfolk, sparked largely by their consternation over his emerging popularity as a teacher of wisdom and worker of miracles. Such activity, while attractive to his followers, is a source of considerable alarm (has he gone mad?) and resentment (who does he think he is?) for his relatives flabbergasted by Jesus' public deviation from his humble Nazareth roots. As a result, Jesus expands his family circle beyond biological boundaries, embracing all who seek to do God's will as his true, spiritual kin, at the same time he finds his ministry curtailed and power diminished by his hometown's unbelief.

While Matthew and Luke mitigate the tension somewhat between Jesus and his family by dropping the matter of Jesus' alleged insanity, Luke also exacerbates the conflict in other ways. Rocky relations with distraught parents are projected back into Jesus' adolescence in the famous disputation scene with the temple scholars. Although the episode ends with Jesus' submissive return home to Nazareth, it establishes a clear line of demarcation between the young Jesus and his mother and father, long before Jesus leaves home for good to pursue his itinerant mission. From age twelve Jesus asserts in no uncertain terms (although his parents are far from certain about what he means) that he "must" attend to family "business" dictated by an exalted "Father," apart from Mary and Joseph's knowledge or consent.

Following Jesus' baptism and anointing with the Spirit around age thirty, familial misunderstanding, frustration, and resentment escalate into homicidal rage, as the Nazareth assembly attempts to hurl their pretentious native son—this "son of Joseph" daring to assume a prophetic-messianic identity and to promote an inclusive mission beyond ethnocentric borders—off the village cliff. Rather than lingering in an effort to defend himself or to endure the violence against him, Jesus escapes his hometown, "pass[ing] on his way," never to return again.

The Gospel of John continues to emphasize the primacy of Jesus' commitment to his heavenly Father's work and schedule over his earthly parents' wishes and interests, although in the wedding incident at Cana, Jesus and his mother eventually collaborate in solving a beverage crisis and salvaging the family's honor. And whatever tensions persist between Jesus and his "own" over the course of his public ministry, at the end of his life, his mother is there—at the foot of the cross—and in turn Jesus makes arrangements for her care and comfort in the home of the beloved disciple. Jesus thus fulfills his duty, as best he can under the tragic circumstances, to honor and provide for his mother in her advancing years.

NOTES

1. See Exod 20:12, 14, 17, and Deut 5:16, 18, 21.

2. I owe this particular citation to Dr. Douglas Aldrich, presented in a sermon at First Baptist Church, Monroe, N.C., and confirmed in correspondence (5 July 2000). In another place, Mother Teresa similarly states: "There is so much suffering all over the world. . . . We pray to the Holy Family (Mary, Joseph, and Jesus) for our family. We say: Heavenly Father, You have given us a model of life in the Holy Family of Nazareth. Help us, O loving Father, to make our family

another Nazareth where love, peace, and joy reign" (Mother Teresa, *A Simple Path* [compiled by Lucinda Vardey; New York: Ballantine, 1995], 20).

3. In a list of five commandments from the second half of the Decalogue, Jesus cites "honor your father and mother" last (because of its importance?) in the synoptic tradition (Mark 10:19//Matt 19:18–19//Luke 18:20).

4. A standard component of household codes, e.g., "Do not speak harshly to an older man, but speak to him as a father" (1 Tim 5:1); "you who are younger must accept the authority of those who are older [elders]" (1 Pet 5:5).

5. *Euthys* ("immediately," "as soon as," "now") is a favorite term of Mark's, conveying the strong sense of urgency with which Jesus carries out his mission. "The time is fulfilled, and the kingdom of God is at hand" (1:15); thus, there is no time to waste.

6. The shared tradition between Matthew and Luke doesn't even allow Jesus a temporary residence: "Foxes have holes, and birds of the air have nests; but the Son of Man has nowhere to lay his head" (Luke 9:58//Matt 8:20). See the discussion of this passage in chapter 5.

7. The verb used here, *krateo,* can carry the strong connotation of "arrest by force," as in the case of the authorities arresting Jesus before his trial and crucifixion (see Mark 12:12; 14:1, 44, 46, 49).

8. In other words, the one who confounds others (transitive use of *existemi*) may in turn be thought to "be confounded, confused" (intransitive use of *existemi,* as Mark 3:21) by virtue of his strange, extraordinary (as in "out of the ordinary") behavior.

9. In the highly stratified Greco-Roman world, a premium was placed on knowing and fulfilling one's place in the hierarchy in order to maintain social stability. Reflecting acceptance of this established pecking order, notice the centurion's announcement to Jesus: "For I also am a man set under authority, with soldiers under me" (Luke 7:8//Matt 8:9); and Paul's advice not to rock the social boat: "Let each of you remain in the condition [race and class] in which you were called" (1 Cor 7:20; cf. 7:17–24). For a discussion of the ancient Mediterranean world as a "limited-good, closed society with its contentment and status-maintenance orientation," see Malina, *The New Testament World,* 90–116 (citation from p. 105); K. C. Hanson and Douglas E. Oakman, *Palestine in the Time of Jesus: Social Structures and Social Conflicts* (Minneapolis, Minn.: Fortress, 1998), 70–72; Richard L. Rohrbaugh, "The Pre-Industrial City," in *The Social Sciences and New Testament Interpretation* (ed. R. L. Rohrbaugh; Peabody, Mass.: Hendrickson, 1996), 109–12.

10. See Mark Alan Powell, *Fortress Introduction to the Gospels,* 42; Luke Timothy Johnson, *The Writings of the New Testament: An Interpretation* (rev. ed.; Minneapolis, Minn.: Fortress, 1999), 162–64.

11. No mention is made of Jesus' father. Is he perhaps dead (leaving Jesus' mother a widow) or about other business back home or elsewhere? Also some early manuscripts lack an explicit reference to Jesus' "sisters" in 3:32. Mark 6:3

confirms that Jesus has sisters, but we cannot be certain that they accompanied their mother and brothers on this occasion.

12. See Julian Pitt-Rivers, "Pseudo-Kinship," in *The International Encyclopedia of the Social Sciences* (New York: Free Press, 1968), 408–13; Hanson and Oakman, *Palestine in the Time of Jesus,* 80–82, 126–28. The term "surrogate family" conveys the same idea; cf. Bruce J. Malina and Richard L. Rohrbaugh, *Social-Science Commentary on the Synoptic Gospels* (Minneapolis, Minn.: Fortress, 1992), 201–2.

13. Compare Pheme Perkins, "The Gospel of Mark," in *The New Interpreter's Bible,* vol. 7 (Nashville, Tenn.: Abingdon, 1995), 566–67.

14. Although we are not concerned primarily with issues of historicity, Mark's candid account of Jesus' family conflicts lays strong claim to being authentic precisely because of its potential for embarrassment. What would the writer of Mark gain from "inventing" a story about Jesus' alleged lunacy? On the criterion of embarrassment or "dissimilarity" in historical Jesus studies, see Bart D. Ehrman, *Jesus: Apocalyptic Prophet of the New Millenium,* 91–94; Mark Allan Powell, *Jesus as a Figure in History: How Modern Historians View the Man from Galilee* (Louisville, Ky.: Westminster/John Knox, 1998), 47–48.

15. Generally a *tektōn* designated any artisan skilled at handcrafting with wood, metal, or stone. On Jesus' profession as "woodworker," see John P. Meier, *A Marginal Jew: Rethinking the Historical Jesus,* vol. 1 (Anchor Bible Reference Library; New York: Doubleday, 1991), 280–85.

16. "They took offense at him" (6:3) could literally be rendered, "They were scandalized (*skandalizō*) by him."

17. "And he *could do no deed* of power there, except that he laid his hands on a few sick people and cured them. And *he was amazed* at their unbelief" (Mark 6:5–6a).

"And he *did not do many deeds* of power there, because of their unbelief" (Matt 13:58).

18. Four times in a short space, Luke explicitly stresses strict compliance with the Law (2:22, 23, 24, 27; cf. 2:39, "When they had finished everything required by the law of the Lord . . .").

19. The so-called "apocryphal" gospels supply numerous tales from Jesus' childhood, including a close parallel to Luke's account of the twelve-year-old Jesus in the temple in *Infancy Gospel of Thomas* 19.

20. I owe the *Home Alone* illustration to a conversation with Professor Amy-Jill Levine.

21. *Odynaomai,* used exclusively by Luke in the New Testament. Compare Luke 16:24—"He [the rich man] called out, 'Father Abraham, have mercy on me, and send Lazarus to dip the tip of his finger in water and cool my tongue; for *I am in agony* (*odynōmai*) in these flames'"; and Acts 20:37–38, "There was much weeping among them all; they embraced Paul and kissed him, *grieving* (*odynōmenoi*) especially because of what he had said, that they would not see him again."

22. See Sir 3:2, "For the Lord honored the father above the children, and he confirmed the right of the mother over her sons" (cf. 3:2–16); and Sir 4:10, "Be like a father to orphans, and instead of a husband to their mother; you will then be like a son of the Most High, and he will love you more than does your mother." Bruce J. Malina, *Windows on the World of Jesus: Time Travel to Ancient Judea* (Louisville, Ky.: Westminster/John Knox, 1993), 82–84; Malina, "Mary— Mediterranean Woman: Mother and Son," *Biblical Theology Bulletin* 20 (1990): 54–64; Malina and Rohrbaugh, *Social-Science Commentary on the Gospel of John* (Minneapolis, Minn.: Fortress, 1998), 272–73. For a perspective drawing on the insights of modern psychology, see Miller, *Jesus at Thirty,* 47–54.

23. See Suzanne Dixon, *The Roman Mother* (London: Croom Helm, 1988), 193–99.

24. Exemplified in the request of Mrs. Zebedee that Jesus grant her sons (James and John) the top positions in the kingdom at his right and left hand (Matt 20:20–28); cf. Malina, *Windows,* 85–87.

25. See Gen 12:10–20; 20:1–18; 26:1–11; Rudolf Pesch, "'Kind, warum hast du so an uns getan?' (Lk 2:48)," *Biblische Zeitschrift* 12 (1968): 245–48.

26. See Gen 20:9–10.

27. Note again the standard household code incumbent upon bishops and deacons and, indeed, upon any pious father in the early church: "He must manage his own household well, keeping his children submissive and respectful in every way" (1 Tim 3:4); "let them manage their children and their households well" (1 Tim 3:12). Compare Malina and Rohrbaugh, *Social-Science Commentary on the Synoptic Gospels,* 299.

28. The ambiguous Greek phrase simply contains the preposition *en* ("in") followed by a dative masculine or neuter plural article, *tois* ("the ones" or "the things") without an accompanying noun. Hence, a literal rendering of Jesus' reply would run something like: "I must be *in the things* of my Father," leaving the interpreter to determine exactly what those "things" are.

29. This statement is part of the shared tradition in Matt 10:37//Luke 14:25 (Matthew softens the "hate" dimension somewhat) and *Gos. Thom.* 55, 101.

30. Luke 18:29–30; cf. Mark 10:29–31//Matt 19:27–30.

31. Jesus' famous parable of the prodigal or lost son is found only in Luke 15:11–32. Robert W. Funk, among others, suggests that this story "has autobiographical overtones" related to Jesus' conflicts with his own family (*Honest to Jesus: Jesus for a New Millennium* [New York: HarperCollins, 1996], 189); cf. Stephen L. Harris, *Understanding the Bible* (5th ed.; Mountain View, Calif.: Mayfield, 2000), 436–37.

32. Raymond E. Brown, *The Birth of the Messiah: A Commentary on the Infancy Narratives in Matthew and Luke* (London: Geoffrey Chapman, 1978), 493–95.

33. Richard Bauckham overlooks this simmering tension between Jesus and his family in Luke and draws too sharp a contrast with Mark's presentation: "[U]nlike Matthew and Mark, Luke's Gospel contains *no indication of a breach*

between Jesus and his family . . . on the general question of Jesus' relationship with his family . . . Mark give[s] the impression of a complete rift, Luke of *complete harmony* between Jesus and his relatives" (emphasis added) (*Gospel Women: Studies of the Named Women in the Gospels* [Grand Rapids, Mich.: Eerdmans, 2002], 221). Luke modulates some of Mark's harsher tones but hardly creates a picture of "complete harmony."

34. Tales of extraordinary births, remarkable childhood feats, and precocious intelligence were typical of Hellenistic biographies or encomia of ancient heroes, such as Plutarch's life of Alexander the Great and Philostratus's of Apollonius of Tyana. See Bruce J. Malina and Jerome H. Neyrey, *Portraits of Paul: An Archaeology of Ancient Personality* (Louisville, Ky.: Westminster/John Knox, 1996), 19–63; Funk, *Honest to Jesus,* 281–85.

35. Luke's account of Jesus' rejection at Nazareth (4:16–30) is over twice as long as Mark's and has been shifted back to the strategic position of Jesus' first public act of ministry. It clearly serves a programmatic function in Luke's narrative.

36. The particular Elijah and Elisha stories which Jesus cites—dealing with the destitute Sidonian widow at Zarephath and the leprous Syrian official, Naaman (4:25–27)—cover the social spectrum of female/male and poor/rich, as well as non-Israelites. For a similar neutralizing of race, class, and gender distinctions among the people of God, see the classic Pauline formulation in Gal 3:27: "There is no longer Jew or Greek, there is no longer slave or free, there is no longer male and female; for all of you are one in Christ Jesus."

37. Acts 12:17; 15:13–21; 21:17–26; 1 Cor 15:3–7; Gal 2:9–12.

38. See Miller, *Jesus at Thirty,* 11–17.

39. Part of the shared tradition between Matthew (10:34–36) and Luke (12:51–53).

40. See Malina and Rohrbaugh, *Social-Science Commentary on the Gospel of John,* 70–72.

41. I am calling her "Mary" for convenience's sake, although the fourth gospel never mentions her by name, only as "the mother of Jesus." This general designation may have something to do with her symbolic function in the narrative (see below).

42. Jesus also uses the same respectful form of address to the Samaritan woman in 4:21. Adele Reinhartz ("The Gospel of John," in *Searching the Scriptures: A Feminist Commentary* [ed. E. S. Fiorenza; New York: Crossroad, 1994], 568–70) notes that, apart from these examples of Jesus' direct use of "Woman," the only other figure whom the Johannine Jesus addresses in a vocative form is God as "Father" (11:41; 12:28; 17:1, 5, 11, 24, 25), a term of obvious honor and intimacy.

43. On the importance of synchronizing all of Jesus' work in John (culminating in Jesus' death) with the divinely appointed "hour," see 4:23, 52–53; 7:30; 8:20; 12:23, 27; 13:1; 16:25, 32; 17:1; 19:27.

44. See Gail R. O'Day, "John," in *Woman's Bible Commentary* (rev. ed.; ed. Carol A. Newsom and Sharon H. Ringe; Louisville, Ky.: Westminster/John Knox, 1998), 383; Reinhartz ("Gospel of John," 569–70) even suggests that Jesus' mother, "who knows of Jesus' powers and instructs others to obey him, is to be seen as an apostolic figure."

45. He also tells stories about wedding festivals, especially in Matthew (9:14–15; 22:1–14; 25:1–13), to illustrate the kingdom of God.

46. He deals with the synagogue ruler, Jairus, and his wife over the death of their twelve-year-old daughter (Mark 5:40–42//Luke 8:51–56). For the most part, throughout the gospels Jesus reaches out to single, unattached, displaced people.

47. See Mark 10:1–12; Matt 5:27–32; 19:1–12.

48. Of course, the argument from silence can run the other way: since the Gospels also never say explicitly that Jesus wasn't married, can't we assume that he probably was—like most everyone else? (cf. the works of William E. Phipps, *Was Jesus Married?: The Distortion of Sexuality in the Christian Tradition* [New York: Harper & Row, 1970]; *The Sexuality of Jesus* [Cleveland: Pilgrim Press, 1996]). Perhaps, but Jesus' strong sense of apocalyptic urgency and statements about becoming "eunuchs for the kingdom of heaven" (Matt 19:10–12) suggest an ascetic orientation appropriate to the crisis at hand. In any case, I do not think that the gospels are covering up Jesus' marriage to Mary Magdalene (or anyone else) out of some misogynistic goal to promote a celibate male clergy. That is a problem for a later period; the New Testament, from the early Pauline letters to the Pastorals, has no quibble with married apostles, bishops, deacons, or other church officials (see Rom 16:3, 7; 1 Cor 9:3; 1 Tim 3:1–2, 12). See further discussion below and in chapter 4 on Jesus' treatment of his body.

49. Similar to Paul's perspective reflected in 1 Corinthians 7, in light of "the impending crisis" (7:26) and awareness that "the appointed time has grown short" (7:29).

50. See Luke 14:26.

51. In the synoptics, the women reappear in the narrative to care for Jesus' body at the tomb; only in the fourth gospel do women witness Jesus' crucifixion.

52. See Craig R. Koester, *Symbolism in the Fourth Gospel: Meaning, Mystery, Community* (Minneapolis, Minn.: Fortress, 1995); and R. Alan Culpepper, *Anatomy of the Fourth Gospel: A Study in Literary Design* (Philadelphia, Pa.: Fortress, 1983), 151–202.

53. Contra Powell, *Fortress Introduction to the Gospels,* 136.

54 See O'Day, "The Gospel of John," in *The New Interpreter's Bible,* vol. 9 (Nashville, Tenn.: Abingdon, 1995), 831–32; and Raymond E. Brown, *The Community of the Beloved Disciple: The Life, Loves, and Hates of an Individual Church in New Testament Times* (London: Geoffrey Chapman, 1979), 196–98.

55 Compare O'Day, "Gospel of John," 832.

56. I am drawing here on the language of the Lord's Prayer in Matt 6:9–13//Luke 11:1–4.

57. John 3:1–6; 7:37–39; cf. also 1 Cor 12:13, "For in the one Spirit we were all baptized into one body—Jews or Greeks, slaves or free—and we were all made to drink of one Spirit."

3

Friendship Bonds

One of the most popular and longest running sit-coms of the past decade on American television has featured the developing relationships among six close-knit, young adult friends, three men and three women making their way in New York City. Of the principal characters on the Emmy-winning show, simply titled *Friends,* two are brother and sister and two eventually marry each other; but on the whole, their primary bond is to each other as friends and confidants. Peer friendship predominates over family ties; in fact, the six friends function very much like a family, or in other terms, like a committed fictive kinship group. The series resonates with a deep-seated human desire for nurture and companionship outside the biological family unit. However strong and stimulating one's family roots might be, most people, young and old, seek out external relationships for further enrichment. And certainly when family relations become strained or abusive in some way, sympathetic bonds of friendship take on even greater importance.

While our current era of unprecedented mobility and family dislocation places special value on building and maintaining friendship networks, the emphasis on social amity is scarcely a modern invention. The ideal of friendship has held an honored place in the history of Western civilization, anchored in ancient Greco-Roman philosophy as well as in the Jewish and Christian Scriptures. Aristotle extolled the virtue of friendship as a model of intimacy and hospitality: "Moreover, all the proverbs agree with this; for example, 'Friends have one soul between them,' and 'Friends' goods are common property.'"[1] Epicurus and Cicero concurred in assessing that "of all the things which wisdom acquires to

produce the blessedness of the complete life, far the greatest is the possession of friendship."[2] The Hellenistic Jewish sage, Jesus ben Sira, highly
prized faithful friends—as opposed to fair-weather friends—who support each other through thick and thin: "There are friends who are such
when it suits them, but they will not stand by you in time of trouble. . . .
Faithful friends are a sturdy shelter: whoever finds one has found a trea-
sure" (Sir 6: 8, 14). Such wisdom is undergirded by the Old Testament
Book of Proverbs, which regards the succor of friends as comparable if
not superior to that of relatives: "A friend loves at all times, and kinsfolk
are born to share adversity" (17:17). "Some friends play at friendship,
but a true friend sticks closer than one's nearest kin" (18:24).

Jesus of Nazareth also acknowledged the social significance of friends,
especially in a cluster of parables in the central section of Luke's gospel.
One story highlights the duty of friends to share their goods and provide
hospitality even at inconvenient times as a paradigm of God's benevolence to his petitioning children (11:5–13). Another parable assumes a
conventional quartet of invited dinner guests comprised of friends,
brothers, relatives, and wealthy neighbors—all of whom can be expected
to reciprocate the host's efforts—as a foil for Jesus' radical expansion of
table fellowship to include four other, less congenial groups with nothing
to offer in return: the poor, the crippled, the lame, and the blind
(14:12–14). As with his approach to family matters, Jesus is not opposed
to the practice of friendship as such, only to its narrow application to an
exclusive clique. The three "lost" parables in Luke 15 envisage a special
celebration among friends and neighbors upon recovering the missing
item (sheep, coin, or son), a pattern that Jesus regards as analogous to
the angels' rejoicing in heaven over a "lost" sinner who repents (15:6–7,
9–10, 29). Finally, in the parable of the dishonest manager (or unjust
steward), Jesus trades on the typical patron-client model of "making
friends" through the granting of financial favors (in other words, "buying friends").[3] On one level he admires the fraudulent manager for
"shrewdly" creating a network of indebted, loyal friends, although Jesus'
ultimate concern is with the faithful disposition of the "true riches" of
God's kingdom (16:8–13).

While Jesus is obviously familiar with conventions of friendship, it is
not so clear in the gospels who his personal friends are or how he treats
them. As a magnanimous feeder, healer, and broker of divine blessings,

Jesus attracts large numbers of client-friends among the impoverished and infirm. He even develops quite a reputation as a "friend of sinners" (Matt 11:19//Luke 7:34). But these alliances, however central to Jesus' identity and mission, hardly qualify as intimate peer liaisons. In fact, the gospels' patent elevation of Jesus as Israel's lord, master, and messiah—indeed the Son of God and viceroy of God's kingdom[4]—emphasizes his unique, superior status—without peer. While many grateful beneficiaries of Jesus' largesse may happily call him their friend, this does not necessarily mean that Jesus pursues their amiable counsel or companionship, any more than the emperor buddied up to the many subjects who regarded themselves as "friends of Caesar."[5] It is lonely and risky at the top; true friends must be chosen and handled with care.

Only a handful of gospel figures enjoy what might be deemed a "close" relationship with Jesus, involving some sense of being his associate and confidant as well as his subordinate and client. We will explore three possible friendship ties: (1) the singular case of John the Baptist, whom the fourth gospel dubs "the friend of the bridegroom" (3:29); (2) among Jesus' disciples, the inner circle of Peter, James, and John in the Synoptic Gospels, and the enigmatic figure of the "beloved disciple" in the fourth gospel; and (3) the sisters Martha and Mary of Bethany, who enjoy a mutual relationship of give and take with Jesus in the Lukan and Johannine narratives (the latter gospel also features the women's brother, Lazarus, whom Jesus calls "our friend," 11:11).

Best Man

All four gospels concur that Jesus enjoyed a special bond with John the Baptist. However, the precise contours of this relationship are difficult to trace, largely because of the tightrope on which the gospel writers walk—admiring John's prophetic mission, on the one side, but insuring that he does not upstage Jesus, on the other. John is great, but Jesus is greater—even though Jesus is baptized by John and, to some extent, builds on John's foundation. Each gospel has its own distinctive way of dealing with the problem. Based on scriptural prophecy and John's own testimony, Mark casts the Baptist in the role of forerunner of the "more powerful" messiah Jesus (1:1–11). Matthew and Luke both elaborate on this model, the former by accentuating John's reluctance to baptize Jesus; the latter, by removing John from the scene before narrating Jesus' baptism.[6] The fourth gospel omits Jesus' baptism altogether and presents John as Jesus' witness who "must decrease" in order that Jesus may be lifted up (1:6–9, 19–34; 3:22–30).

In addition to focusing on Jesus' connection to John's preaching and baptizing, the Synoptic Gospels also disclose Jesus' reaction to John's imprisonment and beheading. The context of suffering provides a key opportunity to assess the quality of Jesus' friendship with John. Will it hold up under fire? Will Jesus "stick closer than a brother" when John needs it most?[7] Again we detect a degree of ambiguity in Jesus' relationship with John, exemplified in Jesus' puzzling appraisal during John's detention in Herod's custody: "I tell you, among those born of women no one is greater than John; yet the least in the kingdom of God is greater than he" (Matt 11:11//Luke 7:28). Initially this sounds like high praise, but by the end of the statement, we're not so sure.

Before proceeding to investigate more fully the adult relationship between John and Jesus revolving around John's baptismal mission and political trials, we should note that Luke alone tracks the connection between John and Jesus all the way back to their infancies. The Lukan birth narrative announces not only Jesus' miraculous conception within Mary's virgin womb but also John's surprising conception within Elizabeth's barren womb six months earlier. What is more, the two mothers are further linked together as "relatives" or "kinswomen" (1:36), who share their experiences of pregnancy in Elizabeth's home (1:39–56).[8] Of course, this association also implies that John and Jesus are related (as cousins) and spend some time together during their childhoods. But Luke provides no details concerning this relationship. When Jesus appears in the Jerusalem temple at age twelve, John is nowhere to be found.

John's Preaching and Baptizing

True friendship in the ancient world involved not only an intimate sharing of mutual interests but also a candid exposing of personal flaws for the friend's genuine good (the goal is character improvement, not public embarrassment). Proverbs advises: "Better is open rebuke than hidden love. Well meant are the wounds a friend afflicts" (27:5–6). In *How to Tell a Flatterer from a Friend*, Plutarch admonishes:

> We ought to keep close watch upon our friends not only when they go wrong but also when they are right, and indeed the first step should be commendation cheerfully bestowed. Then later, just as steel is made compact by cooling, and takes on a temper as the result of having first been relaxed and softened by heat, so when our friends have become mollified and warmed by our commendations we should give them an application of frankness like a tempering bath. . . . For as a kindhearted physician would prefer to relieve a sick man's ailment by sleep and diet rather than by castor and scammony, so a kindly friend, a good father, and a teacher, take pleasure in using commendation rather than blame for the correction of character.[9]

In this context of friendship, we wonder: to what extent and in what way does Jesus endorse and/or criticize John's ministry of preaching and baptism?

By seeking John out and submitting to his baptism, Jesus obviously associates himself with John's mission in a positive way. But in due course Jesus also strikes out on his own path. How does this move affect his relationship with John? If "imitation is the sincerest form of flattery," then Jesus continues to support John by replicating John's basic message. Mark's summary of the "good news" that Jesus proclaims throughout Galilee, with its call to repentance in the face of an imminent, apocalyptic manifestation of God's rule, is wholly consistent with John's proclamation: "The time is fulfilled, and the kingdom of God has come near; repent, and believe the good news" (1:14–15).[10] Also, certain ethical and devotional elements of John's agenda disclosed in Luke, such as demanding financial generosity and integrity from inquirers (3:10–14) and instructing his disciples in the proper modes of prayer (11:1), find clear echoes in the teachings of Jesus.[11]

As for Jesus' furtherance of the rite of baptism, the Synoptic Gospels offer no evidence, except for Jesus' final commission in Matthew that future disciples be baptized in the name of the triune God (28:19). The fourth gospel, however, provides an alternative witness to an early Judean phase of Jesus' ministry in which both he and his disciples "spent some time" baptizing, concurrent with John's activity (3:22–23). In fact, we discover that "Jesus is making and baptizing more disciples than John" (4:1). While such a report boosts Jesus' reputation above John's, it also confirms a basic affinity between their respective missions.[12]

However much Jesus initially mirrors John's work, he soon sets out on his own independent course distinct from John's in certain ways. The goals remain the same, but the strategy changes. Whatever Jesus' early commitment to immersing followers, baptism does not remain a major thrust of his mission as it develops. Jesus does not stay anchored in the Judean wilderness near the Jordan River, as John does, but rather roams among the towns and villages proximate to the Sea of Galilee as an itinerant preacher. Jesus takes his message to the people, whereas John calls the people to come to him. Jesus not only teaches the people; he heals, feeds and feasts with them, whereas John performs no miracles, as far as we know, and is devoted to fasting and a strict ascetic lifestyle.

Do these distinctions in religious practice betray a rift in the fellowship between Jesus and John? By going his own way, is Jesus effectively criticizing his friend John, and if so, in what spirit does he carry out this corrective action? We discover important clues to these questions in two passages highlighting the contrast in dietary habits already mentioned.

First, in all three Synoptic Gospels, Jesus is asked to explain why he does not promote the practice of fasting among his disciples as John the Baptist and the Pharisees do among their followers (Matt 9:14–15// Mark 2:18–20//Luke 5:33–35). In Matthew and Luke, the charge stresses the frequency of these other groups' fasting: "They fast a lot— why then, Jesus, do your followers not fast at all?"[13] In response, Jesus never denigrates the act of fasting (it was an established expression of Jewish piety) or those who advocate it, but simply defends the non-fasting of his disciples as appropriate to the moment: their close association with the messianic agent of God's kingdom, depicted as a bridegroom, calls for banquet-style celebration, not deprivation. Jesus also assumes, however, that when he, the bridegroom, is no longer present, his followers will resume the discipline of fasting. Thus, Jesus recognizes a current distinction in eating habits between his adherents and those associated with the Baptist and the Pharisees, but this scarcely amounts to a critical point of division in Jesus' view. John remains an honored "best man" or "friend of the bridegroom" (to borrow the language of the fourth gospel, 3:29), whatever his dietary preferences. The present discussion turns on the dining activity of Jesus' disciples, not Jesus himself. This leaves the door open for the possibility that, while Jesus does not encourage others to fast, he himself may do so from time to time. The gospels recount only one particular occasion of fasting in Jesus' life, but it is especially noteworthy for both the location and duration of the experience. Just after his own baptism by John, Jesus abides in the Judean wilderness for an intense forty-day fast in which, as Luke describes it, "he ate nothing at all." Not surprisingly, after this ordeal, both Matthew and Luke report that Jesus "was famished."[14]

While Jesus may have fasted now and again, he is known primarily for his festive eating and drinking, as reflected in a second passage, shared by Matthew and Luke, contrasting Jesus' habits with John's: "For John the Baptist has come eating no bread and drinking no wine, and you say, 'He has a demon'; the Son of Man has come eating and drinking, and you say, 'Look, a glutton and a drunkard, a friend of tax collectors and sinners'" (Matt 11:18–19//Luke 7:33–34). We will have more to say in the next chapter concerning Jesus' notoriety as "a glutton and drunkard," but for now we simply register that, despite the obvious differences between John's fasting and Jesus' feasting, Jesus cites these distinctive characteristics to emphasize the solidarity between these two men as fellow targets of unfair criticism. However divergent their respective dietary practices, Jesus and John, each in his own way, fulfill their sacred calling as authentic prophets of God and "children of wisdom."[15]

This text also introduces another potential wedge in the friendship between Jesus and John beyond the issue of food and drink. Jesus is also infamous for being a "friend of sinners." Is it possible to be a friend of John, with his fiery message of repentance, and a friend of sinners at the same time? Part of the issue hinges on the extent to which Jesus demands that sinners must reform or repent to enter the kingdom of God. E. P. Sanders, a leading Jesus scholar and historian of early Judaism, has suggested that, while Jesus clearly encourages repentance (primarily in Luke, much less so in Matthew and Mark), he does not always insist upon it, as John the Baptist does, as a precondition of fellowship. John appears to require seekers to demonstrate concrete evidence of repentance ("bear fruit worthy of repentance," Matt 3:7–10//Luke 3:7–9) before he will baptize them. In contrast to the Baptist's imperative agenda, Jesus' mission focuses more on the declarative gospel of God's gracious acceptance of sinners, regardless of their condition.[16] Still, however looser and wider Jesus' communion with sinners may be, he continues into the final week of his life to commend John's more stringent reform movement against his critics. In the synoptic passion narratives, the first three evangelists present a debate between Jesus and the temple elites in which Jesus subtly but surely associates his own divine authority with that of John's (Matt 21:23–27//Mark 11:27–33//Luke 20:1–8). In Matthew's elaborated account, Jesus' ultimate endorsement of John is transparent: "Truly I tell you, the tax collectors and the prostitutes are going into the kingdom of God ahead of you. For John came to you in the way of righteousness and you did not believe him, but the tax collectors and the prostitutes believed him; and even after you saw it, you did not change your minds and believe him" (21:31–32).

Jesus himself may not always require tax collectors and prostitutes to change their ways before dining with them or announcing the good news of God's love, but he is happy to underwrite John's stricter policy, nonetheless, and to encourage the religious authorities to change their minds about John's legitimacy. If anyone needs to repent, it is the (self-)righteous leaders.

John's Imprisonment and Beheading

We have already hinted at some of Jesus' reactions to the detention and eventual execution of John the Baptist by order of Herod Antipas. We now test more thoroughly the mettle of Jesus' friendship in the face of John's crisis. John had politically threatened Herod's rule in two possible ways, one documented in Josephus's writings, the other in the Synoptic Gospels. Josephus reports Herod's concern that John's surging popularity with and influence over large crowds "might lead to some form of sedition." Better to nip the problem in the bud, from Herod's perspective, and get John off the scene.[17] The gospels focus more precisely on John's denunciation of Herod's illicit, adulterous marriage to his brother Philip's wife, Herodias.[18] Both accounts provide a reasonable motivation for Herod's actions against John and are not mutually exclusive: politics and ethics were often intertwined in first-century Palestine.[19]

Jesus never directly addresses Herod's hostile treatment of John in the gospels, but he does offer some indirect support for his beleaguered friend. For one thing, Jesus' hard line against adultery and divorce amounts to an implicit critique of Herod's marital maneuvers. Also, Luke reports that Jesus conveys a pointed message of protest to "that fox" Herod.[20] Here, Jesus scoffs at Herod's plot to kill him (Jesus), not John the Baptist, but in any case, Jesus shows himself to be no friend of Herod and his murderous schemes. Finally, in the material common to Matthew and Luke, when the imprisoned John dispatches messengers to inquire about Jesus' mission, Jesus seizes the occasion to express publicly his views about John. In affirming John's role as a true prophet of God in the mold of the great Elijah, Jesus deliberately contrasts John with "a reed shaken by the wind" and "a man dressed in soft robes . . . in royal palaces" (Matt 11:7–14//Luke 7:24–29). Why use these particular images to demonstrate John's stability (no wispy reed) and strength (no weak robe)? Jesus may well be drawing a subtle (or not so subtle, given the politically charged atmosphere of the time) and satirical comparison between John the Baptist and Herod Antipas, whose coins featured the picture of a reed on one side—the symbol of Herod's new capital of Tiberias on the shores of the Sea of Galilee[21]—and who, though technically not a king, proudly wrapped himself in royal garb. For Jesus the choice is clear: despite appearances and present circumstances, the true kingdom of God is mediated through the "desert-dwelling prophet" John, not the "palace-dwelling 'man'" Antipas.[22]

Amid these expressions of unqualified support for John's prophetic vocation, Jesus interjects a more ambivalent judgment: "Among those born of women no one is greater than John; yet the least in the kingdom of God is greater than he" (Matthew 11:11//Luke 7:28). Does this statement represent Jesus' decisive break with John over key matters pertaining to the manifestation of God's kingdom?[23] Not necessarily. The first part of the statement suggests that Jesus continues to hold John in the highest esteem. The second part, while seeming to undo the first, betrays Jesus' penchant for paradox and hyperbole.[24] Jesus commonly equates the "last" or "least" with the "first" or "greatest" in charting the inclusive scope of God's kingdom. He stakes out a level playing field in which dynamic prophets like John have no greater claim on the kingdom than pathetic prostitutes. Just as the wealthy and powerful Antipas has no

social advantage over John in Jesus' community, so the righteous and rigorous John has no spiritual monopoly on God's blessing over "tax collectors and sinners." Jesus' purpose is not to discount or dismiss John, but
rather to welcome all who embrace his gospel into the fellowship of
God's people.

While Jesus publicly voices his support for his imprisoned friend John,
what does he do upon learning of John's beheading and burial? Immediately following the account of John's violent end, Mark reports that Jesus
"went away in the boat to a deserted place" with his apostles (6:30–32).
No explicit connection is made, however, between this retreat and John's
execution. The move has more to do with debriefing the Twelve after their
recent Galilean mission (6:30; cf. 6:6–13).[25] In Matthew, however,
Jesus' withdrawal is directly tied to his knowledge of John's fate. After
the Baptist's disciples bury their master's body, "they went and told Jesus"
(14:12). And "when Jesus heard this [the news of John's death and inter-
ment], he withdrew from there in a boat to a deserted place by himself"
(14:13). Unlike Mark, Matthew focuses on Jesus' personal reaction to
John's demise.

Does Matthew's Jesus abandon his friend John in his direst hour, as
Jesus' own disciples will eventually desert him when the authorities press
in? Is Jesus motivated perhaps by a measure of fear and foreboding? After
all, he has been associated with John, and reports soon circulate that a
paranoid Antipas suspects that Jesus might be a reincarnated John come
back to haunt the ruler (Matt 14:1–2//Mark 6:14–16//Luke 9:7–9). Not
a good time to be politically active in Galilee; better to lay low for a
while. Anyway, what can Jesus do to help John now? Still, while there
may be some concern on Jesus' part to dissociate himself from the rebel
John, this is not the only way to interpret Jesus' hasty retreat in Matthew.
The fact that he withdraws alone to a "deserted place" (or desert
region)[26] suggests a strong, renewed identification with John's desert-
based mission. In the wake of John's tragic death, Jesus returns to the
roots of John's mission—and to his own beginnings as a Spirit-anointed
prophet linked to his baptism by John. Perhaps this is a time for Jesus to
reassess his vocation, to undergo another period of wilderness testing, to
take up the mantle left by John with clarified vision and revitalized
commitment. In any case, Jesus does not go to the desert to hide or to
quit his work. The crowds flock to him there—as they previously did to

John—and "he had compassion for them" (14:14). While he does not baptize them, as far as we know, he does mediate God's redemptive rule to the people through his dual ministry of healing and feeding.[27] Not the way John would have done it, but continuing the restorative thrust of John's work, nonetheless.

As Jesus returns from the desert and resumes his itinerant mission, he retains his memory of and respect for his departed friend John. Beset by mounting opposition in his final days, Jesus recalls the heaven-ordained, prophetic authority of John the Baptist, still acknowledged by many, and implicitly aligns his own divinely authorized mission with John's (Matt 21:21–32//Mark 11:27–33//Luke 20:1–8). He then proceeds, through the synoptic parable of the wicked tenants, to indict the political establishment in Israel for its repeated beating and spurning of God's messengers as an ominous prelude to the ultimate crime of murdering God's "beloved son." Mark's Jesus, however, further reports that the authorities have already killed other emissaries, just as they will the son (12:4–5). This may be a veiled reference to the recent execution of John the Baptist, who is clearly on Jesus' mind at this critical time. While Jesus may not have rushed to John's defense in Herod's court, he proudly waves John's banner during his own trying ordeal, anticipating his own imminent execution. One might say that Jesus dies for his friend John, carrying on John's noble prophetic tradition of martyrdom. There is "no greater love than this, to lay down one's life for one's friend."[28]

Fishing Buddies

We have previously observed in Mark's story that Jesus first chooses two pairs of fishermen-brothers to be his followers: Simon/Andrew and James/John (1:16–20). When Jesus expands his apostolic circle to twelve, these original disciples still occupy the top four positions, although Andrew is split from his brother and placed in the fourth slot after Simon (Peter), James, and John (3:14–19).[29] This prepares the reader for several incidents in which Peter, James, and John continue to enjoy a special intimacy with Jesus, comprising an inner nucleus of three confidants among the Twelve and approximating a bond of personal friendship between master and students. On several occasions—such as in

Jairus's home, on the Mount of Olives, or in Gethsemane—Jesus draws these three aside for key moments of demonstration, instruction, or intercession.[30]

This privileged bond does not mean, however, that Jesus pampers or indulges his three closest disciples as "teacher's pets." In fact, more often than not, Peter, James, and John find themselves being chided by Jesus for their lapses in spiritual perception and devotion. Mark perhaps overplays the disciples' dullness for effect (they almost never get the point), but the other gospels concur that Jesus' relationship with his followers, including the inner three, involves some measure of correction: disciples must be disciplined.

Ancient codes of friendship encouraged the sharing of constructive criticism over empty flattery. However, such critical sharpening of friends' characters was expected to be mutual and best carried out in a private setting for purposes of edification rather than humiliation. As Plutarch advised:

> But another opportunity for admonition arises when people, having been reviled by others for their errors, have become submissive and downcast. The tactful man will make an adept use of this, by rebuffing and dispersing the revilers, and *by taking hold of his friend in private* and reminding him that, if there is not other reason for his being circumspect, he should at least try to keep his enemies from being bold. . . .
>
> One other point: *we must be very careful about the frank speech toward a friend before a large company.* . . . For error should be treated as a foul disease, and all admonition and disclosure should be *in secret,* with nothing of show or display in it to attract a crowd of witnesses and spectators. *For it is not like friendship, but sophistry, to seek for glory in other men's faults.*[31]

We now turn to explore the ways in which Jesus, Peter, James, and John both correct and support each other, particularly surrounding the crisis of Jesus' impending death. Does Jesus take criticism as well as give it? How and when does Jesus choose to rebuke his disciple-friends?

Jesus Predicts His Death

A cluster of stories in Mark 8–10 revolve around three instances in which Jesus begins to alert the disciples to his anticipated suffering and execution at the hands of religious authorities. Such news falls largely on deaf ears, however, creating an atmosphere of tension between Jesus and the Twelve, represented by Peter, James, and John. The first episode features Peter's response to Jesus' passion prediction. Peter has just properly identified Jesus as God's Messiah (8:29), but Peter's concept of messiahship apparently has no room for negative talk about persecution and martyrdom. Victory, deliverance, salvation: yes; defeat, distress, death: no. And, so, "Peter took him [Jesus] aside and began to rebuke him" (8:32)—a private offer of criticism thoroughly in keeping with the duty of friendship.

How does Jesus respond? He counterpunches with an especially vivid—and some might say, even vicious—retort, directed at Peter but with his body turned and eye trained on the other disciples: "Get behind me, Satan! For you are setting your mind not on divine things but on human things" (8:33). Luke omits this unpleasant exchange altogether, and Matthew keeps the matter exclusively between Jesus and Peter (16:23). Mark's Jesus certainly stretches the bond of friendship closer to the breaking point, but perhaps not so severely as it might appear. By rebuking Peter in front of the other disciples ("turning and looking at" them implies but does not state whether they actually hear Jesus' remarks), Jesus is not exactly blaring his critique of Peter in a public forum. Jesus does not "call the crowd" together until after he deals with Peter (8:34), and the Twelve are a close-knit group for whom Peter often speaks as leader: they need to know what Jesus thinks of Peter's opinions. Still, isn't labeling the man "Satan" a bit extreme, particularly for a friend? Possibly, but we may also discern here a hint of face-saving for the impulsive Peter. In Jesus' view, Peter is not acting like himself but rather as one unwittingly commandeered by the enemy. When he comes back to his senses, to his right mind and true self, he will acknowledge once again the divine purpose guiding Jesus' destiny.

Jesus' continuing interest in Peter is evident when, "six days later," he takes his Satan-duped apostle along with James and John up to a "high mountain apart, by themselves" (9:2). Soon, however, the solemn, private scene is transformed into an extraordinary drama featuring the brilliant shining of Jesus' countenance and clothes and the reincarnation of two of Israel's greatest heroes, Moses and Elijah, engaging Jesus in conversation. In some fashion, the three disciples share this remarkable epiphany with Jesus.[32] To be sure, they do not quite know what to make of it (which still doesn't keep Peter from trying to control the situation; he has no problem plowing ahead where angels fear to tread),[33] but, nonetheless, they remain the objects of Jesus' special attention and participants in Jesus' most intense religious experiences.

The second time Jesus forecasts his tragic fate in Mark, the entire company of twelve disciples misses the point completely by jockeying among themselves for position as "the greatest" in sacrifice and service. He has already offered the shocking "take up your cross" as the motto for his movement (8:34–37); now he presents a "little child" as the mascot (9:35–37). This is scarcely the macho model the disciples were looking for. Infants and small children were often ignored and dismissed in ancient Mediterranean society (what could they do for you but get in the way and be a burden?),[34] not embraced and welcomed as honored guests (as one should welcome Jesus himself and God who sent him, no less). Shifting the focus away from the child and back to proper status-oriented concerns, John (not Peter this time) complains to Jesus about some independent exorcist using Jesus' name without due authorization. It is apparent, however, that John is less concerned about Jesus' reputation than his own and that of the other eleven "official" representatives of Jesus' kingdom. This outsider poses a competitive threat to their honor, and, thus, "we tried to stop him, because he was not following us" (9:38). How dare this maverick! He has no official Jesus membership card and doesn't know the secret apostolic handshake! Jesus will not be party, however, to this exclusive club mentality. He flatly puts John and the other apostles in their place with the sweeping judgment: "Whoever is not against us is for us" (9:40). This does not deny that John enjoys certain privileges as one of Jesus' closest disciples, but it does deny John the right to circumscribe the boundaries of Jesus' associates. As with family ties, Jesus conceives of friendship bonds in broad, inclusive terms; the welcome mat is out for "whoever" receives a child, drives out a demon, or does anything worthwhile in Jesus' name.

Jesus' third passion prediction in Mark elicits a response from both James and John, distinctive but no more enlightened than the previous responses of Peter and John. The matter still turns around the axis of honor and ambition. Virtually ignoring Jesus' elaborate description of his forthcoming trials (perhaps recalling the futility of Peter's earlier objection), the two sons of Zebedee proceed brazenly to ask Jesus for the cherished seats at Jesus' right and left hand in his glorious kingdom (10:35–37). Jesus once again candidly corrects his misguided friends, noting that they are asking both more than they realize (flanking Jesus' right and left will land them on a Roman cross rather than in a royal court!) and more than Jesus can give (grants of honor are God's business) (10:38–40). While the conversation between Jesus and Zebedee's sons appears to be private, the ten other disciples soon get wind of the discussion and become angry with James and John. Striving and scheming for position inevitably creates tension among friends. The conflict provides yet another occasion for Jesus to stress the primacy of humility, service, and sacrifice as marks of true greatness and friendship (10:41–45).

Jesus Prepares for Death

During his tumultuous final week, culminating in crucifixion, Jesus needs the support of friends as never before. Unfortunately, his colleagues let him down miserably. At the critical moment of his arrest—arranged by Judas, a traitor within the apostolic circle—all the other "disciples deserted him and fled."[35] Both before and after this pivotal event, two synoptic incidents further expose the fickleness of Jesus' followers, focusing again on the not-so-illustrious triumvirate of Peter, James, and John. The first episode features their soporific abandonment of Jesus during his intense struggle with God's will at Gethsemane. The second recounts Peter's famous denials of Jesus in the high priest's courtyard. While the failings of Jesus' friends are on parade in these stories, our concern is more with Jesus' reactions to his drowsy and cowardly disciples. How far does Jesus carry the duty of loyal friendship in the face of betrayal and denial?

According to Matthew and Mark, upon arriving at "a place called Gethsemane" with his disciples (minus Judas), Jesus draws aside Peter, James, and John from the group to accompany him while he prays. Once isolated with his three friends, he pulls apart from them "a little farther" in order to wrestle with Father-God alone concerning his fate. While instructing the larger company of disciples simply to "sit here while I pray," Jesus informs Peter, James, and John of his intense anguish over his impending death and implores them to "remain here and stay awake with me." Although choosing to pray by himself, Jesus wants his companions to keep alert and attuned to his struggle. Contrary to Jesus' desire, however, the three colleagues succumb to slumber: three times Jesus checks up on them, and each time he finds them asleep (Matt 26:36–45//Mark 14:32–41).

How does Jesus respond to his friends' disappointing behavior? Matthew and Mark both reveal Jesus' frustration, although, as usual, Mark's version is somewhat harsher toward the disciples. For example, whereas Matthew continues to use the label "disciples" for the sleepers, Mark uses the more impersonal and distancing "them" (since they are scarcely acting like faithful disciples).[36] The first time Jesus discovers his drowsy friends, he both expresses his annoyance ("Could you not stay awake with me one hour?"—every preacher and teacher knows exactly how Jesus feels)[37] and encourages them again to do his bidding ("Keep awake"). Notice Jesus' persisting compassion. Even though his personal crisis is weighing heavy upon him and his friends are providing little succor, Jesus is more concerned for their welfare than his own ("Pray that you may not come into the time of trial") and even willing to give them credit for good intentions ("the spirit is willing, but the flesh is weak," Matt 26:40–41//Mark 14:38–39). While Jesus himself says nothing the second time he finds his followers knocked out, the Markan narrator highlights their inexcusable shame by remarking that "they did not know what to say to him" ("Sorry" might have been a good place to start) (14:40).

The third time Jesus returns, he is incredulous that Peter, James, and John are "still sleeping" and then, according to Mark, abruptly utters the single word, *apechei*. The meaning of this term is disputed. The New Revised Standard Version (NRSV) and the New International Version (NIV) both opt for the translation "Enough!" implying that Jesus has "had it" with his pathetic attendants and is tired of prodding them to do the right thing. Another possible rendering for *apechei* in this context is "that is a hindrance,"[38] indicating that the disciples are actually hurting rather than helping Jesus by their lethargy. Yet another interpretation shifts the focus away from the somnolent Peter, James, and John to the traitorous Judas. Well-attested economic uses of the verb suggest a reading such as "the account is settled" or "the money is paid," referring to the deal that Judas recently struck to betray Jesus "into the hands of sinners."[39] After praying in Gethsemane, Mark's Jesus knows that his arrest is irrevocable and imminent (14:41–43). As Judas comes into the spotlight, some of the heat is taken off Peter, James, and John for the moment. However we render *apechei* and however strongly we color Jesus' disgust with his three lazy friends (I think it's pretty strong), he does not dismiss these cherished confidants nor discount their basic loyalty. He continues to demand their companionship ("Get up, let us be going"—he could have just left them lying there!) and to distinguish them from the real villain among his disciples ("See, my betrayer [Judas] is at hand," 14:42).

Even with these hints of continuing amity between Jesus, Peter, James, and John, some readers remain uncomfortable with Jesus' harsh treatment of his sluggish companions in Mark. We have already pointed out some subtle ways in which Matthew tones down Mark's presentation while retaining an atmosphere of tension. A glance at Luke's gospel, however, reveals a much more sweeping revision. Luke does not separate out Peter, James, and John from the group; Jesus checks on his followers only once, not three times, and his rebuke is both briefer and softer—"Why are you sleeping?" (22:46); and, most uniquely, Luke goes a long way toward exonerating the disciples by commenting that they are "sleeping because of grief" (22:45). The problem is not callousness, complacency, or weakness of the flesh (Luke omits this point), but rather deep sorrow. This scenario is quite plausible: intense grief and depression can induce sleep as a means of coping with the unbearable. But Mark's messier account of human frailty and frustration, even among friends, rings just as true. Friends do not always come through as they should during times of crisis, and those let down by friends when they need them most often lash back in anger and exasperation. Remember Job and his so-called friends who railed at each other again and again over Job's terrible ordeal. But we should also recall that Job ultimately "prayed for his friends," even after blasting them for their misjudgment and insensitivity (Job 42:7–10; cf. 2:11–13; 4:1–27:23). Likewise, Jesus both criticizes and cares for his three woeful disciples in the context of prayer and suffering. True friendship thrives best in an honest environment of criticism and conciliation, rebuke and repair.

After Jesus' seizure in Gethsemane, his bond with the disciples is further threatened by the infamous denials of Simon Peter. While others flee the scene, at least Peter hangs around the courtyard of the high priest's residence where Jesus is being detained. But Peter is not up to the challenge of the moment: three times—matching the three times Jesus found him sleeping instead of praying—Peter disavows all knowledge of his imperiled friend.[40] For all the good he does, he might as well have run away with the other disciples.

Again our interest is chiefly in Jesus' response to his fickle friend. All four gospels indicate that Peter's denials scarcely take Jesus by surprise; despite Peter's vehement protests, Jesus had predicted this is exactly what Peter would do when push came to shove.[41] Still, the reality of Peter's abandonment has to hit Jesus hard. What does he do? Eerily, Matthew, Mark, and John report no reaction of Jesus whatsoever. A possible implication is that Jesus, quartered inside the priestly palace, does not hear Peter's words. In any case, Matthew and Mark exclusively highlight Peter's reaction, namely, his bitter breakdown and departure upon realizing what he has done.

Once again, Luke stands out from the other gospels and attempts to patch up the rift between Jesus and Peter. Only Luke clearly places Jesus in Peter's presence during the denials and reports that, following the portentous cock crowing, "the Lord turned and looked at Peter" (22:60–61). No words are exchanged, but that poignant glance (the term connotes "looking straight at" someone) combined with the identification of Jesus as "Lord" unquestionably "heighten the pathos" of the scene.[42] Of course, looks can kill, and it is possible that Jesus shoots Peter a piercing look of profound disappointment or even anger. But the wider context of Luke suggests otherwise. Earlier in the same chapter, when Jesus predicted Peter's failure of nerve, Jesus assured him: "I have prayed for you that your own faith may not fail; and you, when once you have turned back, strengthen your brothers" (22:32). The Lukan Jesus maintains his commitment to Peter's welfare and already has in view Peter's restoration and leadership role in the church (amply fulfilled in the Book of Acts).

Thus, we may read Jesus' response following Peter's denials as a look of forgiveness and compassion, consistent with a pervasive gospel emphasis (not only in Luke) on Jesus as an advocate of love (toward enemies as well as friends), peacemaking, and redemption.[43]

Jesus Previews the Destinies of Peter and the Beloved Disciple

Typical of its "maverick" character,[44] the fourth gospel offers its own distinctive portrait of Jesus' relationship with his disciples. Peter still features prominently in the narrative, but by and large, the importance of the Twelve is minimized, and other early followers of Jesus, such as Nathanael, appear only here in the gospel tradition.[45] The most significant of these unique Johannine disciples is the anonymous "one whom Jesus loved" or "beloved disciple." Perhaps a previous follower of John the Baptist who early on switched his allegiance to Jesus (1:35–42), the beloved disciple becomes especially intimate with Jesus in the latter chapters of the gospel as Jesus faces death.[46] Although Jesus loves all of his followers as "friends," proven by his willingness "to lay down his life" for them (15:12–15), the beloved disciple enjoys a special status as Jesus' faithful friend par excellence.[47] He even surpasses Simon Peter in this respect; in fact, the beloved disciple is typically juxtaposed with Peter in a kind of "one-upmanship" contest.[48]

At the farewell supper, the beloved disciple reclines at the honored right side of Jesus,[49] "lying close to his breast,"[50] when Jesus drops the bombshell that one among them will betray him. Wanting to know the identity of the villain, Peter cannot ask Jesus himself but rather must motion to the beloved disciple who has Jesus' ear. This privileged associate asks the question, and Jesus points the finger at his betrayer (13:21–26). The beloved disciple is thus set apart both from Simon Peter (who must defer to the beloved disciple as chief spokesman) and Judas Iscariot (the exposed traitor). The pattern continues as the hour of crucifixion approaches. Peter thrice denies Jesus after his arrest and disappears from the scene (18:15–27). By contrast, the beloved disciple remains with Jesus until the end, standing with Jesus' mother at the foot of the cross (19:25–27).[51] After Jesus' death, the beloved disciple outraces Peter to the empty tomb and alone among the pair "believes" in Jesus' resurrection

(20:1–10). And finally, when the risen Jesus appears at the lakeshore while the disciples are out in the boat fishing, the beloved disciple recognizes him first and informs Peter, "It is the Lord." Peter is caught with his pants down—actually he is "naked"—not quite the way he wants to be reunited with the master he recently denied. He scrambles "to put on some clothes . . . and jumped into the sea" (21:7), his enthusiasm apparently overwhelming his embarrassment. Peter may physically get to Jesus before anyone else, but spiritually he is outstripped yet again by the disciple whom Jesus loved, who consistently emerges in the fourth gospel as Jesus' closest and most perceptive friend.

How does this competition affect Jesus' treatment of the two companions? The Gospel of John obviously favors the beloved disciple as the ideal community representative.[52] To what extent is this favoritism manifested in the behavior of the Johannine Jesus? At the cross, as we have already seen, Jesus certainly nurtures and honors the beloved disciple by entrusting him and his mother to each other's care. At this touching moment, kinship and friendship converge: Jesus' closest relative and closest associate form the basis of a new family of faith and discipleship. This is not intended, however, as a personal affront to Peter on Jesus' part. Peter is not present to hear Jesus' dying words; presumably, if Peter had been there, he would have been included in Jesus' "last will and testament" in some way.

In any case, the Johannine Jesus is not through with Simon Peter. The final chapter in the fourth gospel recounts an important encounter between the risen Jesus and Peter in the presence of the beloved disciple. Three times Jesus questions whether Peter really loves him. This interrogation is predicated on Jesus' continuing love for his fickle follower (if Jesus does not still love Peter, why bother with him at all?). Jesus is clearly reaching out to Peter and inviting him triply to declare his love to countermand his three previous denials.[53] Forgiveness is proffered; balance restored. Peter is thus poised to pastor the flock of Jesus and even to "follow" (21:19, 22) Jesus' pattern as the Good Shepherd who forfeits his life for his sheep (21:15–19).[54]

Although Peter has been highly honored by Jesus, he can't resist wondering how he stacks up against the beloved disciple: "Lord, what about him?" (21:21). Jealousies and rivalries are common bugbears among friends. Jesus cuts through this petty one-upmanship game by essentially saying, "Don't worry about him; that's none of your concern. You just worry about following me" (21:22). Jesus refuses to play favorites and promote party politics among his friends. He also, however, refuses to flatten his practice of friendship into some rigid, banal framework of "equal treatment" (as in treating everyone exactly the same). If Jesus wants to keep the beloved disciple alive until he comes again (21:22–23), that does not lessen his love for Peter or the significance of Peter's unique vocation as pastor and martyr. While these final portraits of Peter and the beloved disciple clearly have important ecclesiastical implications for the history of the Johannine community, they also, on a more basic level, reveal something of the restorative and dynamic character of Jesus' loving friendship.

Dinner Companions

Outside the twelve apostles in the synoptic tradition and the beloved disciple in the fourth gospel, we know very little about the wider circle of friends and followers around Jesus. Luke names three women in 8:1–3 (Mary Magdalene, Joanna, and Susanna) who supported and journeyed with Jesus and the Twelve (along with "many others"), but we hear nothing more about them until they appear at Jesus' tomb at the end of the gospel (24:10). Luke also refers to a company of seventy messengers dispatched in pairs by Jesus, but provides no names or individual profiles (10:1–12). Within this vacuum, however, one additional group of intimates stands out—another trio, as it happens, the siblings Martha, Mary, and Lazarus of Bethany. These friends are featured in both the third and fourth gospels. Their closeness with Jesus is evident in their hospitality toward him (Luke 10:38–42; John 12:1–8) and his reciprocal concern for their physical and emotional well-being (Luke 10:41–42; John 11:1–44). John's gospel explicitly identifies the two sisters and brother as "ones whom Jesus loved" (11:3, 5)—matching the description of the beloved disciple—and has Jesus specifically label Lazarus as "our friend" (11:11).[55]

The episodes exemplifying Jesus' friendship again focus on various crises and conflicts: (1) Martha's distress over serving chores and her sister's irresponsibility; (2) Lazarus' illness and death and his sisters' consequent bereavement; and (3) Mary's extravagant outpouring of affection upon Jesus (in anticipation of his death), challenged by one of his disciples as a frivolous waste. Our concern is with Jesus' basic responses to his friends' dilemmas.

Martha's Worry

In the brief but well-known Lukan episode involving Martha, Mary, and Jesus, Martha "welcome[s] him [Jesus] into her home" (10:38). Evidently, Martha is the eldest sibling and owner of the residence. As such she is also responsible for hosting Jesus in proper and honorable fashion and becomes quite frustrated when the workload overwhelms her while her sister Mary, fixed at Jesus' feet, scarcely lifts a finger to help. So Martha, somewhat miffed at Jesus ("do you not care?") as well as Mary, implores him to order her sister to get on her feet and do her part. Jealousy also seems to infect the situation, as Martha implies that her friend Jesus is giving preferential treatment to Mary at Martha's expense.

In response, Jesus does not give in to Martha's demands, but neither does he rake her over the coals and put her in her place, as is often assumed. Martha has gotten an unjustifiably bad rap in the history of interpretation, variously functioning as a foil for Mary's superior faith and devotion. For example, some have viewed Martha, disparagingly, as the model of legalistic works-righteousness or mundane, unreflective religious activism. Such opinions reveal more, however, about the theological bias of interpreters than the aims of Luke's narrative.[56] While Jesus does counter Martha's complaint, he does so in a respectful, congenial manner befitting his close friendship with Martha.

Three points are worth noting. First, Jesus addresses Martha by name with a double reference—"Martha, Martha"—a mark of familiarity and endearment. Secondly, Jesus does not question *what* Martha is doing but rather *how* she is going about it. Martha is preoccupied with "much serving (*diakonian*)" (10:40). From a Lukan perspective, it doesn't get much better than this: the Lukan Jesus repeatedly endorses and embodies the greatness of service (*diakonia*)—including table service—and servanthood (*diakonos*). Indeed, he announces candidly to his disciples: "I am among you as one who serves (*ho diakonōn*)" (22:27).[57] It is not Martha's faithful service that concerns Jesus, but her excessive worry and fretting over it: "you are worried and distracted by many things" (10:41). Jesus is not so much rebuking Martha as is he trying to help her set aside the anxiety that is making her miserable. Jesus does not want his friends consumed with worry about the practical necessities of life: "Do not keep striving for what you are to eat and what you are to drink, and do not keep worrying . . . your Father knows that you need them" (12:29–30).

Why, then, if Jesus is so concerned to alleviate Martha's worry, does he not bid Mary to assist her? This brings us to the final point. If Jesus chides Martha for anything, it is for her jealous anger at her sister who appears to be shirking her duty and leaving Martha with an unfair share of the burden. Across the gospels, Jesus has little patience with calculated comparisons of duties and benefits, whether it involves Peter's worry over the beloved disciple's destiny in John ("If it is my will that he remain until I come, what is that to you?" 21:22); laborers' complaints to the landowner concerning those hired late in the day in Matthew's parable of the vineyard ("Am I not allowed to do what I choose with what belongs to me? Or are you envious because I am generous?" 20:15); an elder brother's pouting over a party thrown for his younger sibling in Luke's parable of the lost son (15:25–32); or an elder sister's annoyance with her younger sister's rapt attention to Jesus in the Lukan story of Martha and Mary (10:38–42). Jesus works with an economy of grace and liberality, not competition and strict equality. Mary is doing nothing wrong; indeed, she has chosen "the better part" by listening to Jesus' teaching (10:42). If Jesus chooses to indulge Mary in this time of fellowship, what is that to Martha? Jesus is not trying to get back at Martha or denigrate her in any way by being with Mary. He simply chooses to talk with Mary who chooses to sit at his feet. If Martha chooses to prepare supper, that's fine too; or better yet, since this seems to fluster her so, why not join Mary in attending to Jesus' word? Dinner can wait.

Lazarus' Woe

The fourth gospel introduces brother Lazarus, the third member of Jesus' family of friends from Bethany, with the ominous note that he "was ill" (11:1). The two sisters, Martha and Mary, send word of their brother's

condition to Jesus, who is some distance from Judea at the time. Implied
in this report is an urgent plea that Jesus come and minister to his infirm
beloved friend ASAP. Curiously, however, Jesus tarries where he is two
additional days before heading to Bethany (11:6). In the meantime,
Lazarus dies and is buried; when Jesus finally arrives, Lazarus has been
entombed for four days!

As is typical throughout John's gospel, Jesus is scarcely ruffled by this
disastrous turn of events. He remains fully in control of the situation.
Before coming to Bethany, Jesus had already clued his disciples that (1)
Lazarus' "illness was not unto death" (that is, permanent death) (11:4);
(2) he was going to Judea simply to "awaken" Lazarus who had "fallen
asleep" (11:11–13); and (3) he was actually "glad" he would not be
around to prevent Lazarus' death "for your sake"—that is, the disciples'
sake—since this would enable them to witness a first-class sign of Jesus'
resurrection power (11:14–15).

Good for Jesus and good for the disciples: a wonderful educational
opportunity! But not so good for Martha and Mary who spend four miserable days mourning their brother's loss before Jesus arrives on the
scene. However much Jesus might be helping his other followers grow in
faith, it is difficult to interpret his delay in coming to Bethany as the least
bit beneficial to Martha and Mary—to say nothing of poor Lazarus.
Both sisters flatly let Jesus know of their disappointment, although, true
to form, Martha gets to Jesus first, meeting him out on the road "while
Mary stayed at home" (11:20). In any case, they register the same complaint: "Lord, if you had been here, my brother would not have died"
(11:21, 32). To be sure, they still maintain a tone of respect (addressing
Jesus as "Lord"), and Martha adds multiple statements affirming her
abiding faith in Jesus' life-giving power as God's Son and Messiah
(11:21–27). Moreover, Jesus has dropped unmistakable hints along the
way that he intends to raise Lazarus from the grave. We know where the
story is heading. But for all this, including Martha's marvelous confessions of faith, the stone-cold, pungent reality of Lazarus' death is not so
easily dismissed. Indeed, when Jesus orders the stone removed from her
brother's tomb, Martha's response (her final words in the story) bluntly,
even sarcastically perhaps, brings Jesus back down to earth: "You know,
Lord, after four days in the grave, *he stinks!*" (11:39) Resurrection or not,

Jesus manages to embed in Martha's memory not only the stark fact of her brother's death but the stinking fume of his decay as well. Is this what friends are for? Undoubtedly, this drama of Jesus' restoring a rotting corpse to life is unsurpassed in gospel literature.[58] But at what price?

While from a friendship perspective, Jesus' delay in helping his beloved Lazarus remains a curious and even callous phenomenon, other features in the narrative mitigate against this unsympathetic reading of Jesus' actions and show him to be a genuinely sensitive and compassionate ally. For one thing, his trek to Bethany in Judea—delayed or not—is a risky venture for Jesus himself. As the disciples point out, "Rabbi, the Jews were just now trying to stone you, and you are going there [to Judea] again?" (11:8). From Thomas's viewpoint, Jesus is leading them on a suicide mission: they will soon all be just as dead as Lazarus! (11:16). Thus, Jesus' outreach to Lazarus and his sisters during their season of death and grief represents a serious threat to his own life, yet another example of his willingness to lay down his life for his friends (15:13).

Also, when Jesus deals with Martha and Mary, although he never apologizes for his dilatory response, he takes great pains to assure them and empathize with them. Although Martha doesn't quite get the immediacy of the point, Jesus assures her of the hope of Lazarus' restoration to new life (11:23–27). In Mary's case, Jesus specifically draws her out ("The Teacher is here and is calling for you," 11:28) and identifies with her bereavement in a most touching and remarkable way. When he encounters her mournful weeping, Jesus becomes "greatly disturbed in spirit and deeply moved" and cannot help but weep along with her (11:33–35). The Johannine Jesus—usually so cool, calm, and collected—lets down his guard here in the face of his grieving friend. His emotions are churning here, bordering on anger and frustration ("greatly disturbed") mixed with sorrow and compassion ("See how he loved him!" 11:36).[59] He proceeds to the tomb to solve the crisis and work his miracle of resurrection, but he does not do so in a detached and perfunctory manner. He continues to be "greatly disturbed" by the ordeal (the verb is repeated in 11:38) even as he moves to overcome it. An intense battle is at hand—quite literally a matter of life and death. His close friends have been held in the cold clutches of death for four long days. That ought not to be. Jesus feels the horrible depths of their pain as he musters everything in his power to release them from it: "Lazarus, come out! Unbind him, and let him go" (11:43–44). That's what friends are for.

Mary's Waste

As anticipated by the disciples, Jesus' journey into Judea sparks opposition. In particular, his burgeoning popularity following the raising of Lazarus ignites the authorities' suspicion against him.[60] Thus the threatened Jesus "no longer walked openly among the Judeans" (11:54). He has to be extra careful about the company he keeps.

In this difficult period Jesus knows he can count on his friends from Bethany. "Six days before the Passover," he seeks refuge and refreshment in the home of Martha, Mary, and Lazarus (12:1). Reminiscent of the scene in Luke, once again Martha oversees the provision of food while Mary occupies herself at Jesus' feet. Only on this occasion Mary does not sit passively but rather anoints Jesus' feet with a pound of expensive perfume, using her hair as a towel (12:2–3). Again Mary's conduct elicits an objection, not from Martha this time, but from one of Jesus' disciples, Judas Iscariot: "Why was this perfume not sold for three hundred denarii [about a year's wages] and the money given to the poor?" (12:5). He has a point, even though the Johannine narrator summarily undermines Judas' motives by dubbing him a fraudulent thief and future traitor (12:4, 6). Still, a year's salary for a common laborer down the drain? A little dab of ointment would have sufficed along with a fresh bucket of water. Why this waste? Jesus has been put on the spot here. His concern for the poor and critique of the privileged are well known. How can he justify Mary's extravagant display on his behalf? Is this not an apt moment for Jesus to take his friend aside and correct her misguided behavior?

As it happens, Jesus sharply defends rather than reprimands Mary's actions: "Leave her alone" (12:7). In a rare moment of self-indulgence in the gospel accounts, Jesus welcomes his friend's luxuriant and affectionate gesture. Sometimes the loving bond of friendship trumps all other relationships and responsibilities. This is one of those times. Jesus is not suddenly turning his back on the poor. "You always have the poor with you," he comments—not as a callous dismissal of their plight (the poverty problem will never go away, so forget about it!)—but as a simple state-ment of fact (there will always be ample opportunities for aiding the poor, and normally you must seize them!). By contrast, however, Jesus interjects, "you do not always have me" (12:8). Here he offers an omi-nous hint of his imminent demise and a key point of contact with his beloved Mary. She and apparently she alone understands the gravity of the hour. The clock is ticking; her time with Jesus is coming to an end; her chances to show her love are running out. And so, she pre-anoints Jesus' body, as it were, "for the day of [his] burial" (12:7). Perhaps she recalls the awful stench of her dead brother and tries to forestall this ulti-mate indignity with Jesus by dousing him with pure nard, filling the whole house with its fragrance (12:3). In any event, Jesus gratefully accepts Mary's gracious offering of love.

This moving affirmation of loving service to the dead and dying per-haps provides some balance to one of the most shocking reactions of Jesus in the gospels. In the shared tradition in Matthew and Luke, Jesus refuses to allow a would-be follower first to go home and tend to his deceased father. "Let the dead bury their own dead," Jesus flatly an-nounces to the son, "but as for you, go and proclaim the kingdom of God" (Matt 8:21–22//Luke 9:59–60). The Johannine Jesus seems to soften on this point when his own life is on the line. Friends and family need to stick together to the end. The tender ministrations of devoted loved ones take some of the sting out of the enemy of death.

Conclusion

The favorite gospel hymn, "What A Friend We Have In Jesus," rejoices in the intimate, nurturing bond which believers enjoy with the living Lord Jesus, especially through the medium of prayer ("What a privilege to carry everything to God [through our friend Jesus] in prayer"). In this chapter we have explored what kind of friend the gospel narratives por-tray the earthly Jesus to be in relation to his closest associates: one "bap-tist" preacher (John), four disciples (the trio of Peter, James, and John in the Synoptics, and the anonymous "beloved disciple" in the fourth gospel), and three siblings from Bethany (Martha, Mary, Lazarus). While we have trained the spotlight on this inner circle of Jesus' friends, we should not conclude that Jesus promotes narrow cliques or exclusive boundaries of fellowship. While it does appear that he is closer to some people than to others in the gospels, his reputation as indiscriminate "friend of sinners" is widespread and altogether intentional on Jesus' part.

Three characteristics of Jesus' friendship stand out in our study: he proves himself to be (1) supportive and comforting at the same time he is (2) corrective and disciplining, and ultimately, (3) redemptive and forgiving.

1. By definition, friends should stick with one another during times of crisis. By and large, Jesus fulfills such expectations, although not always in conventional fashion. During John the Baptist's imprisonment at the hands of Herod Antipas, Jesus continues to endorse his friend's mission ("among those born of women, no one is greater than John") and certainly proves to be no friend of "that fox" Herod. He thus risks his own neck by speaking out in favor of a political prisoner. The gospels give no indication, however, that Jesus ever personally visits John during his captivity, a somewhat puzzling omission in light of Jesus' strong advocacy of prison visitation as a distinguishing mark of pious character in Matt 25:31–46 ("I was naked and you gave me clothing, I was sick and you took care of me, I was in prison and you visited me," 25:36; cf. vv. 39, 43). He keeps his distance (perhaps for security reasons), content to communicate to John through messengers (sent by John). Further, Jesus does not attend John's funeral following his brutal execution. John's disciples take care of their master's burial by themselves. Still, Jesus does not sever all ties with John after his death. He continues throughout his own trials to commend his friend's ministry and ultimately follows John in martyrdom for the kingdom of God.

   With respect to Peter, James, and John, Jesus takes the brunt of the hostility directed against his movement, allowing these three and the other disciples to escape seizure and crucifixion (for the moment). But Jesus knows that hard times are soon coming for his followers as well, and thus he attempts to prepare them for his departure. For the most part, however, they remain in wishful denial about the prospects of imminent suffering and persecution. Still, while his predictions and instructions fall largely on deaf ears, Jesus assures Peter (in Luke) that he will pray for his apostle's protection and perseverance. Although not a part of the specific episodes analyzed above, we might add that Jesus further comforts his distraught disciples (the entire company, not just a select few) with the promise of his abiding presence through the Holy Spirit ("another Comforter" in John) after his death.[61] As for sisters Martha and Mary in the fourth gospel, Jesus offers much-needed consolation in a more immediate crisis surrounding their brother Lazarus' illness, death, and burial. He speaks with Martha, weeps with Mary, and ultimately liberates Lazarus from the grave. But he takes his time coming to his friends' aid, deliberately delaying his visit until four days after Lazarus' entombment. While this enhances the power of the miracle, it strains the bonds of friendship. Martha and Mary each complain to Jesus: "Lord, if you had been here, my brother would not have died." What kind of friend tarries four days in a life-and-death situation? Jesus has his rational-theological reasons for such a response, but they fall short of fully satisfying the emotional-interpersonal demands of the moment. Overcome with a poignant mixture of grief and anger at the gravesite before his miraculous display, Jesus shows empathy with his friends' distress and perhaps a touch of regret over prolonging it needlessly.

2. While comforting his friends during times of crisis and confusion, he does not coddle them or cater to their insecurities. Quite the contrary, he takes seriously the responsibility of true friends to evaluate one another honestly (if friends won't "speak the truth in love," who will?), to sharpen one another, to improve one another's characters. Of course, since Jesus is not only friend and confidant, but also master and teacher (even to his closest followers), his duty to correct errant thought and behavior is inescapable. Such critical exhortation does not extend so

much to John the Baptist, since, apart from Jesus' baptism, the gospels do not portray the two figures in direct contact. John has his own coterie of disciples to manage distinct from Jesus' circle. Further, as we have seen, Jesus predominantly defends John's mission from external attacks. Still, some implicit critique—or better, complementary amendment (alongside complimentary approval)—of John's work may be detected in Jesus' striking out on his own path, feasting with and seeking out sinners along the way, whereas John fasted and called penitents to his stationary post in the wilderness.

The corrective, disciplining side of friend Jesus is much more evident in his interaction with his three core disciples and, to a lesser extent, with sisters Mary and Martha. In the midst of their consternation over his impending death, Jesus does not hesitate to chide Peter sharply for his worldly, "satanic" preoccupations, or the brothers Zebedee for their misdirected, opportunistic ambitions, or all three for their propensity to sleep (whether from dullness or grief) when they should be praying for strength. And at the end of the fourth gospel, as Peter continues to jockey with the beloved disciple for "favored friend" status, Jesus basically instructs Peter to mind his own business. Among the human foibles that bother Jesus the most across the gospel tradition, the tendency of friends to envy and compete with one another ranks near the top of the list. Martha's fretting that Mary is not pulling her weight and may be gaining some special advantage with Jesus further exemplifies such petty rivalry and, accordingly, draws Jesus' rebuke.

The goal of Jesus' "friendly" critiques is not faultfinding or point scoring, but rather character building and disciple making. In exposing Martha's excessive preoccupation with "much serving," the Lukan Jesus does not so much brush Martha off as invite her to come and share in his teaching with Mary. And by dismissing Peter's interest in the beloved disciple's fate ("What is that to you?"), the Johannine Jesus is not dismissing Peter himself but rather focusing Peter's attention on his own pastoral vocation ("Feed my sheep"; "Follow me!" 21:15–22).

3. Comforting friends during their stressful times and correcting friends' misguided choices and self-destructive conduct fit typical social expectations: that's what friends are supposed to do. But what about when the shoe is on the other foot—when someone desperately needs to be befriended during a personal crisis but so-called friends are nowhere to be found? Specifically, how does the synoptic Jesus react when his (male-disciple) friends all but abandon him at his bitter hour of trial and execution? Although spoken most directly to his executioners, the stunningly gracious words of Jesus from the cross in Luke reverberate out to his cowering disciples as well: "Father, forgive them, for they do not know what they are doing" (23:34). Again considering Peter, who claims to be Jesus' most loyal friend but proves to be the most disappointing at the moment of truth, he beats himself up with remorse when the cock's crow awakens the horror of what he has done to Jesus. But Jesus never responds in kind. He never betrays Peter or berates him for his cowardice. Knowing full well the fickleness of his friend, Jesus prays for Peter (as Luke reports) that his shaken faith will be restored and that, in turn, he will restore many others. The testimony of Acts and early Christian history confirms a fully rehabilitated Peter, a solid rock[62] (at last) sustained by friend and Lord Jesus' unfailing love and forgiveness.

Notes

1. Aristotle, *Nicomachean Ethics* 9.8.1168b, 6–8; cited in Hans Conzelmann, *Acts of the Apostles* (Hermeneia; Philadelphia: Fortress, 1987), 36; cf. Stanley K. Stowers, *Letter-Writing in Greco-Roman Antiquity* (Library of Early Christianity; Philadelphia: Westminster, 1986), 58–60.

2. Epicurus, *Basic Doctrines* 27; Cicero, *About the Ends of Goods and Evils* 1.65; cited in Wayne A. Meeks, *The Moral World of the First Christians* (London: SPCK, 1986), 57.

3. See Halvor Moxnes, "Patron-Client Relations and the New Community in Luke-Acts," in Neyrey, *The Social World of Luke-Acts: Models for Interpretation*, 241–68.

4. On the role of Jesus as "viceroy" in the kingdom of God, see E. P. Sanders, *Historical Figure of Jesus,* 238–48. Assessing Jesus' understanding of his vocation, Sanders concludes: "Jesus seems to have been quite reluctant to adopt a title for himself. I think that even 'king' is not precisely correct, since Jesus regarded God as king. My own favourite term for his conception of himself is 'viceroy.' God was king, but Jesus represented him and would represent him in the coming kingdom" (p. 248).

5. Compare John 19:12; Wayne A. Meeks, *The Origins of Christian Morality: The First Two Centuries* (New Haven, Conn.: Yale University Press), 39–40. In 1 Macc 2:17–18, the emissaries of Antiochus IV attempted to persuade (bribe) Mattathias the priest to offer sacrifices to the Greek ruler and thus become an honored "friend of the king." They promised that in return the king would shower money and gifts upon Mattathias and his family, but this arrangement (which Mattathias flatly refused) scarcely envisioned the prospect of becoming the king's confidant and colleague. "Friend of the king" more properly meant "indebted client of the king."

6. In Matthew, John's hesitation to baptize Jesus is reflected in his desire to be baptized by Jesus: "I need to be baptized by you, and do you come to me?" Only when Jesus assures him that "it is proper for us in this way to fulfill all righteousness" does John consent to baptize Jesus (3:13–15). Luke recounts the imprisonment of John by Herod just before announcing: "when Jesus also had been baptized and was praying." John's personal involvement in Jesus' baptism is thus diminished; effectively, Jesus appears to baptize himself in the presence of God the Father and the Holy Spirit (3:21–22).

7. The virtue of sticking with and supporting a suffering friend was highly valued in the Hellenistic world. As Burton Mack comments in his annotations to Sirach: "In Greek literature of the time, a friend was one who remained true in times of distress and could therefore be trusted with one's official or private interests and affairs ("Sirach," in *The HarperCollins Study Bible: New Revised Standard Version with the Apocryphal/Deuterocanonical Books* [ed. Wayne A. Meeks; New York: HarperCollins, 1993], 1540).

8. Luke 1:56 indicates that Mary stayed with Elizabeth for three months, suggesting that they were more than mere casual acquaintances or distant relatives.

9. Plutarch, *How to Tell a Flatterer from a Friend,* 73C–74E; cited in Abraham J. Malherbe, *Moral Exhortation, A Greco-Roman Sourcebook* (Library of Early Christianity 4; Philadelphia, Pa.: Westminster, 1986), 53.

10. On the continuity between John and Jesus as apocalyptic prophets demanding repentance, see Ehrman, *Jesus,* 137–52; Hill, *In God's Time,* 142–49.

11. See, e.g., Luke 6:27–36; 11:1–13. In 6:27–36, Jesus does not simply parrot John's mandates about sharing with the needy and treating others fairly, but radically extends them. For example, John's exhortation—"Whoever has two coats must share with anyone who has none" (3:11)—becomes "from anyone who takes away your coat do not withhold even your shirt. Give to everyone who

begs from you" in Jesus' teaching. As L. John Topel puts its, Jesus evinces a "beyondedness" in comparison with "the Baptist's more 'reasonable' ethic" (*Children of a Compassionate God: A Theological Exegesis of Luke* 6:20–49 [Collegeville, Minn.: Liturgical Press, 2001], 238). Still, there is a basic continuity between John and Jesus' agendas.

12. On the overlapping immersing activities of John and Jesus in the fourth gospel and the historical plausibility that Jesus functioned as "the Baptist" in his own right, see Joan E. Taylor, *The Immerser: John the Baptist within Second Temple Judaism* (Grand Rapids, Mich.: Eerdmans, 1997), 294–99.

13. "Why do we and the Pharisees fast often (*polla*), but your disciples do not fast?" (Matt 9:14); "John's disciples, like the disciples of the Pharisees, frequently (*pykna*) fast and pray, but your disciples eat and drink" (Luke 5:33).

14. Matt 4:1–2//Luke 4:1–2. Note the comments of historian E. P. Sanders (*Historical Figure of Jesus,* 112–13) regarding the plausibility of this and other occasions of Jesus' fasting:

> It is intrinsically likely that from time to time Jesus sought solitude for prayer and meditation, that he sometimes felt tempted, and that he fasted before beginning his public activity . . . it is possible that he himself later spoke to his disciples about a fast of forty days. Although no one can live for forty days without food and water, in Jewish usage the word 'fast' does not necessarily mean that one abstains completely from all sustenance. Even Luke, who writes that Jesus 'ate nothing' during the forty days (4.2), does not say that he drank no water. It is reasonable to think that Jesus fasted and prayed several days, with only minimal sustenance. . . .
>
> I assume that Jesus fasted on the Day of Atonement, since this is a biblical commandment and he seems in general to have observed the biblical law. But he and his disciples did not observe other fasts that may have become customary.

15. Compare Jesus' concluding statement of defense against those who would denigrate the prophetic missions of both him and John the Baptist in Luke 7:35, "Nevertheless, wisdom is vindicated by all her children."

16. E. P. Sanders, *Historical Figure of Jesus,* 233:

> But, since Jesus did run into opposition for his behaviour with sinners, I am inclined to think that Jesus is not be *defined* as a preacher of repentance. Jesus favoured repentance, but, if we classify him as a type, and describe how he saw his mission, we shall conclude that he was not a repentance-minded reformer. In the New Testament that title clearly belongs to the Baptist.

See further Sanders, *Jesus and Judaism* (London: SCM, 1985), 200–211.

17. Josephus, *Antiquities* 18.116–119; see Steve Mason, *Josephus and the New Testament* (Peabody, Mass: Hendrickson, 1992), 151–63.

18. Matt 14:3–5//Mark 6:17–19; cf. Luke 3:19–20.

19. See Taylor, *The Immerser,* 213–59; Hanson and Oakman, *Palestine in the Time of Jesus,* 82–86.

20. Luke 13:31. On the negative connotations of Jesus' fox reference, focusing on Herod's "malicious destructiveness" (rather than his fox-like cleverness), see John A. Darr, *On Character Building: The Reader and the Rhetoric of Characterization in Luke-Acts* (Literary Currents in Biblical Interpretation; Louisville, Ky.: Westminster/John Knox, 1992), 127–46.

21. Compare Daniel J. Harrington, *The Gospel of Matthew* (Sacra Pagina 1; Collegeville, Minn.: Liturgical Press, 1991), 156; John J. Rousseau and Rami Arav, *Jesus and His World: An Archaeological and Cultural Dictionary* (Minneapolis, Minn.: Fortress, 1995), 58.

22. Crossan, *Historical Jesus,* 236–37.

23. Ibid., 237–38; Crossan, *Jesus: A Revolutionary Biography,* 44–48.

24. Compare A. E. Harvey, *Strenuous Commands: The Ethic of Jesus* (London: SCM/Philadelphia, Pa.: Trinity Press International, 1990), 8–9, 64, 132–39.

25. Mark splices the lively account of John's imprisonment and beheading (6:14–29) between Jesus' sending of the Twelve (6:6–13), their return as "apostles," and their retreat with Jesus "to a deserted place" (6:30–32). This intercalation portends that Jesus and the apostles will ultimately face similar persecution to that experienced by John. As the Baptist prepared the way for Jesus' gospel mission, so he precedes Jesus in suffering at the hands of violent rulers. See Elizabeth Struthers Malbon, *In the Company of Jesus: Characters in Mark's Gospel* (Louisville, Ky.: Westminster/John Knox, 2000), 29: "The Markan narrative rhetoric discloses a parallelism between the preaching, being rejected and 'handed over,' and death of John, Jesus, and the disciples. At chapter 6 John is dead, Jesus is rejected, and the disciples are preaching. What will happen to Jesus next? What will happen to the disciples?" (cf. pp. 206–7).

26. The "desert" or "wilderness" (*erēmos*) setting is emphasized again in Matt 14:15 through the testimony of the disciples: "This is a deserted place [or, the place is a desert] . . .; send the crowds away so that they may go into the villages and buy food for themselves."

27. In Matt 14:14–21, Jesus manifests extraordinary "compassion" toward the multitude by healing their bodies of illness and infirmity as well as by feeding their bellies with mysteriously multiplied loaves and fishes. This incident thus represents a blended demonstration of "magic and meal," to use Crossan's provocative terms, as the primary poles of Jesus' gracious ministry. See Crossan's full discussion in *Historical Jesus,* 303–53. The gospel writers, however, studiously avoid associating Jesus' mighty deeds with "magic," which carried connotations of trickery, showmanship, and occultism (cf. Acts 8:9–24; 13:6–12; 19:18–19). Perhaps "miracle and meal" represents a more suitable combo ("miracle" suggesting true

divine empowerment). On the miracle/magic distinction, see Meier, *Marginal Jew*, 2:538–52.

28. Here I import the language of the fourth gospel (John 15:13; cf. 1 John 3:16) to reinforce the synoptic tradition.

29. Matt 10:2 and Luke 6:14 list Andrew in the number two position—as Peter's brother—before James and John, but overall Matthew and Luke follow Mark in emphasizing Peter's closer bond to James and John within the band of apostles.

30. We will discuss the incidents at the Mount of Olives and Gethsemane below. For the episode where Jesus permits only Peter, James, and John (among the Twelve) to accompany him into the home of Jairus, the synagogue ruler, whose deceased daughter awaits Jesus' revitalizing touch, see Mark 5:35–43// Luke 8:49–56.

31. Plutarch, *How to Tell a Flatterer from a Friend*, 70D–71C; cited in Malherbe, *Moral Exhortation*, 48–50 (emphasis added). For a similar emphasis in the gospels on settling grievances and correcting a colleague's (church member's) errant behavior in private if at all possible, see Matt 18:15–16.

32. For an exhaustive literary and theological analysis of this epiphany in the Synoptic Gospels, see John Paul Heil, *The Transfiguration of Jesus: Narrative Meaning and Function of Mark* 9:2–8, *Matt* 17:1–8 and *Luke* 9:28–36 (Analecta Biblica 144; Rome: Pontifical Biblical Institute, 2000).

33. Apparently, Peter wants to memorialize and prolong this marvelous event by constructing three booths, one each for Jesus, Moses, and Elijah. But he has hardly thought through the details or implications of this building project. Mark and Luke both stress that Peter is really just speaking off the top of his head, "not knowing what to say" (Mark 9:6//Luke 9:33).

34. For examples of a young child as "a nothing, a nobody, a nonperson in the Mediterranean world of paternal power, absolute in its acceptance or rejection of the newly born infant," see Crossan, *Jesus: A Revolutionary Biography*, 62–64 (the citation is from p. 64), and his *Historical Jesus*, 266–69. This is not to say that child abuse or neglect was a universal phenomenon in the first century. But Jesus' disciples show little regard for infants when they "speak sternly" against Jesus' blessing little children in the next chapter of Mark. Such resistance draws a sharp, "indignant" rebuke from Jesus: "Let the little children come to me; do not stop them; for it is to such as these that the kingdom of God belongs" (Mark 10:13–14; cf. Matt 19:13–14//Luke 18:15–16).

35. Matt 26:56//Mark 14:50. Luke does not explicitly report the disciples' desertion, but Jesus' final hours are still haunted by an absence of supportive followers, except for a group of grieving women on the way to the cross (23:27–31).

36. Matt 26:40//Mark 14:37. Compare Raymond E. Brown, *The Death of the Messiah, From Gethsemane to the Grave: A Commentary on the Passion Narratives in the Four Gospels* (2 vols; Anchor Bible Reference Library; New York: Doubleday, 1994), 1:194.

37. Here I cite Matthew's version, which stresses more explicitly than Mark the personal nature of Jesus' query: "Could you not stay awake with me?" (26:40; cf. the original plea, "stay awake with me" in 26:38).

38. Walter Bauer, William F. Arndt, F. Wilbur Gingrich, and Frederick W. Danker, *A Greek-English Lexicon of the New Testament and Other Early Christian Literature* (2nd ed; Chicago: University of Chicago Press, 1979), 84–85.

39. Brown, *Death of the Messiah,* 1:208–9; 2:1379–83.

40. Matt 26:57–75//Mark 14:53–72//Luke 22:54–71//John 18:15–18, 25–27.

41. Matt 26:30–35//Mark 14:26–31//Luke 22:31–34//John 13:36–38.

42. Luke Timothy Johnson, *The Gospel of Luke* (Sacra Pagina 3; Collegeville, Minn.: Liturgical Press, 1991), 358.

43. In Matt 18:21–22, Jesus answers Peter's question "how often should I forgive?" with a classic response suggesting unlimited forbearance: "Not seven times, but, I tell you, seventy-seven times" (cf. Luke 17:4). This is good news for Peter who himself will need repeated forgiveness from his master.

44. See Robert Kysar, *John, the Maverick Gospel* (Atlanta, Ga.: John Knox, 1976).

45. On Nathanael, see John 1:45–51; John refers to "the twelve" only in 6:70–71 ("'Did I not choose you, the twelve? Yet one of you is a devil.' He was speaking of Judas . . . one of the twelve") and 20:24 ("But Thomas . . . one of the twelve").

46. On the beloved disciple, see Raymond E. Brown, *The Community of the Beloved Disciple,* 31–34, 84; James H. Charlesworth, *The Beloved Disciple* (Valley Forge, Pa.: Trinity Press International, 1995).

47. "In a pre-eminent manner he deserves to be called a friend of Jesus (John 15:15). Indeed the Johannine tradition is fond of representing the intimacy that existed between Jesus and the Beloved Disciple" (Raymond F. Collins, *These Things Have Been Written: Studies on the Fourth Gospel* [Louvain Theological and Pastoral Monographs 2; Louvain: Peeters/Grand Rapids, Mich.: Eerdmans, 1990], 44).

48. See Brown, *Community,* 31–32, 84–87.

49. Following the custom of the day, Jesus is likely reclining on his left side around a U-shaped table. Thus, if the beloved disciple is "reclining next to Jesus" and leaning against his chest (13:23, 25), he must be stationed at Jesus' right. Compare David K. Rensberger, "The Gospel According to John," in *The Harper-Collins Study Bible: The New Revised Standard Version with the Apocryphal/Deuterocanonical Books* (ed. Wayne Meeks; New York: HarperCollins, 1993), 2041.

50. This translation comes from Francis J. Moloney, *The Gospel of John* (Sacra Pagina 4; Collegeville, Minn.: Liturgical Press, 1998), 382, 387. Note further Moloney's explanation: "The physical position of the Beloved Disciple is described twice [13:23, 25]. This close physical proximity is a symbol of both affection and commitment. This description matches the relationship that exists

between the historical Jesus and the Father . . . in 1:18" (p. 387). John 1:18 reads: "It is God the only Son, who is close to the Father's heart [or breast or bosom]."

51. John 18:15 indicates "Simon Peter and another disciple followed Jesus" into the high priest's courtyard. Could this anonymous companion be the beloved disciple?

52. This is not to deny that this figure was also a "real" historical person known to the Johannine community, possibly even its founder.

53. Compare Moloney, *Gospel of John*, 555.

54. Jesus' forecast to Peter, "you will stretch out your hands," may imply that Peter will literally follow Jesus in crucifixion. Church tradition holds that Peter in fact died as a martyr on a Roman cross, albeit upside-down (by his own request).

55. Not surprisingly, Lazarus has been proposed as one of the possible candidates for the beloved disciple in John. However, while he is certainly *a* beloved disciple, he is never identified as *the* beloved disciple, who remains anonymous in the fourth gospel.

56. See Elisabeth Moltmann-Wendel, *The Women Around Jesus* (New York: Crossroad, 1997), 15–48.

57. Compare Luke 4:38–39; 9:10–17; 12:35–42; 17:7–10; 22:14–23; F. Scott Spencer, *The Portrait of Philip in Acts: A Study of Roles and Relations* (Journal for the Study of the New Testament Supplement Series 67; Sheffield, U.K.: Sheffield Academic, 1992), 201–6.

58. In the gospels, Jesus resuscitates two other deceased persons: the daughter of the synagogue ruler, Jairus (Matt 9:23–26//Mark 5:35–43//Luke 8:49–56), and the son of an unnamed widow at Nain (Luke 7:11–17). But in both cases the miracle follows close on the heels of death, before burial.

59. The verb translated in the NRSV as "greatly disturbed" (*embrimaomai*) literally conveys something like "snort with anger" (see Rudolf Schnackenburg, *The Gospel of John* [3 vols.; New York: Crossroad, 1987], 2:335–36). What precisely is Jesus angry at: the horror of death? the apparent triumph of evil? the disbelief of the crowd? perhaps even his own procrastination? Compare my forthcoming article: F. Scott Spencer, "'You Just Don't Understand' (or Do You?)" in *A Feminist Companion to John* (ed. Amy-Jill Levine; Sheffield, U.K.: Sheffield Academic, 2003).

60. Undoubtedly the priestly leaders in Jerusalem are jealous of Jesus' surging fame among the people in light of the Lazarus miracle, but more than that, they are worried about Roman reprisals against the Jewish people at large because of the unpredictable enthusiasm surrounding the Jesus movement. Accordingly, the high priest Caiphas diplomatically reasons, "it is better for you to have one man [Jesus] die for the people than to have the whole nation destroyed" (11:50).

61. See Matt 28:20; Luke 24:49; John 14:16, 25–31; 15:26; 16:4–24. On the role of the Holy Spirit as "Paraclete" (sometimes translated as "Comforter") in

John, in conjunction with Jesus' teaching about friendship, see Sharon H. Ringe, *Wisdom's Friends: Community and Christology in the Fourth Gospel* (Louisville, Ky.: Westminster/John Knox, 1999), 64–92.

62. Matthew highlights "Peter" (*Petros*) as the nickname given to Simon by Jesus, as a token of his role as foundational "rock" (*petra*) of Christ's church: "And I tell you, you are Peter (*Petros*), and on this rock (*petra*) I will build my church, and the gates of hell will not prevail against it" (16:18).

4

Body Treatments

At the end of the previous chapter, we observed Jesus' indulgence of Mary's washing his feet with costly perfume. Is this typical of what we might call a preoccupation on Jesus' part with "good grooming"? Walk into any department store in America today and you will find counter after counter, showcase after showcase, displaying a plethora of cosmetics and fragrances for men as well as women. We are obsessed with looking and smelling our best and will seemingly spare no expense when it comes to beautifying our bodies. The old cynical Jewish sage known as Qoheleth, the author of Ecclesiastes, would appear to endorse such interests as a source of at least momentary pleasure in an otherwise "vain" and gloomy world: "Let your garments always be white; do not let oil be lacking on your head" (the precursor of Brylcreem and Vitalis ads) (9:8). Does Jesus also follow this line of wisdom?

In the case of Jesus' anointing at Bethany, we recall that his primary concern is not with appearances and fragrances but with relationships. Jesus accepts a final expression of lavish love from a dear friend in the face of his impending death and burial. Mary functions more as mortician than beautician. Otherwise, apart from two similar though not identical scenes depicting a woman's anointing Jesus' body and occasional interest in hand and foot washing, the gospels do not feature personal hygiene as a major focus of Jesus' ministry.

Indeed, when it comes to body matters, the gospels present Jesus in some ways as a body-denying, self-disciplining ascetic. Situated historically between the rigorous, desert-dwelling John the Baptist and the celibate, body-beating Paul the apostle, this ascetic tendency within Jesus should come as no surprise.[1] Furthermore, the image of the cross, so central to Jesus' identity and destiny in the gospels, is as vivid an ascetic symbol as one could imagine. And the statement "If any want to become my followers, let them deny themselves and take up their cross and follow me" could well be interpreted as an ascetic manifesto (Matt 16:24//Mark 8:34//Luke 9:23).

Still, that is far from the whole story on Jesus' treatment of his body. Radically shaking, if not shattering, his ascetic image is a hedonistic reputation he acquires as a "glutton and drunkard" (Matt 11:19//Luke 7:34). To be sure, these are pejorative labels promulgated by Jesus' enemies; but there has to be some truth behind them to make them stick. These slurs would never work against a John the Baptist or a Gandhi, but for one who spends as much as time as Jesus does frequenting and talking about dinner parties and banquets, they make a point, even if exaggerated. Where there's smoke (attending feasts), there's fire (excessive feasting). And even on the question of Jesus' sexual practices, while the evidence points to his remaining single and celibate, he does not quarantine himself off from women, like some Essene sectarians,[2] or castrate himself as far as we know, as was fashionable in certain monastic circles (he does, however, make some provocative comments about cutting off appendages and self-made eunuchs in Matthew [see below]). He has contact and conversation with numerous women like Martha and Mary—within proper bounds of modesty, of course, except perhaps for a tantalizing incident in Luke 7 in which Jesus' tolerance of a "sinful woman's" rather intimate advances raises certain eyebrows. Jesus is also notorious for reaching out to prostitutes, although not in the carnal sense (Matt 21:31–32).

We confront a mixed, complex portrait of Jesus' treatment of his body in the gospels on a continuum from abstemious to indulgent, ascetic to hedonistic. In attempting to sort out the puzzle, we concentrate on four dimensions of Jesus' bodily existence: (1) how he deals with the problem of dirt through washings and other cleansing practices; (2) how he manages his diet, that is, the quality and quantity of food and drink he consumes; (3) how he handles the matter of sex and potentially erotic encounters; and (4) how he responds to personal physical pain and suffering. While Jesus has much to say and do in the gospels regarding other people's bodies (healing, cleansing, feeding), our main concern is with Jesus' treatment of his own body. Still, as cultural critics remind us, attitudes and actions related to individual bodies often reflect the core values and structures of the larger social body.[3] In short, the physical body symbolically mirrors the body politic. In focusing on Jesus' body, we must thus keep in view its embeddedness or, better, embodiedness within the wider framework of first-century eastern Mediterranean culture.

Dirt

Defining and dealing with dirt is not so simple a matter as might be assumed. For starters, from a sociocultural perspective, not all dirt is "dirty." The problem is more anthropological than geological. It all depends on established boundaries and codes of conduct: dirt is that which defiles or disrupts the order of things; anything that is "out of place" is dirty.[4] Dirt in the garden and the field—exactly where it should be, essential to sustaining life—is perfectly "clean"; however, dirt that is staining carpets in modern living rooms or soiling sacred vessels and furnishings in ancient temples must be removed. The issue is further complicated by cultic versus hygienic, ritual versus biomedical perspectives. In the modern world, cleanliness is largely defined in terms of health and sanitation. At a university where I worked, I remember notices placed in bathrooms across the campus for several months outlining the "scientific" evidence promoting regular hand washing as a major weapon in fighting disease. It's all about germs, bacteria, and chemistry. In ancient, prescientific societies, however, cleanliness or purity had more to do with conforming to a set of prescribed rituals designed to sustain a divinely established order of creation (variously conceived). Priests, scribes, and other experts in religious law had more to do with monitoring and maintaining purity than physicians, scientists, and health inspectors. This is not to say that every bath, every washing in the ancient world was fraught with religious significance. Swimming and foot washing, for example, were in most cases acts of refreshment and diversion rather than devotion.[5] Still, ancient Jews perceived a close connection between dirt and deviance, purity and piety, cleanliness and godliness,[6] albeit in symbolic-metaphorical rather than substantive-moral terms. Impurity and pollution did not equate with immorality and perversion,[7] but did suggest disorder and dysfunction.

In Jesus' case, as we have already suggested, the gospels do not portray him as overly concerned with the beauty or purity of his own body. While welcoming women's anointing of his head and feet on certain occasions, Jesus does not go around with an entourage of female servants attending to his creaturely comforts. Such is the lot of those aristocrats "liv[ing] in luxury . . . in royal palaces," not of radical prophets like John and Jesus (Matt 11:7–9//Luke 7:24–28). By all accounts, seeking physical comfort is not high on Jesus' list of priorities. Again, while submitting to John's baptism and perhaps pursuing his own baptizing work for a time, ultimately Jesus' mission does not revolve around purification rituals (no one ever calls him Jesus "the Baptist," as far we know).[8] On the other hand, assumptions that Jesus regularly flouts Jewish purity rules and denounces groups like the Pharisees for their scrupulous observance run considerably beyond the gospel evidence. True, Jesus is not reported rushing to the closest immersion pool (*miqveh*)[9] to restore his purity after touching the funeral bier of the widow's son or the corpse of Jairus's daughter.[10] But apart from the weak argument from silence (nothing is said about Jesus not washing—maybe he does), Jesus is not in Jerusalem preparing for temple worship according to strict purity regulations (he's up in Galilee), and, more significantly, in both cases Jesus raises the deceased persons to new life, thus eliminating the problem of corpse impurity. Still, should he not have consulted local priests and scribes on the matter? Perhaps, but these are rather extraordinary circumstances beyond the province of the law (death normally has the last word). In a similar though less spectacular situation, Jesus does display respect for priestly legislation on purity issues. While Jesus himself does not undergo any rite of purification upon healing an unclean leper by touch, he does insist in the synoptic accounts that the leper "go [and] show yourself to the priest, and offer for your cleansing what Moses commanded, as a testimony to them" (Matt 8:4//Mark 1:44//Luke 5:14).[11] Jesus does not go out of his way to undermine Jewish purity laws.[12]

To clarify further Jesus' handling of bodily "dirt" in the context of Jewish purity concerns, we consider various incidents concerning the washing of soiled hands and feet.

Hand Washing

In two separate incidents, certain Pharisaic Jews object to Jesus' apparent carelessness concerning the washing of hands before meals: one, featured in Matthew and Mark, focusing on Jesus' tolerance of his disciples' "dirty" hands (Matt 15:1–2//Mark 7:1–5); and the other, found only in Luke, regarding Jesus' own failure to "wash up" before dinner at a Pharisee's home (11:37–38). Again, we must stress, the issue at hand is "not hygiene but holiness"[13] (holiness as "set-apartness," not sinlessness). It is a matter of compliance with certain Jewish purity traditions marking off the sacred and devout from the profane and deviant. Mark would have us believe that the Pharisees represented universal Jewish custom, that is, "all the Jews [who] do not eat unless they thoroughly wash their hands" (7:3). While historians often privilege Mark's gospel because of its presumed chronological priority, in this case the scholarly consensus is that Mark has exaggerated the point. It would have been difficult to find any religious ritual in the first century that "all the Jews" practiced or even endorsed, much less one with such flimsy scriptural foundation as hand washing before meals. There was Levitical precedent for ritual hand washing in the case of persons defiled by some bodily discharge (they could then touch other persons and objects without polluting them), but nothing explicit about washing before eating (Lev 15:11). This practice apparently arose as part of the oral "tradition of the elders" developed by the Pharisees, and even here, we cannot be certain that "all" Pharisees agreed (what we know more assuredly is that pious first-century Jews within and among various groups debated over the proper ways to live as God's holy people).[14] Matthew's gospel, generally better informed about Jewish customs, omits Mark's entire narrative aside concerning the washing habits of "all the Jews."[15] The most we can say is that some Pharisees and scribes are scrupulous about washing hands (and other things) before meals and occasionally clash with Jesus on this issue in the gospel records.

In the present case, Jesus registers no denial of the Pharisees' charges against him and his disciples, and he makes no apology. But neither does he harp on "freedom from hand washing" as a critical issue. In Mark he drops the matter completely; in Matthew he picks it up in a single verse after a lengthy digression (15:20); and in Luke he moves on to consider the tradition of washing cups and dishes (11:39–40), not hands. Jesus does take the opportunity to put Pharisaic tradition in its place, under the supreme authority of divine (Mosaic) law, and to emphasize the primacy of internal purity, a "clean heart," over merely external cleanliness. But these are not particularly radical ideas. The psalmists and the prophets had blazed a well-worn trail on these matters,[16] and no Pharisee worth his salt would have claimed that scrubbed hands (or cups, plates, or utensils) automatically substituted for a pure heart or obliterated a corrupt one. Quite the contrary, clean hands mirror clean hearts. Still, the gospels seem to reflect some underlying debate as to whether clean hearts necessitate clean hands or whether dirty hands somehow signal a wicked heart. If one wants to monitor the moral condition of a person's heart, Jesus thinks it wiser to listen to the discourse from the mouth than to look for the dirt under the fingernails: "what comes out of the mouth proceeds from the heart, and this is what defiles . . . but to eat with unwashed hands does not defile" (Matt 15:18–20).

While Jesus does not appear to be hyperfastidious in the gospels about washing his hands before eating, he also does not vigorously campaign against the practice by others and certainly does not oppose the goal of purity that it symbolizes (the controversy is over means, not ends). Moreover, while hand washing seems optional for Jesus at ordinary meals, no question is raised about his practice of water-cleansing rituals at more formal occasions—say, at wedding feasts or temple celebrations. In John 2, for example, while Jesus utilizes the water "for the Jewish rites of purification" to make wine at the Cana wedding, he does not smash the water pots (Jeremiah style) or speak to the issue of hand washing in any way.[17] And in the next scene, often mislabeled the "cleansing" of the temple, while Jesus drives out the animal sellers and money changers and upends their tables, he does not attack the bath attendants or drain their pools. While Jesus is clearly upset about some aspects of temple "business," purity practices and washing rituals do not appear on his hit list.

Foot Washing

Distinct from the anointing scene in Bethany, fraught with symbolic significance concerning Jesus' imminent death and burial,[18] Luke presents another incident in which a woman washes Jesus' feet (7:36–50).[19] Once again, the setting is a dinner party in a Pharisee's home where Jesus has been invited. On this occasion, however, the problem, from Simon the Pharisee's viewpoint, is too much inappropriate foot washing rather than too little requisite hand washing before eating. In fact, the issue of hand washing is not even raised here as in Luke 11.[20] Moreover, the practice of foot washing in Jesus' day had more to do with refreshing hospitality than with ritual purity, which did not make it a trivial duty (hospitality was taken very seriously in the ancient world[21]), but did remove it from the realm of religious observance. Here dirt is "real" dirt, not a metaphor for impurity. Treading the dusty roads of Palestine in sandals made one's feet "really" dirty. Washing one's feet (or having one's feet washed by servants) upon entering the house (especially as a guest) would be roughly equivalent in modern terms to removing one's muddy boots before traipsing through the living room.

Thus, the bare fact of Jesus' feet being washed before dinner in his host's residence is unremarkable; indeed, it is exactly what would be expected. The difficulty arises from who does the foot washing (an uninvited, unnamed "sinful woman" from the streets) and how it is carried out (in an extravagant, exhibitionist manner). Simon the Pharisee is appalled that Jesus accepts such service. Possible erotic dimensions of this encounter with the "washing woman" will be considered below in connection with Jesus' sexuality, but for now we focus on the basic duty of foot washing and other physical gestures of hospitality. However shocked Simon might be concerning Jesus' actions, Jesus sharply turns the tables on Simon for his inaction. Who's at fault here? Jesus clearly cites three points of contrast between the woman's and Simon's behavior, and Simon does not come out the better for it:

1. "Simon . . . I entered your house; *you* gave me *no water* for my feet, *but she* has bathed my feet with her tears and dried them with her hair.
2. *You* gave me *no kiss, but* from the time I came in *she* has not stopped kissing my feet.
3. *You* did *not anoint* my head with oil, *but she* has anointed my feet with ointment" (7:44–46).

No water for his feet, no kiss on his cheek, no oil on his head. It's surprising that there is food on the table! These are not superfluities but responsibilities of basic civility and hospitality, and Simon has scorned Jesus and shamed himself by being such a shabby host. The "sinful woman," however much the object of Simon's disdain, has actually shown him up in his own home.[22]

Jesus does not go around in the gospels snapping his fingers at hosts and servants, demanding royal treatment. In fact, Jesus may have never bothered to expose Simon's negligence had Simon himself not raised the issue of the woman's conduct. Nonetheless, Jesus obviously accepts common acts of courtesy and comfort when offered. Whatever else he may have denied his body, he does not deprive it of refreshing water, friendly kisses, and fragrant ointment.

Before leaving the matter of foot washing, we must briefly discuss that most famous of foot-washing incidents in the fourth gospel, where Jesus himself fills the basin, dons the towel, and proceeds to wash the feet of his disciples (13:1–20). This episode clearly confirms Jesus' endorsement of the practice of foot washing, although, interestingly, the washing of his own feet does not come into view here. Jesus plays the role of the washing servant to illustrate the lesson that the disciples should likewise humbly "wash one another's feet" (13:14), but no mention is made of their or anyone's washing Jesus' feet. While this may be an incidental omission, it more likely reflects a point of Johannine Christology. In John 13, foot washing is more than a hospitable gesture; it is also a vivid symbol of spiritual cleansing.[23] As the disciples' "Teacher and Lord" (13:13–14), Jesus is the cleanser, not the one in need of cleansing. As the fountain of "living water," Jesus has come "to wash away the sin of the world."[24] From this lofty christological perspective, the Johannine Jesus need not—must not—have his own feet washed. By contrast, Luke portrays Jesus with his feet more firmly on the ground, so to speak, and thus, as for any human being, in need of washing off the dust and dirt of travel.

Diet

If "you are what you eat," as the saying goes, contemporary American society is bordering on the schizophrenic. Our minds and stomachs are deeply divided. Peruse the nation's major glossy magazines while standing in the checkout line at the supermarket, and you will quickly notice numerous articles and advertisements concerning both the latest techniques for dieting and weight loss as well as the hottest recipes for the most luscious desserts and gourmet dinners—often in the same issue! Likewise, the billion-dollar fast-food industry capitalizes on America's craving for fat-laden triple cheeseburgers and super fries while also offering a "lite" menu of garden salads and grilled-chicken sandwiches to satisfy more virtuous appetites.

The conflict is not really a new one. It is just the peculiarly American variation on the old battle between denial and debauchery, control and consumption. Do we deprive and discipline our bodies to eke out a few more years of existence, or do we stimulate and stuff them to get as much pleasure as we can out of this fleeting, "vain life," as Qoheleth suggests?[25] Or can we settle on some happy medium of moderation?

How does Jesus manage this age-old dietary dilemma with respect to his own body? Interestingly, such a question remains a serious issue for some contemporary Christians working within the "What Would Jesus Do?" ethical paradigm. For example, a medical doctor from Florida has recently authored *What Would Jesus Eat? The Ultimate Program for Eating Well, Feeling Great, and Living Longer,* in which he argues that we would be much better off walking as much as Jesus walked (three to ten miles a day) and eating the way Jesus typically ate (except at special feasts)— light on meat and pastries, heavy on whole grains and fresh vegetables, chased with a moderate daily dose of red wine. Obviously, standard church potlucks in the Bible Belt—featuring fried chicken, rich casseroles, creamy desserts, and sweetened iced tea—offer rather different fare. The food may be blessed in Jesus' name, but hardly matches Jesus' menu.[26]

But does the evidence really allow a full and precise charting of Jesus' diet? As suggested above, the gospels present a somewhat ambiguous picture of Jesus' eating habits, as if he were caught in the tension we have been describing between rigorous abstaining and gluttonous indulging.

We will explore each of these poles in turn in an effort to make a bal-anced assessment of Jesus' diet.

Rigorous Abstaining?

Starting with the most extreme form of dietary asceticism—total absti-nence from food for periods of time—the gospels indicate that while Jesus does not regularly fast nor encourage his disciples to do so (in con-trast to John the Baptist, the Pharisees, and other devout Jews), he does fast at least once for an extended period in the Judean desert, just before launching his public ministry. Moreover, while opposed to insincere, theatrical displays of fasting simply to impress onlookers with one's piety, Jesus does not denigrate the practice of fasting as such. In fact, he regards it as a perfectly acceptable act of religious devotion, alongside almsgiving and prayer, provided it is carried out privately before God "who is in secret" and unobtrusively in public. "When you fast" (notice the assump-tion that fasting will be practiced), Jesus exhorts in Matthew's Sermon on the Mount, rather than walking about with hungry looks and haggard faces, "put oil on your head and wash your face [notice the appreciation of basic grooming again] so that your fasting may not be seen by others" (6:16–18).

While the discipline of fasting is not a major driving force behind Jesus' mission, the gospels also hint at certain points that, in urgently pursuing the purpose of God for his life, eating is the least of Jesus' con-cerns. In one sense, he is simply too busy to eat, too consumed with higher pressing business. In another sense, he resists the temptation to use his power and charisma for his own selfish ends: others he feeds by the thousands; he worries very little about his own nutrition.[27] This eschewing of personal dietary indulgence crops up at the start of Jesus' vocation in the famous temptation scene in the desert (Matt 4:1–11// Luke 4:1–13). Following the lengthy fast (mentioned above), Jesus is naturally "famished." At this vulnerable moment, the devil comes and urges Jesus to transform the desert stones into edible loaves. The prob-lem here is not coaxing Jesus to eat (the fast is over, he's hungry, and it's time to eat), but rather encouraging him to use his extraordinary Spirit-power to meet his own physical needs. This would be the first step toward self-aggrandizement, toward having it all: today, stones into bread; tomorrow, dust into delicacies, sand into castles (real ones), anything and everything into gold—the Midas touch all the way to the top.[28] Even in his hungry state, Jesus recognizes the trap. Drawing on the resources of Deuteronomy forged in another desert, he counters the devil's offer with the emphatic declaration of holy Scripture: "One does not live by bread alone."[29] In other words, there are more important things in life than filling one's belly, such as fulfilling God's will and serving the needs of others. This perspective surfaces again later in the shared tradition between Matthew and Luke, as Jesus asserts: "Do not worry about your life, what you will eat . . . for life is more than food" (Matt 6:25–26//Luke 12:22–24).

More directly reflecting Jesus' attitude toward his own bodily nourishment, the fourth gospel uniquely reports Jesus' jolting response to the disciples' plea that he eat some of the food that they have brought from the city: "I have food to eat that you do not know about. . . . My food is to do the will of him who sent me and to complete his work" (4:32, 34). While these statements correlate with the majestic Johannine portrait of Jesus as God's exalted Son sent "from above" (3:31–36), the "living bread that came down from heaven" (6:22–59), and the "true vine" producing fruit in the Father's vineyard (15:1–8), they also fit the more prosaic synoptic profile of Jesus as a man consumed by his calling, fueled by the urgency of his task, running, as it were, on religious zeal. If eating serves the interests of his mission, that's fine; if not, then eating can wait.

What is on the menu when Jesus does eat and drink? Are there particular restrictions in Jesus' diet, such as Nazirite teetotalism or kosher taboos, or peculiar idiosyncrasies, such as John the Baptist's locusts and wild honey? On the whole, Jesus is presented consuming the staples of bread, fish, water, and wine.[30] While he tells stories about a "great banquet," a "fatted calf," and one "who feasted sumptuously every day,"[31] these are not autobiographical accounts (see more below on Jesus' reputation as a glutton). His basic diet is not that of the elites but that of the masses, with whom he shares loaves and fishes in the famous feeding incidents. His drinking of wine is unremarkable. Wine was not a luxury item in Jesus' day, nor was it prohibited by Jewish law, except when resulting in drunkenness. Nazirite vows involving total abstinence from fermented beverages and all grape products, among other things, were special and voluntary, not incumbent. They were expressions of consecration for set periods of time, except for extraordinary cases of lifelong Nazirite devotion from birth as reported of Samson, Samuel, and John the Baptist.[32] There is no evidence that Jesus himself ever undertakes a temporary Nazirite vow, much less a permanent one. The fact that he is a Nazarene because he hails from the village of Nazareth has nothing whatsoever to do with his being a Nazirite.

Although Jesus does not personally follow strict Nazirite regulations, this does not mean he opposes these superogatory practices—he never criticizes John the Baptist's eating habits—or ignores other dietary restrictions mandated for all devout Jews (kosher laws). The parenthetical comment in Mark 7:19 that Jesus "declared all foods clean" is as exaggerated as the remark earlier in the same chapter that "all the Jews" practiced ritual hand washing. Writing for a Gentile audience, Mark again over-stretches the distance between Jesus and Judaism. Not surprisingly, Matthew omits Mark's note that Jesus categorically accepts the purity of all foods and blunts Mark's emphasis that "nothing" which goes into the mouth can defile a person.[33] Moreover, the letters of Paul and the Book of Acts, written before and after Mark respectively, both attest to persisting, vigorous debate among the followers of Jesus concerning the practice of Jewish dietary laws.[34] Clearly the matter is not as cut-and-dried as Mark suggests.

A test case of Jesus' kosher commitment concerns his treatment of swine, that quintessentially "unclean" species in Jewish law and tradition.[35] The gospels feature two "pig tales" involving Jesus, and in neither does Jesus consume any pork or accord the poor pig any dignity. In fact, in the one synoptic story where Jesus finds himself near a herd of swine, he promptly uses them as a receptacle for a "legion" of expelled demons. These malevolent spirits then propel the entire porcine pack to drown themselves in the Sea of Galilee (Matt 8:28–34//Mark 5:1–20//Luke 8:26–39). A disturbing outcome, to be sure: annihilating the lethal demons is one thing; destroying the "innocent" pigs is another. The way they die forecloses any usefulness to their owners; they are a total loss. However, the uniqueness of this violent tale in the gospel tradition should give us pause about drawing ethical lessons from it. No other gospel story features Jesus' participation in the mass destruction of creature or property.[36] Furthermore, this incident is fraught with symbolic-political significance. The name "Legion" and the pig mascot both signify Roman military occupation. Jesus' assault on the vicious forces of demon possession thus constitutes a powerful protest against oppressive Roman possession of Israel.[37] The story is more about defending human rights than denying animal rights and only incidentally has anything to tell us about Jesus' diet.

The other "pig tale" is one Jesus tells in Luke, in which the pigs and the pods they eat represent "skid row," where a rebellious son has landed in "a distant country," in contrast to the sumptuous "fatted calf" awaiting him upon his return home (15:11–24). Obviously, no great love is lost between Jesus and swine: he seems to accept their "unclean" status without reservation.

Gluttonous Indulging?

We come now to assess the nasty rumor going around about Jesus that he is "a glutton and a drunkard." The source for this information, oddly enough, is Jesus himself: he admits that others are saying such unflattering things about him. We suggested above that there has to be some basis for the charges of Jesus' overeating and inebriation. Such criticism would be pointless against a strict dietary ascetic like John the Baptist. Jesus himself points out, in the tradition shared by Matthew and Luke, that the glutton and drunkard labels follow from the fact that, unlike John, "the Son of Man [Jesus] has come eating and drinking" (Matt 11:19// Luke 7:34). Throughout the gospels, Jesus does participate in and speak about various dinner parties and festive celebrations where abundant food and drink are available. But, of course, that doesn't mean that he actually overindulges on any of these occasions, much less on a regular basis (deviant tags of glutton/drunkard imply a pervasive, obsessive habit). In any case, labels do not have to be completely accurate to stick and do damage: just the rumor of their validity can smear a reputation.[38] And with respect to the fallout from such heinous charges as gluttony and drunkenness against a supposed prophet of God, the damage could be considerable, even fatal. Wisdom texts make clear that the path of overindulgence is foolish and destructive:

Do not be among winebibbers or among gluttonous eaters of meat; for the drunkard and the glutton will come to poverty. (Prov 23:20–21)

Wine drunk at the proper time and in moderation is rejoicing of heart and gladness of soul. Wine drunk to excess leads to bitterness of spirit, to quarrels and stumbling. Drunkenness increases the anger of a fool to his own hurt, reducing his strength and adding wounds. . . . Do not be greedy for every delicacy, and do not eat without restraint; for overeating brings sickness, and gluttony leads to nausea. Many have died of gluttony. (Sir 31:28–30; 37:29–31)

The Book of Deuteronomy—the same source Jesus cited earlier, declaring that "one does not live by bread alone"—exposes the gravity of the problem most sharply by associating "a glutton and a drunkard" with a chronically "stubborn and rebellious son" who must be stoned to death in the public assembly (21:18–21).

While Jesus does come "eating and drinking" at banquet tables with little regard for others' opinions about his habits, certain aspects of Jesus' conduct put the matter in perspective and neutralize his gluttonous and drunken reputation. For one, Jesus directly parallels the calumnies regarding his food obsession with the ridiculous gossip concerning John's demon possession. Both charges are on the same low level: vicious in intent and vacuous in content. Whatever others might think, Jesus places himself in league with John as a fellow doer (Matthew) and descendant (Luke) of true wisdom. Secondly, while numerous gospel stories feature Jesus' interest in table fellowship, he does not appear as some party-hopping socialite hobnobbing with the wealthy elite of first-century Palestine. We will have more to say about Jesus' socioeconomic status in the next chapter, but suffice it to say that Jesus is no aristocrat. He frequently chides the rich for their indulgent lifestyles, including their profligate feasting. Two parables in Luke come down hard on opulent, self-absorbed consumers—one, a prominent land baron who adopted an "eat, drink and be merry" motto for his life (12:13–21), and the other, a wealthy gentleman "who feasted sumptuously every day" at a gourmet table (16:19–31). Both men face the harsh reality of death and judgment and find their food and other goods providing little comfort at the end of the day.

If Jesus is so critically disposed toward lavish consumers, why does he frequent banquets and talk about them so much? Is there not a tinge of hypocrisy here? Certain special occasions such as weddings and religious festivals call for little comment since people of all classes would gorge themselves during such events. But why accept invitations from well-to-do hosts and speak about "great dinners" from time to time? Here is perhaps the most important clue to Jesus' dining habits: he regularly uses table fellowship as a site of service to all types of people, not just elites, and as a sign of God's kingdom drawing near. Jesus eats and drinks in the homes of businessmen (tax collectors) and legal experts (Pharisees) not so much to be nourished or entertained, but to reach out and help others— more often than not, assorted "sinners" and other needy persons who happen to gather at the meals or whom Jesus insists should be invited.[39] In a particularly bold move at a banquet given by a leading Pharisee in Luke, Jesus takes note of the assembled guests and promptly exhorts his host to invite "the poor, the crippled, the lame, and the blind," who can offer nothing but gratitude in return, instead of family, friends and rich cronies (14:12–14). He punctuates this admonition with a parable concerning a "great dinner" (14:15–24), promoting the same emphasis on inclusive table fellowship or "open commensality."[40] In Jesus' eyes, such meals illustrate God's gracious care for the poor and disadvantaged and foreshadow the great messianic banquet at the end of the age, when "people will come from east and west, from north and south, and will eat in the kingdom of God" (Matt 8:11//Luke 13:29).

In summary, Jesus appears to maintain an interesting balance in his eating and drinking. He resists the extreme stereotypes of the fanatical diet-conscious ascetic, on the one end, and "the proverbial party animal,"[41] on the other. Flowing from his philosophy that "life is more than food," Jesus could dine lavishly or lightly, sumptuously or simply, but always in the interest of furthering his mission as the agent of God's merciful kingdom. Whether fasting or feasting, he aims to subordinate his own desires and needs to the will of God and the needs of others.

Although most likely kosher observant, he never judges people on
dietary grounds (as apparently some folks judge him), except for the
wealthy stockpilers who cared less about sharing their food with the
poor. All in all, Jesus happily consumes food and drink when offered, but
is not consumed by them.

Before leaving the matter of what Jesus does and does not eat in the
gospels, this is a good place to discuss briefly the "hungry" Jesus' strange
act of cursing the barren fig tree, resulting in its withering to death (Matt
21:8–22//Mark 11:12–14, 20–24). No gospel story presents Jesus actually eating figs, but this one intimates that he strongly craves some for
breakfast (Matthew sets the scene "in the morning"). There is nothing
unusual in this desire: figs, along with dates and olives, were common
fruit staples in ancient Palestine, and Jesus periodically appeals to fig
trees as object lessons for his teaching (Matt 24:32–35//Mark
13:28–31//Luke 21:29–33; Luke 13:6–9). What is extraordinary is this
one occasion where Jesus miraculously destroys a fig tree for not yielding
the desired fruit. How strange that this Jesus, who refused to use his
power to manipulate nature to create food for himself by changing
stones to bread at the outset of his ministry, now, at the end of his career,
uses his power to annihilate nature when it fails to satisfy his fancy.
Again, as with the slaughter of the swine, we must appreciate the uniqueness of this incident in the gospels. Jesus makes no more a habit of cursing figs than he does of drowning pigs. These are particular singular acts
with political-symbolic meanings. As the downfall of the Legion-infested
swine typifies Jesus' protest against the diabolical injustice of Roman
occupation, so, it seems, the withering of the fruitless fig tree signifies
Jesus' challenge against the ineffectual and opportunistic temple authorities in Jerusalem. The incident is closely connected with Jesus' dramatic
denunciation of the temple as "a den of robbers." Hebrew prophets Isaiah, Jeremiah, and Hosea, among others, used unproductive fig trees and
grape vines as metaphors for a decaying Israel courting national disaster.[42] God had planted and cultivated them in the promised land to show
forth God's character in the world. Failing this mission, they faced the
tragic prospect of being uprooted or cut down. In classic prophetic
mode, Jesus issues a similar warning to the faithless and fruitless religious
establishment of his day. Thus, Jesus' eccentric attack on the fig tree has

less to do with his growling stomach than his burning heart for the renewal of God's people, his passionate "hunger for righteousness."[43]

Sex

In recent years the Catholic Church in America has been beset by sexual scandal, focusing on priestly abuse of male youth. Married clergy in the Protestant tradition are scarcely exempt from sexual misconduct, as witnessed in certain high-profile exposés of philandering televangelists. Such scandals do nothing to help the cause of Christianity in the modern world. They bring much shame and raise many questions, not least of which is "What Would Jesus Do?" A recent *Newsweek* cover story on the Catholic crisis was entitled just that.[44]

Our question is more fundamental: What did Jesus do with respect to his own sexuality? Thus far we have seen in the gospels that Jesus complies with basic Jewish obligations concerning washing and feeding the body, but not with the stringent demands of full-blown asceticism. When it comes to sexual conduct, however, Jesus moves much closer to the ascetic model.[45] In considering Jesus' family ties (chapter 1), we pointed out that the gospels provide no evidence that Jesus ever courted or married. While affirming the Genesis ideal of faithful marital union between a man and a woman for life,[46] Jesus himself chooses to remain single and celibate—a controversial choice, to be sure, but wholly consistent with his urgent eschatological hope. With the advent of God's kingdom at hand, there isn't time or energy for normal family entanglements, which in any case would soon be irrelevant in the new heavenly order where there would be "no marrying or giving in marriage."[47]

Certain strands of Jesus' teaching vividly reinforce the practice of sexual asceticism. In Matthew, after speaking of the sanctity of marriage, Jesus also affirms the value of celibacy for a select group ("only those to whom it [the gift of celibacy] is given") "who have made themselves eunuchs for the sake of the kingdom of heaven" (19:1–12). In the Sermon on the Mount, he cuts more deeply to the heart of the matter, imploring a man to pluck out his right eye or chop off his right hand if they cause him not only to commit an illicit sexual act (adultery), but even to fantasize about it (lust) (5:27–30).[48] While it is highly doubtful that Jesus advocates literal amputation of eye, hand, or penis,[49] he does call for radical disciplining and denial of body parts associated with sexual pleasure.

Apart from the major decision not to marry, does Jesus' conduct always evince a complete abnegation and repression of his own sexuality? He certainly does not avoid social intercourse with women altogether, even in the potentially compromising situations of private dinners (as in the home of Martha and Mary) or public journeys.[50] But, of course, though no doubt raising a few eyebrows, acts of eating, talking, and traveling with women do not in themselves constitute or automatically set the stage for sexual impropriety, any more than wandering and working closely with a group of men (like the twelve apostles) imply any homosexual activity. And besides, not all forms of rigorous sexual asceticism demand total isolation from the human race, or at least that part of it which might tempt one to stumble; indeed, one's self-control might be best honed and showcased in the heat of "normal," everyday life. In short, Jesus' association with women, while demonstrating that he is not a misogynist, settles nothing in and of itself concerning his sexual conduct. In the absence of any explicit romantic or erotic elements in the scenes depicting Jesus' encounters with women, coupled with his strict teaching on the matter, we assume his lifelong celibacy.[51] The burden of proof is on those who suggest otherwise, interpreting the gospels—without warrant, in my judgment—as puritanical tabloids mounting a colossal cover-up of Jesus' sexual exploits. Ultimately we have to wrestle with what the gospel writers do provide us, rather than overspeculate about what they might have omitted or whitewashed.

That being said, while the majority of stories involving Jesus and women are sexually "innocent," there are a couple of provocative episodes that, as presented in the gospels, reveal a degree of erotic tension. Both incidents—one in Luke, the other in John—feature Jesus' interaction with individual, anonymous women bearing containers of liquid: one, a jar of ointment; the other, a jug of water. The "wetness" of the scenes contributes to their sensual undertones. To say they are "drenched in sexual intimations," as one writer describes a related scene,[52] may be extreme, but there is at least a suggestive "mist" in the air.

Jesus and a Sinful Woman in the City

We return to Luke's story of a woman's anointing Jesus' feet in the house of Simon the Pharisee, focusing now, however, not on the basic act of foot washing, but more particularly on who performs the act and how it is carried out. Both elements are crystallized in Simon's response to the spectacle: "If this man [Jesus] were a prophet, he would have known who and what kind of woman this is who is touching him" (7:39).

This is not a standard scene of a household servant washing a guest's feet with towel and water—amenities that, we may recall, Simon fails to provide Jesus. Into this vacuum walks a known "sinner-woman" from the streets of "the city," uninvited, unwelcome—except by Jesus—and uninhibited in her attention to Jesus' feet. Commentators often assume that the lady fits the profile of a notorious prostitute, but this is far from certain. She is a "sinner," yes, falling short of the highest standards of righteousness, but not all "sinners" are hard-core criminals or good-for-nothings. And, to narrow the point, all wayward women, despite the stereotype, are not whores. The woman in Luke 7 is an outcast, an undesirable from the city's streets and alleys, but she shares company with "the poor, the crippled, the lame and the blind" (cf. 14:13, 21) as much as with the prostitute; in any case, Luke never labels her as such. Still, for all our uncertainty about her precise identity, as a known sinner crashing a Pharisee's dinner party, she is certainly not Simon's idea of a model citizen or of the type of person a reputed holy teacher like Jesus should tolerate touching him at the table.

Here's the real rub: this business of "touching" Jesus while he is reclining at the dinner table, that is, stretched out on his left side in the typical banqueting posture.[53] Of course, one can scarcely wash someone's feet without touching him or her, but there are modest conventions governing such contact, which the woman transgresses. There is touching, and then there is *touching*. The word which Simon uses (*haptō*) can connote explicitly sexual touching leading to and including intercourse, as in Paul the Pharisee's (and/or certain Corinthians') notorious maxim: "It is well for a man not to touch (*haptesthai*) a woman" (1 Cor 7:1). Modifying the statement slightly, Simon might well be thinking of the scene he witnesses: "It is well for a holy man not to allow himself to be touched—in that way—by a woman, a sinful woman at that."

Yet the reclining Jesus does allow himself to be touched repeatedly on his feet by the woman's tears, lips, and hair, combined in what one scholar calls a "messy mixture" with the ointment of myrrh.[54] Delicious ambiguity surrounds each item, leaving the scene bristling with double entendre. The object of the woman's affection, Jesus' feet—mentioned no fewer than seven times in the story—may accent her humble gratitude for Jesus' compassion and willing submission to his authority; on the other hand (or foot!), a woman's attention to a man's feet could betray euphemistically more phallic interests, as with Ruth's famous uncovering of Boaz's feet on the threshing floor. The "dirtiness" of man's lowest, "least honorable" appendages can cut two ways: dirty as in "dusty" or dirty as in "risqué" (as in a "dirty" joke).[55]

With her flood of tears, the woman may be expressing deep sorrow over her past life of sin, but such intense display of emotion may also convey a wellspring of love and passion for Jesus; in any case, the tearful flow represents a lavish personal gift to Jesus from the woman's own inner recesses, from her bodily "waters." A polite kiss of greeting—usually on the hand or cheek—accompanied by a refreshing anointing—usually with household olive oil applied to the guest's head—constituted common practices of hospitality in the ancient world.[56] But prolonged, continuous kissing of the feet and dousing them with expensive perfume goes well beyond the call of duty and perhaps the code of decency.

Then there's the matter of the woman's letting her hair down and wrapping its tresses around Jesus' feet. Is this just a resourceful act of making do in the absence of a towel? Or is this disheveling of hair another exhibition of mourning over flagrant transgression, concomitant with the woman's tears and the rending of garments in Levitical legislation?[57] Or yet again, is this more of a sensuous display, the unbound, free-flowing, tousled look of lovemaking, more appropriate to the private marital bedroom than to the public fraternal banquet?[58] While I do not think we can go so far, as one commentator does, to equate any woman's public unpinning of her hair with going topless in modern America,[59] I do think it represented at least a potentially immodest act, especially when such loosened locks became entwined around a man's body, as in the story in Luke 7.

Taken individually, any of the sinful woman's gestures may be explicable within "acceptable" parameters of behavior. But the woman's extended personal wetting, kissing, perfuming, and wiping of Jesus' feet with her hair comprise excessive, deviant "public display of affection" (PDA) by almost anyone's standards, ancient or modern. That being said, we still are not compelled to label the woman a whore or regard her actions as lewd. To state the obvious, all demonstrably affectionate women are not harlots; all female sexuality is not prostitution; and all erotica is not pornography. Simon may be appalled at what he perceives to be the woman's whore-like conduct and may even extrapolate from this that she had regularly approached other men in such wanton fashion, but that is not a necessary conclusion from the evidence at hand. Deviance is in the eye of the beholder.[60] Jesus, for his part, takes a very different view of the proceedings, thoroughly "neutralizing" Simon's deviant labeling of the woman.[61] Jesus in fact never calls the woman anything but "this woman," whom he invites Simon to see in a different light (7:44). While agreeing that she has committed many sins, Jesus never brands her as an inveterate "sinner" of any stripe nor exhorts her to "go and sin no more," as in the case of the woman caught in adultery.[62] Point by point, as we have seen above, Jesus contrasts the woman's extravagant hospitality with Simon's utterly deficient response (no water, no kiss, no oil). This sinful woman, far from being a deviant in Jesus' eyes, thoroughly outshines Simon the Pharisee as a model of faith, love, and wholeness (7:44–50).

We cannot get around the fact, however, that in accepting and commending this woman's "great love" for him (7:47), Jesus is accepting and commending the particular form this lovemaking takes, with its unmistakably erotic as well as emotional dimensions. Jesus makes no attempt (as countless interpreters have done) to desexualize the woman or himself on this occasion. This does not mean that Jesus regularly goes around seeking erotic encounters (he doesn't seek this one; the woman comes to him), still less that this is the beginning of some sort of romantic affair with this affectionate woman. An appreciation of the sensual elements of the scene in Luke 7 in no way compromises Jesus' commitment to celibacy. It does, however, mitigate an extremist view of Jesus' asceticism as some kind of body-hating, sex-repressing, woman-fearing fanaticism (certain forms of asceticism border on such mania). God made no mistake when he created humankind, male and female. As the agent of an imminent new order that would transcend gender distinctions, Jesus

himself remains single and celibate, but in the meantime, alongside his
warnings against unbridled lust, adultery, and fornication,[63] he affirms
by precept and example the legitimacy of human sexuality, properly
expressed, as a vital channel of sincere love in the present world—perhaps
even a hint of the passionate, divine love encompassing God's kingdom.[64]

Jesus and a Samaritan Woman at a Well

On the surface, Jesus' encounter with the Samaritan woman in John 4 is
quite different from his engagement with the sinful woman in Luke 7.
The Johannine scene takes place outdoors rather than within a home,
and involves extensive conversation but no physical contact between
Jesus and the woman. Still, there is once again something surprising,
even shocking, about Jesus' conduct, focalized this time through his
own followers: "Just then his disciples came. They were astonished that
he was speaking with a woman, but no one said, 'What do you want?'
or, 'Why are you speaking with her?'" (4:27). Reluctant to voice their
criticism (unlike Simon the Pharisee), they, nonetheless, question the
propriety of Jesus' action. After the disciples arrive on the scene, the
woman, too, evidently senses the awkwardness of the situation, as she
immediately rushes back into the city, leaving behind her water jar
(4:28).

What is the problem here? More than simply talking with a woman
in the open, the tension is heightened by where the conversation takes
place. Location can be everything, and there are few places in Jewish lore
more laden with significance than a well of water, Jacob's well at that
(4:12). A man and a woman talking alone beside a well could only mean
one thing: love is in the air, intimate talk is being shared, marriage is on
the horizon. It was at a well, amid discussions of water drawing, that
Abraham's servant discovered Rebekah and arranged for her marriage to
Isaac (Gen 24:10–61), that Jacob fell in love with Rachel who would
become his wife (Gen 29:1–12), and that Moses wooed and won his
wife, Zipporah, in the land of Midian (Exod 2:15–22). There are no precise modern equivalents for this familiar biblical-type scene,[65] but it
approximates a young couple talking over a candlelight dinner in an ele-
gant restaurant: you don't expect them to be chatting about the weather
or the price of eggs at the supermarket. Something's going on!

Of course, things are not always as they appear. Is there anything internal to the discussion between Jesus and the woman at the well supporting the stereotype? As it happens, Jesus makes the first move with a direct and personal request to the woman: "Give me a drink" (4:7). This goes beyond a casual asking for the time of day or the way to town. It involves a more intimate solicitation of an essential substance—the very water of life—to be taken in through Jesus' lips into the depths of his being. The woman is understandably taken aback by Jesus' request: "How is that you, a Jew, ask a drink of me, a woman of Samaria?" (4:9). While the narrator parenthetically highlights the ethnic boundary that Jesus crosses ("Jews do not share things in common with Samaritans," 4:9), the gender gap is also evident in the self-designation of Jesus' interlocutor as "a woman (*gynaikos*) of Samaria."

After his surprising opening gambit, Jesus quickly turns the discussion to the "living water . . . gushing up to eternal life," which he can give to the woman (4:10–14). This line of talk is no less perplexing to the woman but does take some of the sexual edge off the encounter. She now becomes intrigued with both the awkward mechanics ("Sir, you have no bucket and the well is deep") and blatant audacity ("Are you greater than our ancestor Jacob who gave us this well?") of Jesus' hydraulic proposition (4:11–12).[66] But then Jesus proceeds explicitly to bring up the woman's marital state: "Go, call your husband, and come back" (4:16). Is this Jesus' way of finding out if the woman is available or not? In fact, we soon learn that she is available ("I have no husband," 4:17), thus seemingly setting the stage for what typically happens around wells in the Bible. But rather than pursuing any personal romantic interest in the woman, Jesus begins, somewhat sarcastically, to expose the woman's complete marital history. It is not a pretty picture: "You are right in saying, 'I have no husband'; for you have had five husbands, and the one you have now is not your husband. What you have said is true!" (4:17–18). Interpreters have often inferred from this information that the woman was loose and immoral, no doubt a prostitute and a pathetic "five-time loser,"[67] and that Jesus' purpose was to expose her sinfulness and reform her. But that is neither how the woman takes it nor how Jesus means it. There is no call for repentance here (again, no "Go and sin no more," as with the adulteress in 8:1–11), and there are other explanations for the woman's past. While having lived a difficult life, it

was not necessarily a decadent one. Perhaps she had been tragically widowed on five occasions (the Sadducees pose a presumably plausible scenario to Jesus concerning a seven-time widow [Matt 22:23–33//Mark
12:18–27//Luke 20:27–40]) and was now living with (not sleeping
with!) her closest male relative. We just don't know. In any case, the
woman responds to Jesus' disclosure not with remorse or shame but with
recognition of Jesus' prophetic authority (he "told me everything I have
ever done!"), which spurs her to engage Jesus in theological debate and
ultimately to acknowledge and testify to his role as God's Messiah
(4:19–30).

All along, it seems, this is Jesus' goal: to bring this woman to faith in
his life-giving power as God's anointed prophet and Messiah.[68] His
intentions are thoroughly religious and spiritual, not romantic or sexual.
Yet, Jesus does not hesitate to use a romantic setting and intimate
knowledge of the woman's sexual history without prejudice to capture
her attention and lead her to the truth. Here again we have important
evidence suggesting that while Jesus himself does not seek to satisfy personal sexual desires, he is neither afraid nor ashamed of sexuality as a
vital part of the human condition.

Pain

No pain, no gain. Such a motto drives all sorts of activities in our body-
conscious age relative to physical fitness and athletic prowess: hitting
the weights, running the extra laps, straining the muscles, sweating
the pores, pushing the limits—all to look better, feel better, play better.
You've got to work the body long and hard to attain peak performance.
While the equipment is fancier and the standards are higher, the basic
commitment to body discipline is nothing new. The apostle Paul aptly
sums up the competitive spirit in ancient Greco-Roman society: "Athletes exercise self-control in all things." He then proceeds to trumpet his
personal dedication to such discipline, albeit in the interest of fulfilling
God's will rather than winning an Olympic laurel: "I punish my body
and enslave it, so that after proclaiming to others I myself should not be
disqualified" (1Cor 9:24–27). While Paul is no doubt engaging in a bit

of metaphorical exaggeration, he has plenty of literal physical hardship to back up his claim: "labors . . . imprisonments . . . countless floggings . . . often near death. Five times I have received . . . the forty lashes minus one. Three times I was beaten with rods. Once I received a stoning"— and on and on he goes. Of course, persecutors, not Paul himself, inflicted these bodily bruises. But Paul submitted to these indignities willingly enough and regarded them with some pride as badges of honor and means of enhancing spiritual strength: "[The Lord] said to me . . . 'power is made perfect in weakness.' So I will boast all the more gladly of my weaknesses, so that the power of Christ may dwell in me. Therefore, I am content with weaknesses, insults, hardships, persecutions, and calamities for the sake of Christ; for whenever I am weak, then I am strong" (2 Cor 11:23–29; 12:9–10).

Whereas Paul, in the service of Christ, approximates a strict ascetical model of bodily self-discipline (minus the whips and hair shirts),[69] Jesus himself does not fit the mold so neatly. While he lives an austere life with minimal concern for creaturely comforts (see chapter 5 on possessions), Jesus does not go out of his way to whip his body into shape, to squash his physical desires, to tame the evil propensities of the flesh. He values the discipline of prayer (perhaps along with occasional periods of fasting) as a deterrent to the "weakness of the flesh" and speaks paradoxically of the need to "lose" one's life in order to "save" it,[70] but he does not, as far we know, view personal pain and punishment as a means to piety. He suffers plenty the last few days of his life, culminating on the cross, but before that, he has no record of imprisonments, beatings, stonings, and other physical tortures to "boast" about, as Paul does. Jesus is no stranger to bodily suffering, which afflicts others all around him, but rather than reveling in their disease and disability as some sort of means of grace, he endeavors to alleviate the pain whenever possible, to bring healing and restoration to broken and battered bodies.

A closer look at both Jesus' ministry of healing and his ultimate martyrdom on a Roman cross will refine our assessment of Jesus' perspective on bodily pain, especially his own.

The Ministry of Jesus: Healing the Sick

If Jesus was ever ill or otherwise incapacitated before the final days of his life, the gospels never mention it. He is plagued by no "thorn in the flesh" or other "physical infirmity," as was Paul by his own admission (2 Cor 12:7–10; Gal 4:13–14). Simply put, until his violent death, the gospels do not focus on Jesus' own ailments but rather on his sensitivity to the afflictions of others. The four evangelists unanimously agree that Jesus heals the blind, the lame, the leprous, and other diseased persons.

In Luke's account of the synagogue crisis in Nazareth (discussed in chapter 2), hometown mockers of Jesus' mounting reputation as a healer issue the challenge: "Doctor, cure yourself" (4:23). Implicit in this taunt may be an assumption that Jesus was something of a sideshow magician who must perform personal tricks to prove his power. In any event, Jesus does not take the bait here or anywhere else in the gospels. He does not employ his power to promote his own health or popularity.[71] He juggles no venomous snakes to demonstrate his control over lethal diseases;[72] he jumps from no dangerous peaks to excite the crowds and project an aura of invincibility, as the devil had tempted him to do (Matt 4:5–7//Luke 4:9–12). Later, as he approaches death, the hecklers again hurl their insults: "He saved others; he cannot save himself" (Matt 27:42//Mark 15:31//Luke 23:35). The pattern of Jesus' ministry effectively supports this charge. He lives for others; he heals others. Whether or not he could have saved himself, he seems to have cared little about it.

Perhaps until those final, fateful days leading to the cross, Jesus had little cause to be concerned about his own physical well-being. By all accounts, he was a healthy, vigorous young man, tirelessly proclaiming the good news of God's kingdom day and night throughout the villages of Galilee. What does he know personally about pain? A couple of passages in Matthew suggest more than a detached, professional interest in alleviating others' suffering. According to these texts, Jesus "feels their pain" deeply and genuinely (not in the trivial sense that, unfortunately, came to be associated with President Clinton's rhetoric in the 1990s). More than that, Matthew contends, the healing Jesus quite literally fulfills the mission of Isaiah's suffering servant in that "he took our infirmities and bore our diseases"—that is, in some sense, empathically transferred the ailments to himself (Isa 53:4//Matt 8:17). Whatever the full theological import of this scriptural link (Isaiah 53 was a fertile source of early Christian reflection), it certainly highlights a vital dimension of Jesus' well-known compassion for others: his ability to be passionately, poignantly moved on a "gut level" by others' pain.[73]

This strong identification with suffering humanity is conveyed most vividly by Matthew's Jesus in a parable dealing with the ethical standards that ultimately separate the sheep from the goats, the good from the evil, the blessed from the judged. The good, the blessed, the honored will be those who have ministered to the physical needs of the Father's Son (the Son of Man): "For I [the Son of Man] was hungry and you gave me food, I was thirsty and you gave me something to drink, I was a stranger and you welcomed me, I was naked and you gave me clothing, I was sick and you took care of me, I was in prison and you visited me" (25:35–36). How can everyone be judged fairly by their treatment of Jesus, the Son of Man? However important he might be as God's emissary, he is but one man limited by time and space. How can everyone be expected to minister to his needs? Simple: "Just as you did it to one of the least of these who are members of my family, you did it to me" (25:40). In other words, Jesus is saying, "Every time you feed a hungry person, tend to a sick body, and so on, it's as if you are helping me; I am Everyone." While obviously spinning a metaphor here, it seems more than a mere illustration Jesus spouts off the top of his head. It springs from acute, personal sensitivity to the ills and aches of embodied humanity. To borrow another metaphor from the apostle Paul, when one member of the corporate body of human beings hurts, the incarnate Jesus hurts with him or her (1 Cor 12:26; 1 Cor 1:6–7).

The Martyrdom of Jesus: Drinking the Cup

However much Jesus may have empathized with others' pain over the course of his ministry, he has plenty of his own pain to deal with in experiencing the horrors of Roman crucifixion. To some degree, all four gospels present Jesus as a noble martyr facing the hour of death with heroic resolve, courage, even equanimity. Such conduct validates his innocence and vindicates his death as part of God's salvific plan outlined in sacred Scripture and overriding his enemies' diabolical plot. However, in the midst of these highly stylized gospel "passion narratives"[74] trumpeting Jesus' valiant martyrdom, a solemn strain remains suggesting Jesus' very real struggle with the painful fate he must endure.

This struggle revolves around the rich, recurring image of "drinking the cup [of wine]." While an appropriate symbol of joyous celebration, as in toasting a milestone or victory, "drinking the cup" also signifies woeful misery, as in drowning one's sorrows or downing the bitter dregs of judgment.[75] The image first appears in Jesus' response to James and John's lobbying for the honored positions at Jesus' right and left hands, reported in Matthew and Mark (Matt 20:20–23//Mark 10:35–40). Jesus wonders if they have any idea what they're really asking for, since Jesus' destiny, as he has repeatedly informed them, involves considerable suffering, including violent death. Can James and John drink the bitter cup of woe and undergo the engulfing baptism of fire that awaits Jesus? They say they can, but given their selfish ambitions, it's hard to take them seriously or know what kind of wine and water they have in mind. Jesus, by contrast, is under no illusions about his fate. The wine he takes in and distributes to his disciples at the Passover feast, for example, all too vividly impresses upon him the image of his own blood soon to be "poured out" of his crucified body. While at this moment of celebration Jesus "gives thanks" for the cup and envisions, beyond the suffering, a future, triumphant toast of God's renewing kingdom, later that evening he is not so confident. "Distressed and agitated . . . deeply grieved, even unto death," as Mark describes his emotional state, Jesus withdraws with his three closest disciples to wrestle with God in prayer concerning his impending demise. He even dares to ask his all-powerful heavenly Father to "remove this cup from me." A suitably pious, submissive addendum follows—"yet, not what I want, but what you want"—maintaining Jesus' stature as a heroic martyr; but, nonetheless, a very human recoiling from suffering and death persists in Jesus' request (14:32–36). He is not a glutton for punishment; if there were a way to fulfill his calling and avoid intense physical anguish, he would naturally prefer that.

The Christian tradition has not always been comfortable with Jesus' seeming "weakness" here, however understandable it might be from a human standpoint. Even within the other gospels, we observe a tendency to tone down Mark's emphasis.[76] The Markan Jesus pleads with his Father to "remove this cup" in the strongest terms, using an intimate

double address—"Abba, Father"—and a sweeping affirmation of his
Father's sovereignty—"for you all things are possible" (in other words,
"I know you are more than capable of altering my fate") (14:38). By
contrast, both Matthew and Luke abbreviate the plea and couch it in
more conditional ("if") and thus, submissive, terms: "My Father, if it is
possible . . ."; "Father, if you are willing . . ." (Matt 26:39//Luke 22:42).
And the fourth gospel all but turns the tradition on its head by having
Jesus theoretically consider the option of asking God for a reprieve only
to reject it as unthinkable: "Now my soul is troubled. And what should I
say—'Father, save me from this hour'? No, it is for this reason that I have
come to this hour" (12:27). While the other evangelists attempt to "spin"
the Markan Jesus' plea for deliverance in order to accentuate his courage
and obedience to God's will, Mark's account remains as a compelling
canonical witness to Jesus' serious wrestling with alternatives to martyrdom, pursuing a path of lesser pain if possible.[77]

But ultimately such a path is not possible in the intersection of clash-
ing agendas between the prophet Jesus and the Roman-Judean political
establishment. To maintain the status quo, Jesus must be eliminated,
must die on a cross, must drink the cup of torturous pain. His reaction
to this bitter metaphorical cup may be explored in relation to a literal
cup of wine proffered to him as a dying man. All four gospels indicate
that either the attending "soldiers" or some unspecified "bystanders"
offer Jesus a drink of "sour/vinegary wine" (*oxos*) as he hangs on the cross
(Matt 27:47–48//Mark 15:35–36//Luke 23:36–37//John 19:28–30). Two
questions emerge regarding this gesture: Why is Jesus given this libation
and does he drink it? Is this a conventional, even somewhat charitable
gesture, designed to quench the dying Jesus' thirst or blunt his pain, if
only momentarily? Or is it a pure act of mockery, as Luke suggests most
clearly (23:36–37), a bitter final taste in the mouth to punctuate a panoply
of brutal physical sensations accompanying crucifixion? Or, as John presents it (19:28–29), is it an almost-mechanical fulfillment of biblical
prophecy, specifically Psalm 69:21 ("for my thirst they gave me vinegar
to drink")? Only the fourth gospel stipulates that Jesus actually requested
("I am thirsty") and "received the wine" (19:28, 30). But, again, this is
not due to any frailty on Jesus' part or desire for anesthesia: it is simply
part of the scriptural plan that Jesus must execute.[78] The Synoptics

remain mute about whether Jesus accepts the drink or not. In the scenario where the soldiers mock Jesus' suffering by offering him bitter wine, the presumption is that Jesus refuses it.

For our interest in how Jesus deals with his own bodily pain, the key issue is whether he imbibes wine of any kind as a painkiller. Conventional wisdom permitted, even encouraged, alcoholic numbing in the face of intense, hopeless suffering: "Give strong drink to one who is perishing, and wine to those in bitter distress; let them drink and forget their poverty and remember their misery no more" (Prov 31:6–7). As we have just seen, however, the only text (John) explicitly indicating that Jesus drank wine on the cross has nothing to do with pain relief. Additional texts in Matthew and Mark suggest a second offering of wine to Jesus just before he is hoisted up on the cross (Matt 27:33–4//Mark 15:22–23). Here the beverage is a sweet wine (*oinos*) laced with other substances: gall in Matthew's case, which turns the mixture sour and again echoes Psalm 69:21, and myrrh in Mark's account, which adds a pleasing, aromatic dimension and may well reflect a final indulgence to a condemned man (the proverbial "last meal"). Whatever the concoction, Jesus resolutely "did not take it." The language is strongest in Mark (Matthew's Jesus at least tastes the drink before declining it) and perhaps connects symbolically with Jesus' ultimate acceptance of God's will in Gethsemane: determined—after considerable struggle—to drink fully the cup of woe and suffering ordained by his sovereign Father, he refuses to drink the cup of momentary joy and relief offered by the insolent soldiers.[79]

Within this complex gospel tradition, it is difficult to sort out exactly what kind of drink(s) Jesus is offered at what moment(s) and for what reason(s). But consistent with the custom of the day, Jesus clearly has the opportunity to drink some kind of fermented beverage in the hours surrounding his crucifixion. And, except in the fourth gospel, where Jesus drinks to fulfill God's plan (not to dull his pain), the tradition agrees that Jesus declines to drink, choosing instead to face the full horrors of unjust execution without benefit of anesthetic, to die a martyr's death bravely, stoically, even ascetically, one might say. A joyous consumer of wine throughout his ministry as a means of reaching out to needy persons, this is a different occasion. This is no "happy hour," but rather an hour or reckoning, a moment of truth. There is "a time for every matter under heaven": a time to live and a time to die; a time to drink and a time to thirst; a time to indulge and a time to abstain.[80] Jesus has a good sense of timing.

Conclusion

It is common for health professionals in our society to stress the importance of a balanced diet, a well-rounded lifestyle, and moderate exercise—a happy medium of bodily care. While such language is ours and not the gospels' and while Jesus never espouses the *via media* as a philosophical principle, his treatment of his own body, as portrayed in the gospels, does fall for the most part somewhere between the extreme poles of strict asceticism and unabashed hedonism.

In response to dirt, Jesus bathes others' feet and permits his own head and feet to be refreshed but seems unconcerned about washing his hands before dinner. Impurity, ritual or otherwise, is not the unpardonable sin for Jesus (or for most Jews in Jesus' day; impurity is easily remedied), but neither is pettifogging legalism. Jesus worries about the priorities of those who might take cleanliness matters too far, but he's not on the warpath against the whole Jewish purity system. To state the obvious (but sometimes overlooked): overall, Jesus, like most devout Jews, acts like bodily purity is a good thing, but not the only thing that matters.

In terms of diet, Jesus appears to follow a typical first-century Jewish menu, abstaining from pork and other "unclean" items, fasting on occasion but not as a rule, and feasting at many more times. While the balance here may tilt toward surfeit more than restraint, it is important to recall the gospels' repeated emphasis that meals, banquets, and the like are more means to an end than focal activities for Jesus. Though the gospels frequently place Jesus at dinner gatherings, they never describe his savoring a delectable meal. Jesus is no culinary connoisseur. He eats for the fellowship, not for the food. He uses the meal table as a meeting table to spread the good news of God's gracious kingdom.

As for Jesus' sexual conduct, the balance undoubtedly shifts toward the pole of abstinence. But such behavior is grossly distorted if interpreted as a sign of denigrating human sexuality as a base pursuit or the root of all evil. Not only Jesus' teaching on the sanctity of sex and marriage grounded in God's good creation, but also his personal interaction with women, demonstrate that Jesus is neither gynophobic nor anti-sex. Two close encounters, with a "sinful" woman in Luke and a Samaritan woman in John, especially confirm his comfort with erotic language, feelings, and even contact, while he remains celibate. Jesus' ethics of love cannot be reduced to some "pure ideal" divorced from human bodily existence. The woman in Luke whom Jesus commends for showing him "much love" shows that love through her body—lips, hair, hands, tears—in intimate, (com)passionate contact with his body.

With regard to Jesus' experience of pain, the focus naturally falls on the events surrounding his crucifixion, reported in excruciating detail by all four evangelists. While the gospels assess the level of Jesus' discomfort in distinctive ways, none attempts to deny (as some dualistic "gnostics" would have it) that he suffers real bodily torture as a victim of brutal execution. The Synoptic Gospels portray Jesus as flinching at first (in varying degrees) from such an ordeal, but as ultimately accepting his fate head-on (without anesthesia) as part of God's will for his life. The fourth gospel stresses Jesus' bold resolve (no hesitation here) to offer himself voluntarily as a redemptive sacrifice for God's people. So the incarnate Jesus knows pain, feels pain, and heroically endures pain as a means to achieving his God-ordained mission. Put another way, pain—more specifically, avoiding or alleviating pain—is not the primary determinant of Jesus' personal conduct. But neither does Jesus seek to "mortify the flesh" through self-flagellation or other painful expressions of bodily discipline. There is no virtue in pain for its own sake. In fact, Jesus' actions are typically driven by the impulse to relieve pain and suffering, to bring peace and comfort to the weak and infirm. The pain he must accept at the end of his life, when there's no other way, he accepts not as part of some rigorous self-improvement plan, still less as part of some perverse masochistic sport, but as part of his unshakeable commitment to resist all oppressive forces threatening the well-being of God's people. In the language of the gospels, "he took our infirmities and bore our diseases"; he came "to give his life a ransom for many"; as "the good shepherd [he] lays down his life for the sheep" (Matt 8:17; Mark 10:45; John 10:11).

NOTES

1. On John the Baptist, see Mark 1:2–6; Matt 11:7–19//Luke 7:24–35; on Paul, see 1 Cor 7:1–40; 9:24–27. On the whole issue of asceticism, see the stimulating collection of essays in Leif E. Vaage and Vincent L. Wimbush, eds., *Asceticism and the New Testament* (New York: Routledge, 1999).

2. See Pliny, *Natural History* 5.73; Josephus, *Jewish War* 2.120. On the connections between these Essenes and the sect at Qumran known through the Dead Sea Scrolls, see James C. Vanderkam, *The Dead Sea Scrolls Today* (London: SPCK; Grand Rapids, Mich.: Eerdmans, 1994), 71–75; 90–91; and Geza Vermes, *An Introduction to the Complete Dead Sea Scrolls* (Minneapolis, Minn.: Fortress, 1999), 122–26, 162–63, 187–88.

3. See, e.g., Mary Douglas, *Purity and Danger: An Analysis of Concepts of Pollution and Taboo* (London: Routledge & Kegan Paul, 1966), and her *Natural Symbols: Explorations in Cosmology* (New York: Pantheon, 1982), 65–81; Elaine Scarry, *The Body in Pain: The Making and Unmaking of the World* (New York: Oxford University, 1985).

4. Compare Malina, *New Testament World*, 28, 164–65.

5. Wealthy aristocrats in Roman Palestine commonly had swimming pools for recreational purposes; see E. P. Sanders, *Judaism: Practice and Belief: 63 BCE–66 CE* (London: SCM; Harrisburg, Pa.: Trinity Press International, 1992), 225.

6. The old adage "cleanliness is next to godliness" is still in circulation but sounds more like a quaint relic of the past: no one takes it very seriously these days. Now the notion of "dirt" is much more connected with disease than with deviance.

7. "[T]he Jewish concepts of pure and impure, clean and unclean cannot be equated with virtue and vice, good and evil. Instead, purity is a symbolic framework connected with the Temple, the divine presence there, and, more broadly, with the experience of bodily life and bodily death" (Reed and Crossan, 128; cf. pp. 128–30). Compare Christian E. Hauer and William A. Young, *An Introduction to the Bible: A Journey into Three Worlds* (5th ed.; Upper Saddle River, N.J.: Prentice-Hall, 2001), 222–23.

8. The only indication in the gospels that Jesus promoted the ritual of baptism prior to his resurrection appears in John 3:22 and 4:1–2. In the latter reference, however, the evangelist makes clear that Jesus himself did not do the baptizing: "Now when Jesus had learned that the Pharisees had heard, 'Jesus is making and baptizing more disciples than John'—although it was not Jesus himself but his disciples who baptized—he left Judea."

9. See Sanders, *Judaism,* 222–29, for a detailed description of these immersion pools common throughout Roman Palestine across the social spectrum.

10. The first incident is found only in Luke 7:11–17; the latter is a synoptic story in Matt 9:18–26//Mark 5:21–43//Luke 8:40–56. On the matter of corpse impurity, see Lev 21:1–2, 11; Num 6:6–12; 9:6–10; 19:11–22.

11. Similarly, in the unique Lukan report of Jesus' curing ten lepers, he instructs them all to "Go and show yourselves to the priests" (17:14).

12. See the trenchant analyses of Paula Fredriksen, *Jesus of Nazareth,* 105–10, 197–214; "Did Jesus Oppose the Purity Laws?" *Bible Review* 11 (1995): 20–25, 42–47; and "What You See Is What You Get: Context and Content in Current Research on the Historical Jesus," *Theology Today* 52 (1995): 75–97.

13. Borg, *Conflict,* 110.

14. In addition to his comprehensive *Judaism,* see E. P. Sanders' helpful "thumbnail sketch" of Jewish religion in Jesus' day, noting both the common beliefs and practices of most Jews as well as points of dispute, in *Historical Figure of Jesus,* 33–48.

15. Matt 15:2; note the helpful analysis of Daniel J. Harrington, *Gospel of Matthew,* 229–34.

16. E.g., Ps 51:6–17; 139:23–24; Jer 31:31–34; Ezek 11:19–20; 36:26–27.

17. True, Jesus transforms the "holy water" at the wedding into wine, but he does not thereby undermine the practice of hand washing. Presumably, the guests had already "washed up" by this point of the festivities, and in any case, Jesus does nothing dramatic—like pour the water out or shatter the pots—before creating the wine. In John 7, moreover, at the Feast of Tabernacles or Booths in Jerusalem—which included various water rituals—Jesus speaks of the "rivers of living water" which the Spirit will impart (7:37–39); but again, while perhaps exploiting the symbolic ambience of the occasion, Jesus in no way denigrates the temple water ceremonies to make his point.

18. In Mark 14:3–9, an unnamed woman anoints Jesus in the house of Simon the leper; in John 12:1–8, Mary, sister to Martha and Lazarus, anoints Jesus in her own home. Both accounts take place in Bethany and note the connection with Jesus' upcoming burial.

19. Although it has been common to view this story as a distinct-but-parallel version of the same anointing incident in Mark and John, I think that its distinctive elements outweigh its similarities and thus treat it as a separate episode altogether.

20. This further suggests that hand washing is only an occasional—not a persisting—problem dogging Jesus' mission.

21. On foot washing and other hospitality requirements assumed in this scene, see Kenneth E. Bailey, "Through Peasant Eyes," in *Poet & Peasant and Through Peasant Eyes: A Literary-Cultural Approach to the Parables in Luke* (comb. ed.; Grand Rapids, Mich.: Eerdmans, 1980), 1–21.

22. Compare Joel B. Green, *The Gospel of Luke* (Grand Rapids, Mich.: Eerdmans, 1997), 312–13.

23. The exchange between Jesus and Peter in 13:6–11 makes clear the link between foot washing and spiritual cleansing in this scene. Not surprisingly, some interpreters have viewed it as a "baptismal" episode.

24. I am mixing the Johannine metaphors of Jesus as "the Lamb of God who takes away the sin of the world" (1:29) and Jesus as the source of "a spring of water gushing up to eternal life" (4:14). We could also add the picture of 15:2, "You have already been cleansed by the word that I have spoken to you." Whatever the image of Jesus—as Lamb, water, or Word of God—he purifies his sinful followers.

25. Qoheleth's philosophy of life disclosed in the book of Ecclesiastes is deeply ambivalent: he claims to have tried the path of self-indulgence and found it wanting ("vain") but still concludes that the best one can do in this crazy life is to "eat your bread with enjoyment and drink your wine with a merry heart" (see Eccl 1:12–2:26; 3:9–13; 5:18–20; 8:14–15; 9:7–10).

26. The book was written by Dr. Don Colbert (Nashville, Tenn.: Thomas Nelson, 2000). A summary of the book and interview with the author may be found in Don O'Briant, "W.W.J.E.? (What *would* Jesus eat?)," *Atlanta Journal Constitution,* 9 March 2002, B1–2.

27. In the story of Jesus' feeding the multitude—one of the few incidents from his ministry reported in all four gospels (Matt 14:13–21//Mark 6:30–44; 8:1–10//Luke 9:10–17//John 6:1–15)—the emphasis falls squarely on Jesus' concern for others' nourishment. Presumably, he himself also ate on this occasion, but that is beside the point in the gospel narratives. The fourth gospel further stresses that Jesus resists exploiting this incident simply to enhance his own popularity: "When Jesus realized that they were about to come and take him by force to make him king, he withdrew again to the mountain by himself" (6:15).

28. This push for personal power is at the heart of the other two temptations as well: dazzling the crowds by flying off the temple mount and gaining "all the kingdoms of the world" by bowing down before the devil. See further discussion on Jesus' management of his honor in chapter 7.

29. The citation is from Deut 8:3, recalling Moses' review of Israel's forty-year trial period in the wilderness. Luke's version has Jesus quote only the part "One does not live by bread alone" (4:4), thus emphasizing (as is typical in Luke) Jesus' focus on physical and material matters. Matthew provides an extra spiritual touch by including the next Deuteronomic statement, "but by every word that comes from the mouth of God" (4:4).

30. See, e.g., Matt 7:9–10; 14:13–21; 26:26–29; Mark 6:30–44; 8:1–10; 14:22–25; Luke 9:10–17; 11:11; 22:14–23; 24:28–30, 41–43; John 2:1–11; 6:1–13; 21:1–14. Jesus' reference in Luke 11:12 to a child's common request for an "egg" may suggest that this had also been a regular part of his diet.

31. All in Luke: see 14:15–24; 15:23–30; 16:19.

32. See Num 6:1–21; Judg 13:1–14; 1 Sam 1:11; Luke 1:13–15.

33. If Matthew 15 is utilizing Mark 7 as a source, it jumps from Mark 7:1 to 7:5, thus eliminating Mark's assessment of standard Jewish behavior. Matt 15:17 also omits the parenthetical comment in Mark 7:19, "he [Jesus] declared all foods clean." Contrast further Mark 7:15, "there is nothing outside a person that by

going in can defile, but the things that come out are what defile," with Matt 15:11, "it is not what goes into the mouth that defiles a person, but it is what comes out of the mouth that defiles." See Harrington, *Gospel of Matthew,* 229–30.

34. See Gal 2:11–14; Acts 10:1–11:18; 15:1–35; Sanders, *Historical Figure of Jesus,* 218–23; Harrington, *Gospel of Matthew,* 231–4.

35. See, e.g., Lev 11:1–8; Deut 14:3–8; Isa 65:1–4; 66:17; 1 Macc 1:47; 2 Macc 6:18–7:42. In this last text, Eleazar and a family of seven brothers and their mother are all tortured and killed for refusing to eat pork during the anti-Judaic pogrom of Antiochus IV.

36. While the demons represent the primary destructive agents in this incident, Jesus does play a secondary role in the massacre of the herd of swine.

37. Compare Richard A. Horsley, *Jesus and Empire: The Kingdom of God and the New World Disorder* (Minneapolis, Minn.: Fortress, 2003), 101: "As Jesus exorcized the alien forces that had possessed the people it was possible to recognize the identity of those alien occupying forces, that is, the Roman armies. By implication, in Jesus' exorcisms those Roman soldiers, Legion, were being sent to their destruction in the sea" (see further, pp. 98–103). On the "pig" as "a symbol of the Tenth *Fretensis* Legion stationed in Syria, which fought against Jerusalem in the 66–70 war," see Warren Carter, *Matthew and the Margins: A Sociopolitical and Religious Reading* (Maryknoll, N.Y.: Orbis, 2000), 212–13. Carter also comments, "The subsequent destruction of the pigs is not only an economic loss, but suggests a coded depiction of Rome's demise" (p. 213).

38. On the issue of labeling deviance in gospel narratives, see the incisive studies of Malina and Neyrey, *Calling Jesus Names: The Social Value of Labels in Matthew* (Sonoma, Calif.: Polebridge, 1988), and their "Conflict in Luke-Acts: Labeling and Deviance Theory," in *Social World of Luke-Acts,* 97–124.

39. See Matt 9:10–13//Mark 2:15–17//Luke 5:29–32; Luke 15:1–32; 19:1–10.

40. Emphasis on Jesus' "open commensality" is a major component of Crossan's portrait of the historical Jesus (see *Historical Jesus,* 332–53; *Jesus: A Revolutionary Biography,* 66–74). On Luke 14, see the excellent study by Richard L. Rohrbaugh, "The Pre-Industrial City in Luke-Acts: Urban Social Relations," in *The Social World of Luke-Acts,* 125–50.

41. The phrase comes from a Jesus Seminar fellow, as reported with affirmation by Robert W. Funk, *Honest to Jesus: Jesus for a New Millennium* (New York: HarperCollins, 1996), 208–9. See the balanced assessment of Jesus as a "millenarian ascetic" with respect to diet in Allison, *Jesus of Nazareth,* 172–74.

42. See Isa 5:1–7; Jer 8:13; Ezek 15:1–8; Hosea 9:10–17; Mic 7:1–7.

43. Compare Matt 5:6, "Blessed are those who hunger and thirst after righteousness, for they will be filled."

44. The cover headline of *Newsweek,* 6 May 2002, reads: "What Would Jesus Do?: Beyond the Priest Scandal: Christianity at a Crossroads." The principal article is by John Meacham, "Sex and the Church: A Case for Change," pp. 22–32.

45. Asceticism was not an all-or-nothing package deal; one could follow strict standards of self-denial in one or more areas of life, but not others. Notice, again, the sensitive treatment of the issue by Allison, *Jesus of Nazareth,* 172–216.

46. Jesus never directly addresses the issue of same-sex relations, positively or negatively, in the gospels.

47. Allison, *Jesus of Nazareth,* 182–216.

48. See also Matthew 18:6–9//Mark 9:42–48, where the focus is not on sexual conduct as such, but rather on curtailing any personal action of hand, foot, and eye that might cause others to "stumble."

49. Practices of dismemberment and castration for religious reasons were known in the ancient world (including the self-castration of the early church father, Origen). But Jesus knows a good metaphor when he sees one and likely does not intend his followers to carry matters this far. To anticipate the next section in this chapter, Jesus does not advocate the infliction of bodily pain as a means of spiritual growth.

50. See Mary Ann Tolbert, "Asceticism and Mark's Gospel," in *Asceticism and the New Testament* (ed. Vaage and Wimbush), 39–41; cf. Luke 8:1–3 and 10:38–42.

51. See Allison, *Jesus of Nazareth,* 211–16.

52. Tolbert, "Asceticism," 41, applied specifically to the anointing scene in Mark 14:3–9. I will be considering below the related but distinctive anointing episode in Luke 7:36–50, which is actually more erotically charged than its Markan counterpart.

53. This scenario explains why the woman comes up "behind him" to wash his feet (they would be stretched out and angled back from the U-shaped table surrounded by couches where Jesus reclines on one hand and eats with the other). See Green, *Gospel of Luke,* 309–10.

54. Turid Karlsen Seim, *The Double Message: Patterns of Gender in Luke & Acts* (Nashville, Tenn.: Abingdon, 1994), 93–94.

55. See Ruth 3:4, 7–10; Amy-Jill Levine, "Ruth," in *Women's Bible Commentary* (exp. ed.; ed. Carol A. Newsom and Sharon H. Ringe; Louisville, Ky.: Westminster/John Knox, 1998), 88–89. First Corinthians 12:21–23 appears to correlate the feet and genitals as "members of the body that seem to be weaker" or "less honorable" (in need of covering) but in fact "are indispensable" to the body's well-being.

56. See Bailey, *Through Peasant Eyes,* 6–10.

57. Lev 10:6; 13:45; 21:10; cf. Num 5:18.

58. According to Num 5:11–32, a wife suspected of being unfaithful to her husband is to be brought to trial before the Lord's priest, who will "dishevel her hair" and compel her to drink "the water of bitterness that brings the curse." If the water treatment (torture?) has no effect, she is deemed innocent. Because of the sexual focus of this ordeal, Alice Bach suggests that the hair-messing gesture functions less as a sign of mourning than as a public reenactment of the woman's

alleged immorality: "The half-disrobed woman with disheveled hair, appearing as though she had been caught in an intimate act . . ." ("Introduction to a Case History: Numbers 5:11–31," in *Women in the Hebrew Bible: A Reader* [ed. Alice Bach; New York: Routledge, 1999], 461.)

59. Green, *Gospel of Luke,* 310.

60. See John M. G. Barclay, "Deviance and Apostasy: Some Applications of Deviance Theory to First-Century Judaism and Christianity," in *Modeling Early Christianity: Social-Scientific Studies of the New Testament in its Context* (ed. Philip F. Esler; New York: Routledge, 1995), 114–27.

61. On the process of "neutralizing" deviant labels, see Malina and Neyrey, "Conflict in Luke-Acts," 108–22.

62. This story appears in the fourth gospel (John 8:1–11) in most manuscripts and versions, although there is some evidence of its placement in Luke's gospel.

63. See the litany of vices in Matt 15:19//Mark 7:21–22.

64. The Jewish wisdom tradition stresses not only the destructive potential of sexual misconduct, but also the joyous vitality of sexual pleasure, properly experienced according to God's design (see Prov 5:15–19). The explicit erotic poems of the Song of Solomon especially underscore this affirmation of sexual enjoyment. In the history of interpretation, fastidious Jews and Christians have often allegorized these poems as depicting God's intimate love for Israel and/or the church. However, while pointing secondarily to the depths of divine love, these songs are first and foremost exactly what they appear to be: lyrical expressions of conjugal passion. Jesus sings no romantic love song, but he does seem to embrace the spirit of Solomon's canticles in his acceptance of the affectionate woman in Luke 7.

65. See Robert Alter, *The Art of Biblical Narrative* (New York: Basic Books, 1981), 47–62.

66. For a brilliant and creative treatment of the "hydraulic" and other "liquid" dimensions of this story, see Stephen D. Moore, *Poststructuralism and the New Testament: Derrida and Foucault at the Foot of the Cross* (Minneapolis, Minn.: Fortress, 1994), 43–64.

67. Paul Duke, *Irony in the Fourth Gospel* (Atlanta, Ga.: John Knox, 1985), 102–3.

68. This emphasis on faith/belief is central to Jesus' encounters with various individuals throughout the fourth gospel: in addition to the present episode, see, e.g., 3:1–21 (Nicodemus), 9:1–41 (man born blind), 11:1–44 (Lazarus, Mary, and Martha), 14:1–14 (disciples), 20:24–29 (Thomas).

69. On Paul as "the model ascetic," see Calvin Roetzel, *Paul: The Man and the Myth* (Minneapolis, Minn.: Fortress, 1999), and the articles in parts 2 and 3 of Vaage and Wimbush, eds., *Asceticism and the New Testament,* 157–328.

70. Represented both in the synoptic tradition—Matt 16:24–25//Mark 8:34–35//Luke 9:23–24 (cf. John 12:25)—and in the shared material between Matthew and Luke—Matt 10:37–39//Luke 14:26–27 (cf. Luke 17:33).

71. A common tendency among itinerant magicians and wonder workers, like Simon Magus criticized in Acts 8:8–24, and various self-promoting quacks and wizards "addicted to magical art" chided by Philostratus in his account of the exemplary philosopher, Apollonius of Tyana (*Life of Apollonius* 8.7). See Spencer, *The Portrait of Philip in Acts,* 92–107; Howard Clark Kee, *Miracle in the Early Christian World: A Study in Sociohistorical Method* (New Haven: Yale University Press, 1983), 252–89.

72. Compare Mark 16:18; Acts 28:3–6. Jesus' statement in Luke 10:19, "See, I have given you authority to tread on snakes and scorpions," is clearly meant in the context as a metaphor for overcoming "all the power of the enemy."

73. The word repeatedly referring to Jesus' "compassion" in Matthew (*splanchnizomai*) connotes a sense of pity and sympathy for the harassed (9:36), the hungry (14:14), and the blind (20:34) from the depths ("bowels," *splanchna*) of his inner being.

74. The term "passion narrative" typically designates the account of Jesus' final week in Jerusalem culminating in his crucifixion and burial. All four gospels devote major attention to these events: see Matt 21:1–27:66; Mark 11:1–15:47; Luke 19:28–23:56; John 12:1–19:42. Scholars generally agree that the evangelists have shaped these accounts of Jesus' death for their own pastoral and theological aims, but the extent of this creative impulse is debated. Arguing for a more sober blend of history and theology, tradition and redaction, see the magisterial, two-volume study by Raymond E. Brown, *Death of the Messiah.* On the side of thoroughgoing revisionism ("prophecy historicized"), see John Dominic Crossan, *Who Killed Jesus? Exposing the Roots of Anti-Semitism in the Gospel Story of the Death of Jesus* (New York: HarperCollins, 1995).

75. See Ps 11:6; Isa 51:17, 22; Jer 25:15–29; Hab 2:15–16.

76. See Brown, *Death of the Messiah,* 1:171–2.

77. In a textually disputed statement (not found in some early manuscripts), Luke elaborates on Jesus' agony: "In his anguish (*agonia*) he prayed more earnestly, and his sweat became like great drops of blood falling down on the ground" (22:44). While this provides a brutally graphic portrayal of Jesus' intense struggle, it does not mean here that he is praying for relief. His heavy "sweating" is reminiscent of an athlete "pumped" for competition or a warrior primed for battle. Thus, Jesus is likely praying for strength (cf. 22:43) to face the impending ordeal. See the discussion in Brown, *Death of the Messiah,* 1:179–90, and in chapter 6 below.

78. John places further scriptural significance on this scene by noting that Jesus was offered a sponge-full of wine attached to a "branch of hyssop." Hyssop was associated with various rituals in the Old Testament (Lev 14:4–6, 49–52; Num 19:6, 18; Ps 51:7), especially the sprinkling of lamb's blood on the doorposts at the first Passover (Exod 12:22). See Rensberger, "The Gospel According to John," 2051.

79. See Brown, *Death of Messiah,* 2:940–4.

80. Compare Eccl 3:1–8.

5

Money Matters

The famous scriptural warning against the diabolical threat of greed—"the love of money is the root of all evil" (1 Tim 6:10)—does not come from the lips of Jesus, but it might as well have. This sweeping critique of consumerism is redolent of numerous opinions that Jesus does register in the gospels:

You cannot serve God and wealth. (Matt 6:24)

Be on your guard against all kinds of greed. (Luke 12:15)

How hard it is for those who have wealth to enter the kingdom of God! (Mark 10:23)

None of you can become my disciple if you do not give up all your possessions. (Luke 14:33).

By all accounts, Jesus offers little comfort to merchants and financiers. To put it mildly, his words would find little welcome on modern Wall Street; indeed, they would be repudiated.

But rhetoric can be overblown, talk can be cheap—especially when it comes to ministers and money, preachers and prosperity. In a powerful position to call upon their followers to "give 'til it hurts" in God's name, charismatic religious figures can easily succumb to temptations to exploit gullible masses for their own personal gain. This is not a problem unique to contemporary televangelists; it's been around a long time, at least as long as Simon the Magician tried to capitalize on the apostles' ability to impart the Spirit (Acts 8:9–24). The apostle Paul was so sensitive to the prospect of being perceived as a mercenary missionary, only in it for the money, that he "worked night and day" at a blue-collar profession (tent making) to support himself, even though he had "the right" to receive material aid from the churches he had founded.[1]

What about Jesus? How do his personal financial dealings square with his tough talk about corruptible earthly treasures? The gospels offer hints that Jesus learned his father's trade of woodworking (Mark 6:3; Matt 13:55),[2] but they nowhere suggest that he continues to practice the profession alongside his public ministry. Apparently, he does not adopt Paul's "bi-vocational" approach to ministry; he seems unemployed except as the traveling agent of God's kingdom. How then does he live? How is he supported? The temptation scene at the outset of Jesus' ministry categorically denies that he is materially sustained by supernatural means: he feeds others but does not lift a finger to stock his own cupboard with bread fashioned from stones. Obviously, then, he must depend on the hospitality and generosity of others. But to what extent? As a dynamic, apocalyptic prophet and healer, Jesus exerts enormous influence over his followers to forsake everything on behalf of God's kingdom. What does Jesus personally expect to get out of this campaign? The potential for exploitation and self-aggrandizement cannot be ignored.

Precisely because of this optimal scenario for selfish gain and abuse of power, Jesus' disinterest in material acquisition stands out all the more. As one recent biographer points out concerning Jesus, "As a rural Galilean Jew he distrusted and even detested money."[3] While, as we have seen, Jesus is not depicted as a thoroughgoing ascetic—he enjoys his food and drink and other bodily comforts—nonetheless, he owns no property, occupies no palace, earns no paycheck, and accumulates no possessions, as far as the gospel evidence indicates. Whatever he aims to realize in the kingdom of God, it is not a personal fortune. Whatever sacrifices he demands of his disciples, he demands no less of himself.

Such a radical renunciation of financial entanglements may suit Jesus' pressing eschatological agenda, but it seems impractical, if not absurd, for twenty-first century American Christians in a capitalist culture with college, retirement, and medical bills to pay for. Of course, as Christians we are free (even obligated?) to buck the prevailing culture in Jesus' name, but greed tends not to be one of those top headline sins that rouses our indignation. Many of our churches—the successful ones!—are big-budget operations with the lion's share going to staff and buildings. Mother Teresa inspires wonderful sermon illustrations but few lifestyle changes. Her attraction is in her uniqueness, her quaintness, her foreign-ness—sort of like Jesus. Although we are loath to admit it, Jesus and Mother Teresa are profoundly un-American.

Maybe this is putting the matter too strongly. Maybe Jesus is a good bit more "practical" and financially savvy than a quick reading of the gospels might suggest—more like Paul of Tarsus than Francis of Assisi or Teresa of Calcutta. Maybe there are other sides of the coin to Jesus' business dealings, more congenial to Wall Street concerns, which need to be appreciated. At any rate, a closer look at Jesus' economic activity is in order, focusing on his personal involvement with property, money, and material goods, assessing to what extent Jesus conducts his public life and ministry, as portions of the gospels intimate, with no place, no purse, and no possessions of his own.

No Place

In a sweeping confession of his vagabond existence, in contrast even to foxes and birds with their natural habitats, Jesus announces in the tradition shared by Matthew and Luke: "the Son of Man has nowhere to lay his head" (Matt 8:20//Luke 9:58). This habit stands out in comparison with the early Christians' pattern of establishing religious communities within their homes, so-called "house churches."[4] Strikingly, Jesus gives the impression that he is constantly on the move and cannot afford, either for economic or security reasons, to settle down anywhere. He is no traveling merchant or dignitary lodging at five-star inns or aristocratic villas. When night falls, he either continues his itinerant ministry or sleeps where he can—under the stars, perhaps, or in a cave, on the streets, in a stable? Jesus claims he has nowhere to lay his head.

How does this statement square with the gospel portraits of Jesus' activity? It is certainly fair to say that all four gospels are more interested in charting Jesus' ministerial movements and actions than his leisurely pursuits or sleeping arrangements. In fact, the only time Jesus is depicted being "asleep" occurs in a boat with his disciples on the turbulent Sea of Galilee—a scene which dramatically underscores that Jesus "lays down his head" only in the most unconventional, not to mention uncomfortable, places in carrying out his itinerant mission (Matt 8:24//Mark 4:38//Luke 8:23). In the final hours of his life as he wrestles with his ominous fate, Jesus eschews sleep in favor of watchful prayer, which is more than can be said for his weary trio of followers. As we observed in chapter 3, Jesus repeatedly finds Peter, James, and John napping on duty during his hour of crisis and admonishes them: "Stay awake and pray that you may not come into the time of trial" (Matt 26:41//Mark 14:38). Such seems to have been a kind of motto for Jesus' entire mission: the imminent breakthrough of God's kingdom, which consumes Jesus' attention and controls his every action, demands constant vigilance and diligence. Resting and nesting are not high on Jesus' agenda.

Still, it would be stretching the point to envision Jesus as utterly homeless, living exclusively "on the streets" as a wandering beggar, à la certain radical philosophers of the day.[5] In sending out the twelve apostles on their own missionary circuit, Jesus exhorts them to "enter" and "stay" in houses of receptive hearers "until you leave the place" (Matt 10:11//Mark 6:10//Luke 9:4). This coincides with Jesus' own pattern of accepting hospitality and using others' homes as a base of fellowship and ministry, whether those of devoted followers and friends in Capernaum and Bethany or of well-to-do Pharisees like Simon and tax collectors like Levi and Zacchaeus.[6] Jesus celebrates his final Passover meal with his disciples in a "guest room" in Jerusalem prepared by the unnamed "owner of the house"—a "large room upstairs," as it turns out, "already furnished and ready" for occupancy (Mark 14:14–16//Luke 22:11–13). Thus Jesus does not always "rough it": from time to time, he enjoys sumptuous banquets and comfortable lodgings as an honored guest in others' residences. But these sojourns are consistently brief and intermittent; he never lingers and wears out his welcome. Moreover, as we have seen, Jesus' aim in his various house-calls is benevolent, not self-indulgent. He gives more than he receives, not in terms of money and material goods, but in terms of teaching, healing, and brokering the kingdom of God. In this sense he "earns" his keep, consistent with his viewpoint that "the laborer deserves to be paid."[7] The gospels report numerous charges—both true and false—that Jesus' critics level against him, but freeloading, moneygrubbing, and thievery are never cited.

So while Jesus does not literally and totally have nowhere to lay his head, the gospel evidence supports his generally itinerant lifestyle. We might aptly call him a "drifter," except that such a label implies aimlessness and irresponsibility—and Jesus is anything but that. There is a method to his meandering, maybe multiple methods. Matthew and Luke provide related yet distinctive interpretations of Jesus' wandering by placing his claim to have no resting place in different narrative contexts.

Matthew: No Rest for the Weary

Matthew incorporates Jesus' self-portrait of restlessness in a discussion concerning the rigors of discipleship: to follow Jesus is to follow an uncertain, unsettled path (8:18–22). The ensuing stories, linked by the catchword "follow," illustrate the dangers and opportunities awaiting the itinerant Jesus and his disciples. Ironically, the very next passage features a scene in which Jesus does lay his head down to sleep. But he reclines on no ordinary bed and ultimately gets little rest, because he sleeps on a sailing boat being battered by a turbulent storm (8:23–27). It is not, however, the accommodations or weather that disturb his nap, but rather his panicky disciples who had "followed him"[8] into the boat without following his example of peaceful reliance on God's protection. At the end of the day, the lesson is clear: the way of Jesus is a way of motion, not rest, through menacing territory. What rest is available is that snatched in transit, in the midst of trouble, by those who trust in God. Unfortunately, the disciples of Jesus have only "little faith" to draw on, hence their distress.

After being stirred by his anxious followers, Jesus proceeds to still the raging storm (8:25–27); but this provides only a temporary lull. There is no indication that Jesus goes back to sleep, and upon arriving at the shore, the sailors immediately face another tumultuous force—this time embodied in "two demoniacs coming out of the tombs" (8:28). There will be no rest in this region until these madmen are tamed. Even then, after Jesus dispatches the demons into a herd of swine who promptly drown themselves in the sea, the townspeople are so rattled by this "bay of pigs" incident that "they beg [Jesus] to leave their neighborhood" (8:34). No warm welcome here.

Although Jesus then crosses the sea again back "to his own town" (9:1), he continues to find precious little repose. First, he reaches out to a man permanently at rest ("paralyzed") and enables him to walk again (9:2–8). Then, instead of settling down in these familiar environs, Jesus resumes his habit of "walking along" and calling recruits, such as the toll collector Matthew, to "follow" him (9:9). He winds up eating in Matthew's home with "many tax collectors and sinners . . . and his disciples" (9:10), but this dinner turns out to be anything but a relaxing affair as Jesus comes under attack for consorting with undesirables (9:11–12). While defending himself against this and other charges, a local synagogue official bursts in and interrupts Jesus,[9] pleading with him to come and cure his stricken daughter. And, in an interesting reversal of the call to follow Jesus, Jesus himself "got up and followed him, with his disciples" (9:18–19). After resuscitating the little girl in the synagogue ruler's house, Jesus does not linger. We are told that he simply "went on from there." But as usual he is not alone: on this occasion "two blind men followed him" into another house, pleading for Jesus' attention and ultimately receiving his healing touch (9:27–29).[10]

Despite his frequent stops in various houses and despite his protestation against advertising his reputation as a miracle worker (9:30), Matthew's Jesus enjoys little solitude. Pressed by both hostile opponents and helpless unfortunates, Jesus remains on the move, following a course chock full of challenges but offering scant chance for rest. Since every place poses some kind of threat or problem for Jesus, there indeed is no place for him to lay his head.

Luke: No Room in the Inn

The Lukan setting for Jesus' statement concerning the Son of Man's homelessness likewise emphasizes the cost of discipleship, but focuses more pointedly on the pattern of rejection. Jesus is forced to wander from place to place because of closed doors and callous dismissals from would-be hosts. The immediately preceding episode, strategically set at the beginning of the major "travel narrative" or "central section" of Luke's gospel,[11] features the refusal of a Samaritan village to accommodate Jesus and his followers even for a single night en route to Jerusalem (the Samaritans venerated Mount Gerizim as God's true sanctuary and thus wanted nothing to do with Jerusalem-honoring Jews) (9:51–56). Jesus takes this rejection in stride (he's used to it) and proceeds on his way—which is more than can be said for his hotheaded disciples James and John, who want to incinerate the village Elijah-style (9:54). Jesus gladly embraces other aspects of Elijah's prophetic ministry, but not this one.[12] His followers have a lot to learn about shaking the dust from their feet and moving on.[13]

Luke's Jesus has learned to accept and expect rejection and dislocation literally from the cradle. The famous Lukan birth story features a double dislodging—first, the inconvenient trek of Joseph and his pregnant wife from Nazareth to Bethlehem (to register for the imperial census), and then, the makeshift settlement in a Bethlehem barn, where the baby Jesus is born and boarded "in a manger, because there was no place for them in the inn" (2:1–7). As his life commences with displacement, so his ministry. Jesus' inaugural public address occurs in his hometown synagogue in Nazareth, where, as we have seen, he encounters virulent opposition. The only place in which Jesus' inhospitable auditors want him to lay his head is at the bottom of a cliff outside the village (4:29). Whether at Bethlehem in Judea, Nazareth in Galilee, or an unnamed town in Samaria, Jesus has become accustomed to closed doors, "no vacancy" signs, and no safe, secure place to settle. This hardship persists throughout his life, culminating in two dramatic final resting places: the cross, where Jesus lays his thorn-crowned head against a splintery beam of wood; and the tomb, which Jesus soon evacuates to ascend to his heavenly abode. From beginning to end, from stable to sepulcher, this world affords Jesus only fragile, fleeting shelter at best, but no lasting home.

Finally, this sense of perpetual movement and displacement is not something Jesus laments, but rather embraces and encourages. In presenting the demands for following him who "has nowhere to lay his head," only Luke's Jesus concludes: "No one who puts a hand to the plow and looks back is fit for the kingdom of God" (9:62). The kingdom of God is ahead not behind, awaiting those who restlessly push forward rather than those who longingly look back and linger in their tracks. Settling down is not always a good thing: "Remember Lot's wife" (17:32).[14]

No Purse

In the Synoptic Gospels, Jesus sends out the Twelve with explicit instructions to "take nothing for their journey . . . no bread, no bag, no money in their belts."[15] Similarly, Luke's Jesus also dispatches a group of seventy delegates with no money or means of collecting any: "Carry no purse, no bag" (10:4). Roving Cynic philosophers were known for their "begging bags" in which appreciative auditors could deposit money (like the empty hat passed by street performers).[16] But not so Jesus' disciples: on these particular missions they may receive basic hospitality (food and lodging) in exchange for preaching and healing, but not monetary payment.

Strangely, however, toward the close of Luke's gospel, Jesus appears to reverse this policy:

> He said to them, "When I sent you out without a purse, bag, or sandals, did you lack anything?" They said, "No, not a thing." He said to them, "*But now, the one who has a purse must take it, and likewise a bag. And the one who has no sword must sell his cloak and buy one.* For I tell you, this scripture must be fulfilled in me, 'And he was counted among the lawless'; and indeed what is written about me is being fulfilled." (22:35–37)

It is difficult to know what to make of this instruction. Perhaps it reflects a concession to later customs of financial support for both resident Christian ministers and itinerant evangelists. In any case, it is hard to take this advice literally in its present context. Jesus endeavors to impress upon his naïve disciples the harsh reality of the "lawless" times they are about to enter, beginning with Jesus' crucifixion. Persecution will be severe; circumstances dire. Even if they do carry purse and bag, what good will it do? Who (but fellow believers) will share anything with them? Likewise, what good will come from selling one's cloak to buy a sword? Their weapons would be no match against Rome's arsenal, and they would just die colder and more destitute without their coats. Thus Jesus appears to be issuing more of a wake-up call to his complacent followers than a concrete plan of action.[17] And whatever Jesus envisions for the disciples' future, he still affirms in this passage the former pattern of providing for their material needs apart from soliciting or begging ("'When I sent you out without a purse [or] bag . . . did you lack anything?' They said, 'No, not a thing.'").

But how typical, how widespread, is this money-less mode of operation for Jesus and his followers? While Jesus often addresses economic issues in his parables and other teachings (usually in a critical vein, challenging the wealthy), financial concerns figure little in his personal life. He does not charge a fee for his ministerial work. A hemorrhaging woman, who had "spent all that she had" on ineffectual physicians, is never asked to pay a penny when Jesus heals her (Mark 5:25–34//Luke 8:43–48). Jesus encourages, even demands, giving money to the poor, but however much he identifies with the poor, he never solicits funds for himself.[18] Moreover, as far as the gospels report, he never even takes up a collection for the poor or anyone else, as does the apostle Paul.[19] Jesus brokers many benefits to the underprivileged, but coins and scrip are not among them.

In short, Jesus scarcely fits the profile of a businessman. He seems to care little about acquiring and managing money for himself. But can he and his followers really survive without any money of their own? Although not a dominant strain in the gospels, there are hints of some financial transactions within the Jesus movement. From the synoptic tradition, we learn that certain wealthy women from Galilee underwrite Jesus' ministry. Matthew and Mark wait to disclose this fact retrospectively from the crucifixion scene: "There were also women looking on from a distance [at the cross]; among them were Mary Magdalene, and Mary the mother of James the younger and of Joses, and Salome. These used to follow him and provided for him when he was in Galilee; and there were many other women who had come up with him to Jerusalem."[20] Luke refers to these supportive women earlier in the narrative and in somewhat greater detail:

Soon afterwards he [Jesus] went on through cities and villages, proclaiming and bringing the good news of the kingdom of God.

The twelve were with him, as well as some women who had been
cured of evil spirits and infirmities: Mary, called Magdalene, from
whom seven demons had gone out, and Joanna, the wife of
Herod's steward Chuza, and Susanna, and many others, who *provided for them out of their resources.* (8:1–3)

In each of these synoptic texts, the verb translated as "provided for" in
the NRSV is the common Greek term for "serving" (*diakoneō*), which can
denote a range of tasks, including menial service (waiting on tables, foot
washing, and the like), financial service (distributing funds, managing
investments), and spiritual service (participating in worship, ministering
to the needy). Women in the ancient world were more commonly associated with the first category (domestic service) but were not restricted to
that form of service exclusively. In the financial arena, aristocratic
women were free to support various causes with their own disposable
wealth. Recent studies have suggested that religious and political reform
parties (like that of the Pharisees) especially benefited from wealthy
female donors. Denied influence through established channels of authority dominated by a male hierarchy, these upper-class women "could support opposition movements over and against their husbands' political
leanings, demonstrating their financial independence by supporting
charities of their choice."[21] Luke's account may reflect just such a scenario. Among the Galilean women who serve Jesus "out of their
resources" (or "with their possessions") is Joanna, the wife of a Herodian
official (Chuza)—an aristocratic woman with means to support Jesus
and perhaps motivation born of some disaffection with Herodian patri-
archs and policies.[22] Luke also supplies another motivation for Joanna's
generosity: Jesus had delivered her, along with Mary Magdalene and
"many other women," from some demonic or medical malady. Still, we
must underscore that these women's contributions are not presented as
required remuneration for services rendered. They are not legally bound
to Jesus as indebted servants; they follow and support Jesus financially as
voluntary expressions of love and gratitude.

While the Synoptics provide some clue to a source of Jesus' income,
the fourth gospel uniquely suggests some system of money management
within the Jesus circle. One reference discloses that "his [Jesus'] disciples
had gone into the city [Sychar] to buy food" (4:8), and two comments

assume their pooling of funds into a "common purse" (or "money box," 12:6; 13:29) for purchasing provisions (e.g., "for the festival") and helping the poor (13:29). The primary purpose behind these brief economic references, however, is not to illustrate the fiscal condition of Jesus' group, but rather to show the sinister reputation of Judas, the group's treasurer. The narrator first mentions the "common purse" to stress that its manager is nothing but a common thief with his sticky hands regularly in the till (12:6). Thus we know what Judas really has in mind when he objects to Mary's expensive "waste" of perfume on Jesus' feet (12:5). The second "purse" reference is embedded in the scene where Jesus identifies Judas as his betrayer, and Judas promptly exits to execute his nefarious plan. In place of the singular episode in the Synoptics where Judas suddenly agrees to deliver Jesus to the authorities for a fee (Matthew quantifies the price as thirty pieces of silver),[23] the fourth gospel exposes a history of Judas's shady business practices as Jesus' greedy accountant.

In summary, the gospels suggest that while Jesus does not charge for his services, beg for support, or worry much at all about personal business matters, he and his disciples still receive some funds through voluntary, charitable offerings. But how far does this money go, and how is it managed (apart from Judas's misappropriations in the fourth gospel)? We turn now to a closer investigation of two areas of Jesus' life where one would expect money to be involved: procuring food and paying taxes. The old adage contends that the two most certain things in anyone's life are death and taxes. True enough, but before death, nothing is more basic to survival than eating. Food and taxes: common concerns of any society, and both (usually) require money.

Buying Food

Neither Jesus nor any of his closest followers appear to be either landowners or tenant farmers. If they did possess land at one time, they abandon it to pursue the mission of God's kingdom.[24] They are thus in no position to grow their own food. Other options for sustenance include: (1) purchasing food in the market, (2) receiving food from donors and/or hosts, (3) foraging for leftovers, and (4) tapping other, nonagricultural food sources, like fishing. Passing references to the first option appear in the fourth gospel, and numerous cases of the second surface across the gospel tradition. That leaves the other two possibilities for consideration—foraging and fishing.

An interesting incident develops in the Synoptic Gospels as Jesus' disciples "pluck heads of grain" while journeying "through the grainfields" of Galilee (Matt 12:1–8//Mark 2:23–28//Luke 6:1–5). Jesus accompanies them during this scavenging expedition, but evidently does not participate. Nevertheless, he defends his followers' action against attacks by certain legal experts (Pharisees). The act of foraging, which may strike modern readers as trespassing on others' property and stealing their possessions, is not the problem. Jewish law encouraged farmers to leave some of their harvest in the fields for the poor and indigent, both native and alien, to "glean." There were quantity limits, to be sure—grain was to be eaten directly hand-to-mouth, not harvested by sickle and hauled off in containers—providing subsistence, not surplus, for the needy.[25] The disciples duly comply with these regulations; the crux is not so much what they do as when they do it. The Pharisees charge them with "doing what is not lawful on the sabbath," that is, laboring (reaping) on the holy day of rest. Our concern at present is not with the fine points of Jesus' position on Sabbath observance. Suffice it to say that he fully endorses the disciples' gleaning as an act befitting their status as poor, wandering strangers in the land. Whatever money is at the disposal of Jesus and his associates, it cannot have been much. If they had a booming portfolio or a brimming cash box or a productive estate to support them, this foraging, on the Sabbath or any other day, would have been unnecessary at best, uncharitable to the truly poor at worst.

The proximity of Jesus' mission to the Sea of Galilee, including travel across the sea itself, combined with the fishing background of some of his disciples, presents a plausible opportunity for self-support. In the absence of farming and the limits of foraging, fishing provides an alternative food supply, abundant and free, not to mention a potentially lucrative export business if carried out on a larger scale.[26] The fact that multiple boats and nets are associated with Peter, Andrew, and the sons of Zebedee may signal that they are men of some means—not aristocrats, to be sure, but not lowly peasants either.[27] Still, it is noteworthy that the only occasions in the gospels which depict these disciples' catching fish or eating fish they have caught is in their first encounters with Jesus, when he calls them to follow (Matt 4:18–22//Mark 1:16–20; Luke 5:1–11), or their last, when he appears to them as risen Lord (despair over Jesus' death seems to drive them back to their former jobs) (Luke 24:41–42; John 21:1–14). In between, they forsake fishing as a commercial enterprise to pursue the urgent missionary vocation of "fishing for people" (Matt 4:19//Mark 1:17; Luke 5:10).[28] It's hard to believe that they ceased fishing for fish altogether, particularly for their own (and Jesus') consumption, but the gospels do not mention it.

Finally, we consider the famous incident(s) in which Jesus supplies bounteous portions of bread and fish for a hungry multitude—one of the few miracles featured in all four gospels.[29] After a long day of teaching the crowds who flock to him in "a deserted place," Jesus intends to feed his hearers before dismissing them. Nice idea—but the disciples want to know how Jesus plans to pull off this extraordinary banquet (for thousands of guests!) at the last minute. Their remote location is scarcely propitious for finding enough food, and a quick poll of the assembly turns up only a handful of loaves and fishes—a negligible amount under the circumstances. That leaves the prospect of going into town and buying food. The disciples suggest in fact that the audience go home (it is already late in the day—"very late," according to Mark 6:36) and "buy food for themselves," but Jesus scotches that proposal. So what now? Are the disciples supposed to do the shopping on their budget? That's a ridiculous notion from their perspective, since it would take some "two hundred denarii" (about six months wages for an average laborer) for everyone to get even a tidbit.[30] By implication, that's either hypothetical money they don't have or, if they do have it, that's both too much to waste on a bunch of strangers and too little to make a difference. Because Jesus does not address the money issue at all, but proceeds to multiply the meager supply of bread and fish, it is likely the disciples do not have the two hundred denarii to spend even if they wanted to (Jesus is never shy about asking people to share their money—all of it!—with the poor).

The significance of this miraculous feeding story may be appreciated in various ways. On one level it appears to mirror the divine provision of bread (manna) during ancient Israel's wandering in the wilderness (desert).[31] Moreover, some have suggested that the "real" miracle is Jesus' ability to persuade peasants, who typically hoard what little food they have for themselves, to share liberally with their neighbors (the lesson: when everyone shares, there's more than enough to go around).[32] In any case, from an ethical viewpoint, it is revealing that Jesus consistently exercises his power, whether creative or persuasive, to serve others, not himself. He refuses to turn a single stone into bread (or money) to satisfy his own hunger.

Paying Taxes

Jewish males over age twenty in first-century Palestine were responsible for paying (among other tolls and fees) the annual *denarius* (average day-laborer's wage) tribute to Rome and the half-shekel (two denarii = *didrachma*) levy to the temple treasury in Jerusalem—both "head" taxes remitted in silver coinage.[33] If Jesus carries no wallet and acquires no money, as certain parts of the gospels suggest, what does he do come tax time? He could, of course, evade the duty either surreptitiously, hoping not to get caught, or blatantly, as a form of protest. There was well-known precedent for the latter response. In 6 C.E. a Galilean named Judas led an ill-fated tax revolt against Rome, refusing on religious principles to pay tribute to any master other than God.[34] Jesus certainly does not shy away from criticizing illegitimate "domination systems,"[35] both political and religious, Roman and Jewish, insisting on God's exclusive priority over all earthly masters, including Mammon/money (Matt 6:24//Luke 16:13). But does this protest extend to tax resistance? Two brief gospel incidents offer our main clues to this question.

First, on the Roman side, we consider the synoptic case in which certain schemers directly ask Jesus: "Is it lawful to pay taxes to the emperor, or not? Should we pay them, or should we not?" (Matt 22:15–22//Mark 12:13–17//Luke 20:20–26). As a creative teacher, Jesus responds not merely with words, but also with a memorable visual aid. He asks his challengers to show him a coin (denarius) used to pay the tax. Why doesn't he simply pull one out of his own bag? Two possibilities present themselves, and I suspect both are in view here: one, Jesus has no denarius of his own, further proof that his pockets are empty; and two, Jesus employs a favorite strategy of turning the question around on his accusers. It's their coin with the image of their emperor engraved on it. To whom does it belong, then? Well, obviously to Caesar; therefore, "give to the emperor the things that are the emperor's, and to God the things that are

God's." This statement is not (as often assumed) a straightforward endorsement of both civic and religious duty (pay your taxes to the state, bring your tithes to God, and don't rock the boat). Jesus' response is more ambiguous and potentially more inflammatory.[36] Perhaps an oblique attack on Caesar?—"Yeah, let's give him what he deserves; give him his just due: it's payback time!"[37] Or a gibe against his challengers?—"What are you doing carrying around a coin etched with the emperor's idolatrous image? Get rid of it; give it back to Caesar; it's his anyway." In either case, there is a critical edge to Jesus' answer, albeit one that stops short of calling for full-scale revolt. Jesus never explicitly instigates a tax rebellion, but he also seems to care little about acquiring his own denarius to support Rome. Caesar's money is none of his business.

On the Jewish side, concerning payment of the temple tax, we turn to one of the strangest incidents in gospel literature, recorded only in Matt 17:24–27. When asked if "your teacher" (Jesus) pays the didrachma to the temple treasury, Peter impetuously answers in the affirmative, thus setting himself up for correction. As Jesus explains to Peter, royal heirs do not pay tribute (they receive it); thus, as children of God's kingdom, Jesus and his followers are "free" (17:26), legally exempt from financing God's house. But such freedom is not absolute. In the face of many within Israel who do not accept or understand Jesus' messianic mission, Jesus enjoins Peter to pay the temple tax "so that we do not give offense to them" (17:27).[38] Jesus does not want to be misjudged as a lawbreaker or temple basher or anything else that might jeopardize his outreach to "the lost sheep of the house of Israel" (10:6).

While Jesus' motive for paying the temple tax is clear and commendable, his means for obtaining the money is another story—a fish story, in fact, which stretches the imagination beyond belief (as fish stories often do: the minnow evolves into a marlin as the tale is repeated). Peter is instructed to check the mouth of the first fish he snags, where he will find deposited a double-didrachma coin (*stater*) to cover both his and Jesus' tax bill.[39] On the one hand, this tale may confirm that Jesus and his followers have no money of their own to spend—or at least none to spare on taxes. On the other hand, however, Jesus' manipulation of nature for his own financial gain represents a bit of profiteering hocus-pocus in the mold of Simon Magus or King Midas. As one commentator poses the conundrum: "Taken literally, the story has problems not only of physics but also of ethics, and it conflicts with other pictures of Jesus, who does not use his miraculous power for his own benefit."[40] Obviously, the best solution is not to take the story literally (fish do not spew silver coins any more than geese lay golden eggs); the "moral" of the story is what counts (freedom is limited at the point where it causes others to stumble). Also, the utter uniqueness of this story within the gospels must again be underscored. It constitutes a response to a special situation—not the norm. Jesus eats fish himself, breaks and distributes fish so others can eat, and maybe even catches fish from time to time. But he wastes no further time checking fishes' mouths for loose change. Matthew's Jesus spins a parable about a merchant finding a pearl of great price, but needless to say, this story is not about promoting the oyster industry or the mining of Mediterranean waters for gold, silver, and precious stones. In fact, it's about selling everything one has for the sake of the kingdom of heaven (the most valuable pearl of all) (13:45–46). So, once again it seems, we find Jesus quite comfortable operating without money.

Before leaving this unusual incident, we must briefly consider another level of interpretation, the other side of the coin, if you will. While in one sense, finding money in a fish's mouth is unparalleled in the gospel writings, in another sense it is symptomatic of numerous episodes in which God miraculously meets human needs through Jesus—including other feats involving fish (either catching or catering them).[41] As God graciously provides food and health for bodily sustenance, so God wondrously supplies money for tax relief (the tax burden could be unbearable for many poor and disabled peasants). But there may be another issue as well—more critical than charitable, more belligerent than beneficent. By demonstrating God's powerful manipulation of nature to produce tax money, Jesus may be underscoring God's sovereign control over the world and its resources and thus God's exclusive right to assess and receive tithes and taxes from God's people. Accordingly, Matthew's Jesus may not be that far from Judas of Galilee and other objectors to oppressive foreign taxation after all. We know that in the period following Rome's destruction of the Jerusalem temple in 70 C.E., Rome cruelly co-opted the annual Jewish half-shekel/didrachma temple tax to support its own rebuilding of the sacred shrine to Jupiter in the imperial capital. By a heinous twist of fate, conquered Jews were now required to underwrite pagan worship. If, as most scholars contend, the final edition of Matthew's gospel was penned in this tumultuous post-70 era, then the story of God's unique provision of the double-drachma coin may carry an implicit protest against Caesar's usurpation of divine prerogative. If God so allows and allocates, God's people may go ahead and pay Caesar's tax in the meantime, but they have no doubts about who is truly Lord or with whom "the buck" ultimately stops.[42]

No Possessions

Since Jesus owns no land or house to stock with animals, farm tools, furniture, or knick-knacks—and since he appears to have no surplus funds to buy these things anyway—that leaves little to discuss in terms of Jesus' possessions. He seems to take quite seriously his dictum, announced in Luke's gospel, that "one's life does not consist in the abundance of possessions" (12:15). Still, however austere one's existence, it's impossible to survive with absolutely nothing. There's the matter of food and drink, which we've already considered; but there are also basic concerns related to clothing[43] and transportation. One does not have to be financing extensive wardrobes and expensive vehicles—major items in modern American budgets—to appreciate the problem. The poorest of the poor, ancient and modern, have to worry about wearing something and getting from here to there.

To be sure, Jesus says, "Why do you worry about clothing?"—but not as a pretext for establishing a nudist colony. He assumes that everyone needs clothing but cautions against becoming preoccupied with obtaining it: God will provide necessary covering as surely as God adorns the lilies of the field and provided coats for the first human couple.[44] Moreover, while walking seems to be Jesus' main mode of travel, it is not suitable for every journey. Ventures across the Sea of Galilee, for example, normally require a vessel. (Jesus walks on the water once to punctuate a special faith lesson for his disciples, not to demonstrate a fancy new means of transport ["Come get your bionic jet skis—the latest in missionary motoring!"]). And at least one time on land, Jesus does not walk but rather rides on an animal's back. So Jesus does possess (or have access to) some clothing and some form of transportation. The question is: How does he obtain these things and how much does he have?

What Jesus Wears

While prohibiting his disciples from taking along any bread, bag, or money, Mark's Jesus permits them to have a few necessities; namely, a staff, a belt (sash), a tunic (*chitōn,* undergarment)—the same one every-day, no extras!—and sandals (6:8–9). The material shared by Matthew and Luke restricts the disciples' kit even further, eliminating both staff and sandals (Matt 10:10//Luke 9:3; 10:4). Thus the fashion image of Jesus and his followers is simple in the extreme: the same, single tunic (presumably washed now and then) worn next to the skin, a belt around the waist, and either sandals or bare feet. Although not as Spartan as John the Baptist's camel-hair shirt and leather belt,[45] this basic outfit conveys a similar no-frills look in contrast to royal dandies, criticized by Jesus, bedecked in "soft robes . . . fine clothing, and . . . luxury" (Matt 11:7//Luke 7:25). Speaking of John, his insistence on being unworthy "to untie the thong of his [the Coming One's] sandals" may imply that Jesus owns sandals and does not (always) go barefoot.[46] But this may also be a standard idiom to denote humility and subservience, irrespective of one's footgear.

Apart from tunic, belt, and sandals, another piece of clothing considered essential in the ancient Mediterranean world was a cloak/coat or outer garment (*himation*), used not only for daytime wear but also as a covering or pillow (rolled up) at night.[47] Although not mentioned in Jesus' missionary instructions, he elsewhere assumes that cloaks are customary attire and even appears in such garb himself. In the Sermon on the Mount/Plain in Matthew/Luke he refers to both *chitōn* and *himation,* but in doing so he radically challenges his hearers to give up these under and outer garments without a fuss to greedy prosecutors (an extreme case of giving someone "the shirt off your back") (Matt 5:40//Luke 6:29). In the first gospel, a woman with a bleeding disorder and others suffering from various ailments seek healing from Jesus by touching the fringes or tassels attached to his *himation* (9:20; 14:36). These fringes, traditionally made of blue cord suspended from the hemmed corners of the cloak, were worn by pious Israelites as reminders of their covenantal obligations to God.[48] Jesus' dress thus exhibits his avowed commitment to fulfilling the law and keeping the commandments (5:17–20). Leather pouches containing Scripture called "phylacteries," strapped to the arm and forehead, served a similar purpose,[49] but the gospels never specify that Jesus dons such accessories. In fact, Matthew's Jesus chides the Pharisees for sporting especially "broad phylacteries" as well as "long fringes" (23:5). While not opposed to sober demonstration of one's devotion to the law, Jesus does recoil from ostentatious display, in clothing as well as in other matters.

The most extensive discussion of Jesus' wardrobe is associated with the final hours of his life, just after he is sentenced to die. Initially, Matthew and Mark provide the most details:[50] the soldiers shamefully strip Jesus of his own clothing and adorn him with a purple robe, a crown of thorns, and a reed scepter in a mock-royal investiture, accompanied by sarcastic adulation ("Hail to the king!") and indignant gestures (spitting in his face, striking his head). Following this spectacle, the soldiers denude Jesus again, re-dress him in his own garb, and lead him to the Place of the Skull (Golgotha/Calvary) for crucifixion. For amusement and profit, they proceed to undress Jesus a third time and to divide his garments. Now the fourth gospel describes the scene most fully: the executioners rip Jesus' cloak (*himation*) into four pieces, one for each of them, and cast lots for his (untorn) tunic (*chitōn*) (19:23–25).[51] Although highlighted as a fulfillment of Scripture from a believer's perspective (John 19:24//Ps 22:18), this is scarcely the soldiers' intent. Recreation, exploitation, and humiliation are their games. Gambling provides a welcome diversion from the morbidity of crucifixion; cloth represents a valuable commodity;[52] and a final stripping and shaming suits any would-be "king" who dares to challenge Rome's hegemony. Let Jesus die naked and utterly destitute—without palace, without servants, without clothing, without anything. What kind of king is that?

The kind of king Jesus represents is in fact a kind of anti-king—a king who wholly sympathizes with and enters the plight of the "least of these," the have-nots, those without food, drink, shelter, freedom, health, and, yes, clothing. In the self-referential language of Jesus' parable in Matthew: "I was hungry . . . I was thirsty . . . I was a stranger . . . I was naked . . . I was sick . . . I was in prison" (25:35–36). The ethical punch of this self-portrait is to elevate merciful action toward the poor and oppressed as the distinguishing mark of God's kingdom: "Come, you that are blessed by my Father, inherit the kingdom prepared for you . . . for I was naked and you gave me clothing" (25:34–36). The wealthy Joseph of Arimathea, who claims Jesus' bare corpse and "wraps it in a clean linen cloth" for burial (27:57–60), literally fulfills this requirement for entering God's royal household. But Joseph is no singular saint. His deed betokens a much wider application: "Truly, I tell you, just as you did it to one of the least of these who are members of my family, you did it to me" (25:40). By clothing the needy, we can replicate Joseph's action; we can clothe Jesus and thus claim our place in God's kingdom.

What Jesus Rides

A contemporary group of American Christian activists known as the Evangelical Environmental Network have recently launched a national campaign promoting the use and manufacture of "the most fuel-efficient and least polluting" modes of transportation. The principal motto (or should we say the driving principle?) behind this project trades on the WWJD? phenomenon with a special twist: "What Would Jesus *Drive?*" Adherents are asked to take the "What Would Jesus Drive Pledge," which affirms that "making transportation choices that threaten millions of human beings violates Jesus' basic commandments: 'Love your neighbor as yourself'; and 'Do to others as you would have them do to you.'" The movement assumes, among other things, that Jesus would likely not be tooling around in a gas-guzzling SUV or high-performance sports car; rather he would "walk, bike, car pool, and use public transportation" whenever possible.[53]

Of course, in his first-century Palestinian milieu reflected in the gospels, the only one of these mobile options available (or conceivable) to Jesus is walking. And by and large, that is how Jesus gets around, covering manageable distances by foot throughout his homeland (the foot-washing scenes discussed in a previous chapter presuppose pedestrian travel). Unlike Paul, for example, Jesus never undertakes major voyages across the Mediterranean or expeditions over Europe and Asia Minor. He does, however, occasionally use two other modes of transportation, which figure little in modern environmental debates but further fill out

Jesus' economic profile. Exceptional gospel scenes depicting Jesus other than as a pedestrian show him riding a boat across the Sea of Galilee or a beast into the city of Jerusalem.

How do Jesus and his followers gain access to a boat? Do they own, rent, or borrow one? Is there a ferry service across the lake? Jesus' earliest followers—the two pairs of brothers, Peter/Andrew and James/John—own boats, nets, and other gear appropriate to their fishing enterprise on the Sea of Galilee; but upon encountering Jesus, they promptly leave their business, boats and all, to pursue a new vocation of catching people for God's kingdom. We are not told, however, what happens to their equipment. Do they sell their boats, destroy them, give them away, leave them in someone's charge (father Zebedee, perhaps?), or just abandon them temporarily? While forsaking all to follow Jesus, might they still use their own boats periodically in the service of their master's mission?

The various gospel accounts placing Jesus and his disciples in a boat as a means of conveyance across the sea or a platform for teaching on the shore never specify whose boat is being used. But a chain of evidence in Mark 3–8 suggests that Jesus uses a single boat likely belonging to one of his disciples. First, as Jesus' popularity and notoriety swell in Galilee, he instructs "his disciples to have a boat ready for him because of the crowd, so that they would not crush him" (3:9). The word for "boat" (*ploiarion*) can signify "little boat" or a "skiff," but seems to be synonymous in Mark with a related term, *ploion*, which assumes no particular size dimensions.[54] At any rate, Jesus' order implies that his disciples have access to a vessel. They appear to fulfill their assignment, since we soon encounter Jesus seated in a boat on the Galilean seaside (4:1). The crowds are there too, just as Jesus suspected, so he uses this opportunity to teach them before making his getaway. It is evening when Jesus and his disciples finally embark on their voyage. Mark's account of the departure, "leaving the crowd behind, they [the disciples] took him [Jesus] with them in the boat" (4:36), reinforces the notion that it is their (the disciples') vessel.[55] Matthew and Luke both adjust the picture somewhat to present either Jesus' leading his disciples into the boat or the whole group stepping in together.[56] These modifications seem designed to avoid any hint that Jesus may have followed his disciples, as if they are his captains, but they do not preclude the possibility that the boat belongs to someone within Jesus' group. Several subsequent references in Mark's narrative chart a series of movements back and forth across the sea on what appears to be the same boat (always "the boat," *to ploion*).[57] Such ready access to this craft over a period of time hints that it is owned by one of Jesus' associates, rather than borrowed or rented from someone outside the circle. This supposition that the disciples never completely abandon their fishing gear meshes with the fourth gospel's portrayal of Simon Peter's return to his boat and net after Jesus' death (21:1–11).

The lone example of Jesus' riding an animal in the gospels is associated with the so-called "triumphal entry" into Jerusalem. Mark and Luke present Jesus mounted on a colt (*pōlos*) of an unspecified beast (it could be a young horse or a donkey) (Mark 11:2–4//Luke 19:30–33). Matthew and John, with explicit allusion to Zech 9:9, designate the animal as a donkey (*onos/onarion*).[58] Either way, Jesus does not enter the holy city with pomp and circumstance: he commands no gilded chariot or noble steed, nor is he carried on a royal litter or servants' shoulders. Rather he rides a humble beast of burden, befitting his affinity with the meek and lowly, but also serving the gospels' loftier theological agenda. Matthew and John's citation of Zechariah's prophecy explicitly links Jesus' entry into Jerusalem with the anticipated arrival of Israel's conquering Messiah-king.[59] Mark and Luke's description of the animal as "a colt that has never been ridden" likely symbolizes the uniqueness of Jesus' messianic mission and his total consecration to God.[60]

Our present concern is with Jesus' economic status. Apart from generally confirming his humble image, what else can we learn about Jesus' attitude toward possessions from the way he procures the donkey's services? In the synoptic tradition, Jesus dispatches two disciples from the Mount of Olives into a nearby village (either Bethphage or Bethany), with instructions to "find" a tethered colt and "bring it here" (Matt 21:1–7//Mark 11:1–7//Luke 19:28–35). How does Jesus know this? Is this a case of supernatural clairvoyance, or does Jesus simply pre-arrange his travel plans? The text doesn't say.[61] The more important issue relates to how the disciples can just walk up and take this animal for a ride (like hotwiring some car on the street and taking it for a spin). Anticipating that questions might be asked, Jesus tells his followers to justify their action with the curt rejoinder, "The Lord needs it." Presumably, the colt's owners (in Luke) or other curious bystanders (in Mark) know who this "Lord" is, intimating that the animal belongs to Jesus' friends or sympathizers. In any case, no money is exchanged; the disciples neither purchase nor lease the colt. In fact, Mark makes an explicit point that the colt is being temporarily borrowed: "The Lord needs it and will send it back here immediately" (11:3). Jesus acquires no possession here; he makes no lasting claim on the beast.

Matthew and Luke leave matters more open, however. Luke says nothing about returning the colt, and Matthew shifts the focus regarding who sends the animal(s) to whom. Matthew reports, "and he [the owner] will send them [the donkey and its foal] immediately"—without Mark's additional "back here"—and thus highlights the owner's willingness to send the donkey/colt to Jesus as well as Jesus' royal prerogative to commandeer another's property.[62] The fourth gospel further accentuates Jesus' unique authority. No questions are asked; no middlemen are involved. John reports only that Jesus himself "found a young donkey and sat on it" (12:14), an act appropriate to Jesus' position as sovereign Lord of all creation.

These brief gospel accounts in which Jesus secures transportation for his final ride into Jerusalem thus reflect a trajectory of increasing economic independence. On the one end, Mark maintains Jesus' reliance on others' generosity and Jesus' personal disinterest in owning material possessions; on the other, John stresses Jesus' absolute claim on any and every earthly commodity and creature. For the fourth evangelist, the psalmist's sweeping declaration—"The earth is the Lord's and all that is in it, the world, and those who live in it" (24:1)—applies as surely to Jesus the Son of God as to the God of Israel.

Conclusion

As with other dimensions of Jesus' life, his dealings with money and material goods do not fit a simple, uniform pattern. It is too extreme to claim that Jesus lives in abject poverty throughout his public ministry; similarly exaggerated are depictions of Jesus as a high-flying socialite. He fits somewhere in between these poles, although not exactly in the middle. On "balance"—to use an accounting term—the gospels place Jesus much closer to the poorer end of the economic spectrum. Put another way, Jesus' financial "balance" is much closer to zero than, say, to the seventy-five pounds of silver (one "talent") featured in one of his parables.[63] Apart from identifying Jesus with the poor, the gospels also give a strong impression that Jesus gives little thought to his own personal economic welfare. In their own way, the poor can be just as materialistic as the rich—that is, preoccupied with material gain. Indeed, simply to survive, the poor have to pour all their energies into acquiring life's necessities. Jesus is not insensitive to this terrible plight and thus spends the great bulk of his energy feeding and healing the impoverished and infirm. But when it comes to his own sustenance and comfort (and that of his disciples), Jesus remains nonplussed, trusting in God's grace and the generosity of others to see him through. In his own language, he "seeks first the kingdom of God" and "takes no thought" for matters of personal survival (Matt 6:25–33 KJV).

Much of Jesus' seeming oblivion to obtaining and managing money and possessions relates to the urgent and itinerant nature of his mission. Whatever his economic status before launching his public ministry (as a "woodworker," he probably was a member of the artisan class—perhaps with some earning potential beyond subsistence laborers, but scarcely wealthy),[64] once he goes "on the road" with his followers proclaiming and enacting the good news of God's kingdom, there is no time for or interest in gainful employment or capital campaigns. Money matters are, at best, a cumbersome distraction. Again, despite spinning a classic story that highlights a "good Samaritan's" willingness to pay the hotel bill for a convalescing "neighbor" (Luke 10:25–37), Jesus worries little about arranging, much less paying, for his own lodging. With no (permanent) place to lay his head, Jesus sleeps where he can during the course of his travels—in a boat on a stormy sea, if necessary, or in the home of a gracious host.

In terms of resources, Jesus does appear to have some money at his disposal. The Synoptics (Luke especially) indicate that certain aristocratic Galilean women contribute to his support, and the fourth gospel refers to a "common purse" or "cash box" managed by Judas for Jesus and his disciples. But we have no idea how much money is available, and no gospel story depicts Jesus himself spending any. He seems to have no purse and not even a single coin to illustrate a point (about paying taxes to Caesar). He doesn't think twice about whether there is enough money to buy food for the five thousand: while his disciples are counting their denarii, Jesus is contemplating a miracle along the lines of God's ancient provision of manna in the wilderness. In the fourth gospel, the Jesus group's financial condition is tainted by the fraudulent oversight of the treacherous Judas—scarcely a model of business ethics. In the main encounter between Judas and Jesus over money, while Judas calculates the three hundred-denarii loss of Mary's spilt perfume, Jesus cares only about Mary's extravagant love.

Constantly on the move preparing for the imminent establishment of God's just and merciful kingdom, Jesus has no interest in accumulating possessions or any "treasures on earth" beyond "catching people" to comprise God's renewed household. For the most part, he seems to travel light, conducting his mission with only the clothes on his back. And at the end of his life, as he is crucified for resisting imperial power and injustice, he doesn't even have these. Naked he comes into the world, and naked he returns; the Lord gives and the Lord takes away—blessed be the name of the Lord.[65]

NOTES

1. See 1 Cor 9:1–18; 1 Thess 2:1–12; cf. Acts 18:1–4.
2. "Is not this the carpenter's son?" (Matt 13:55); "Is not this the carpenter, the son of Mary . . . ?" (Mark 6:3).
3. Bruce Chilton, *Rabbi Jesus: An Intimate Biography* (New York: Doubleday, 2000), 78.
4. See, e.g., Rom 16:5; 1 Cor 16:19; Col 4:15; Acts 2:46; 5:42; 12:12; 16:40; 18:7; 20:20.
5. Among the most famous of these roving, radical philosophers in the Greco-Roman world were the Cynics, founded by Antisthenes (a student of Socrates) and Diogenes of Sinope in the fifth to fourth centuries B.C.E. Cynics (or "Canines") railed against the conventions of polite society on street corners, dramatizing their counter-cultural agenda through their shabby clothing and mendicant lifestyle. Without home or income, they survived by scavenging and begging (the "begging bag" was among their most distinctive gear). While certain affinities may be detected between the teachings of Jesus and the Cynics, some scholars have pressed the connection too far, even suggesting that Jesus was a Cynic. Among other differences, the gospels never portray Jesus begging for support (he advocates generous giving to the beggar, but not becoming a beggar). See the helpful

summary and critique of Cynic-oriented studies of Jesus in N. T. Wright, *Jesus and the Victory of God* (Minneapolis, Minn.: Fortress, 1996), 66–74; and Richard A. Horsley and Neil Asher Silberman, *The Message and the Kingdom: How Jesus and Paul Ignited a Revolution and Transformed the Ancient World* (Minneapolis, Minn.: Fortress, 2002), 58–59, 92–94.

6. See, e.g., Matt 8:14–17//Mark 1:29–34//Luke 4:38–44//Matt 9:9–13// Mark 2:13–17//Luke 5:27–32; Luke 7:36–50; 10:38–42; 19:1–10; John 12:1–8.

7. Luke 10:7. This statement is embedded in Jesus' instructions to a group of seventy disciples he dispatches on a mission of healing and proclamation throughout Galilee: "Remain in the same house, eating and drinking whatever they provide, for the laborer deserves to be paid" (cf. 10:1–12).

8. Unlike Mark's account, which indicates that the disciples "took" (*paralambanō*) Jesus into the boat, Matthew stresses that they "followed" (*akoloutheō*) him into the vessel from the start. Matthew thereby underscores the importance of dutiful discipleship in the story.

9. Following the attack on Jesus' table fellowship (9:9–13) are questions about his views on fasting (9:14–17). Then the synagogue ruler approaches Jesus about his sick daughter (9:18). This entire sequence of events occurs in Matthew's home.

10. This is one of two stories in Matthew in which Jesus heals a pair of anonymous blind men (cf. 20:29–34). The parallel accounts in Mark 10:46–52//Luke 18:35–43 feature the healing of a single blind man (named Bartimaeus in Mark). A similar pattern emerges in Matthew's presentation of two Gadarene demoniacs where Mark and Luke have only one (Mark 5:1–20//Luke 8:26–39). This doubling tendency may reflect Matthew's understanding of these figures as more representative (of needy humanity) than unique.

11. This lengthy section runs from Luke 9:51–19:28 and coheres around a loosely structured journey to Jerusalem. Note the beginning, "When the days drew near for him to be taken up, he set his face to go to Jerusalem" (9:51) and ending, "After he said this, he went on ahead, going up to Jerusalem" (19:28; cf. 13:33–34; 17:11).

12. Luke's Jesus endorses and emulates Elijah's merciful ministry of caring for widows, feeding the hungry, and raising the dead (cf. 4:25–26; 7:11–17; 9:10–17), but not the prophet's fiery response of retribution. On Luke's appropriation of the Elijah/Elisha paradigms, see Craig A. Evans, "The Function of the Elijah/Elisha Narratives in Luke's Ethic of Election," in *Luke and Scripture: The Function of Sacred Tradition in Luke-Acts* (ed. Craig A. Evans and James A. Sanders; Minneapolis, Minn.: Fortress, 1993), 70–83; and Thomas L. Brodie, "Luke-Acts as an Imitation and Emulation of the Elijah-Elisha Narrative," in *New Views on Luke and Acts* (ed. Earl Richard; Collegeville, Minn.: Liturgical Press, 1990), 78–85.

13. See Luke 10:10–12. "Shaking/wiping the dust off one's feet" can be a symbolic gesture of protest against an unreceptive town (sort of like throwing up

one's hands in disgust), but it is clearly a nonviolent act. It may anticipate severe retribution but waits for God to exact final righteous judgment "on that day" ("I tell you, on that day it will be more tolerable for Sodom than for that town," 10:12).

14. Only Luke among the gospels cites this classic biblical example of one whose progress is blocked (Lot's wife literally becomes a salt block) by looking back at a corrupt world (Sodom and Gomorrah) she was instructed to leave behind (see Gen 19:12–26).

15. The citation is from Mark 6:8. See the parallels in Matt 10:9–10//Luke 9:3.

16. See n. 7 above. Note the critical evaluation of the Cynics' beggary by Dio Chrysostom, *Oration* 32.7–12:

> And as for the Cynics, as they are called, it is true that the city contains no small number of that sect, and that, like any other thing, this too has had its crop—persons whose tenets, to be sure, comprise practically nothing spurious or ignoble, yet who must make a living—still, these Cynics, posting themselves at street-corners, in alley-ways, and at temple-gates, pass around the hat and play upon the credulity of lads and sailors and crowds of that sort, stringing together rough jokes and much tittle-tattle and the low badinage that smacks of the market-place (translation from Malherbe, *Moral Exhortation,* 24–25).

17. For more on this passage, especially related to Jesus' peculiar call to arms, see chapter 7.

18. Two stories in Luke 18–19 illustrate the point. First, Jesus challenges the opulent ruler to "sell all that you own and distribute the money to the poor . . . then come, follow me" (18:22). Jesus wants this man's loyalty and obedience ("follow me") but not his money—that must go to the poor. Second, Jesus inspires the wealthy tax collector Zacchaeus to give half of all his possessions to the poor (19:8). However, while accepting Zacchaeus's hospitality, Jesus neither requests nor receives any personal payment of funds.

19. See Rom 15:25–28; 1 Cor 16:1–4; 2 Cor 8–9.

20. The citation is from Mark 15:40–41. Compare the close parallel in Matt 27:55–56.

21. Tal Ilan, *Integrating Women into Second Temple History* (Tübingen: J. C. Mohr [Paul Siebeck], 1999; repr., Peabody, Mass.: Hendrickson, 2001), 33. Ilan further concludes: "Through their financial contributions, such women may have influenced decision and policy making in the opposition parties they chose to support. Such a reconstruction is highly probable for early Christianity and is just as plausible for the Pharisee movement" (p. 33; cf. pp. 11–37).

22. For a comprehensive profile of Joanna in the Gospel of Luke and early Christian history, see Bauckham, *Gospel Women,* 109–202. For a lively, imaginative

reconstruction of Joanna's relationship with Jesus, see Gerd Theissen, *The Shadow of the Galilean* (Philadelphia: Fortress, 1989), 119–27. In this historical novella, Theissen presents an exchange between Joanna and the narrator-investigator:

> I soon turned the conversation towards Jesus. Joanna had been the first person to tell me of him. I couldn't believe my ears when I heard that she supported Jesus. She told me quite openly:
> "I send him money and food. My husband doesn't know. You mustn't tell him. When it's possible, I look for Jesus in order to listen to him."
> All the followers of Jesus whom I had met so far were ordinary people. But Joanna was a member of the upper class. I asked,
> "Do other well-to-do people support him?"
> "A few. He gets support from everywhere. But that doesn't fit what people say. . . ." (pp. 119–20)

23. Matthew 26:14–16//Mark 14:10–11//Luke 22:1–6.

24. See Mark 10:28–30, "Peter began to say to him, 'Look, we have left everything and followed you.' Jesus said, 'Truly I tell you, there is no one who has left house or brothers or sisters or mother or father or children or fields, for my sake and for the sake of the good news . . ." (cf. Matt 19:27–29).

25. See Deut 23:24–25; Ruth 2:1–23; Josephus, *Antiquities* 4.221–237.

26. Processes of salting, smoking, and pickling allowed for exporting fish and fish sauces throughout the Roman Empire. On the bustling and profitable fishing industry connected with the Sea of Galilee during the Herodian period, see Rousseau and Arav, *Jesus and His World*, 25–30, 93–97, 245–48; Horsley and Silberman, *The Message and the Kingdom*, 24–26; Marianne Sawicki, *Crossing Galilee: Architectures of Contact in the Occupied Land of Jesus* (Harrisburg, Pa.: Trinity Press International, 2000), 27–30, 143–47.

27. Matt 4:18–22//Mark 1:16–20; Luke 5:1–11. Mark 1:20 specifies that James and John "left their father Zebedee in the boat with the hired men" to follow Jesus. This suggests a family fishing business of sufficient size to support a crew of employees.

28. Jesus' parable of the dragnet in Matt 13:47–50 compares the outreach of God's kingdom to casting a seine into the sea (of humanity) and attracting a full draught of fish (people) "of every kind." Sorting out the good/righteous from the bad/evil adherents is left to the angels "at the end of the age."

29. The story of the feeding of the five thousand appears in Matt 14:13–21//Mark 6:30–44//Luke 9:10–17//John 6:1–15. Matt 15:32–39//Mark 8:1–10 add a briefer, largely duplicate account of the feeding of four thousand.

30. The two hundred denarii amount is disclosed in Mark 6:37//John 6:7. John alone has Philip voice the disciples' frustration, emphasizing that such an amount "would not buy enough bread for each of them to get a little."

31. While implied in all the gospels, this symbolism is most obvious in Jesus' extended discourse in John 6:22–59 following the miraculous feeding in 6:1–15.

32. See, e.g., Theissen, *Shadow of the Galilean,* 120.

33. Exod 30:11–15 provides the scriptural foundation for the half-shekel tax for the Jewish sanctuary. On taxation in early Roman Palestine, see Hanson and Oakman, *Palestine in the Time of Jesus,* 113–16; Rousseau and Arav, *Jesus and His World,* 275–79, 309–11.

34. Josephus, *Jewish War* 2.118; *Antiquities* 18.3–9, 23–25; see references and discussion in Richard A. Horsley and John S. Hanson, *Bandits, Prophets, and Messiahs: Popular Movements at the Time of Jesus* (New Voices in Biblical Studies; San Francisco, Calif.: Harper & Row, 1985), 190–99.

35. A concept stressed in numerous works by Walter Wink. See, e.g., *When the Powers Fall: Reconciliation in the Healing of Nations* (Minneapolis, Minn.: Fortress, 1998), 4: "Domination System: A social system characterized by hierarchical power relations, economic inequality, oppressive politics, patriarchy, ranking, aristocracy, taxation, standing armies, and war. Violence became the preferred means for adjudicating disputes and getting and holding power."

36. See Wright, *Jesus and the Victory of God,* 502–7; Horsley, *Jesus and Empire,* 98–99.

37. Wright (*Jesus and the Victory of God,* 504–5) suggests that Jesus' response "should be understood as a coded and subversive echo of Mattathias' last words" to his son, Judas Maccabeus, in preparation for overthrowing the oppressive regime of the Greco-Syrian tyrant, Antiochus IV Epiphanes: "Judas Maccabeus has been a mighty warrior from his youth; he shall command the army for you and fight the battle against the peoples. You shall rally around you all who observe the law, and avenge the wrong done to your people. Pay back the Gentiles in full, and obey the commands of the law" (1 Macc 2:66–68).

38. This incident prefaces a block of Jesus' teaching underscoring the importance of avoiding behavior that would cause God's "little ones" to stumble: "If any of you put a stumbling block before one of these little ones who believe in me, it would be better for you if a great millstone were fastened around your neck and you were drowned in the depth of the sea" (18:6; cf. 18:1–14). Notice Jesus' continuing use of the sea as an illustration.

39. Compare David E. Garland, *Reading Matthew: A Literary and Theological Commentary on the First Gospel* (New York: Crossroad, 1993), 186: "The incident ends with what seems to be a whimsical fish story and a highly unusual solution to any cash flow problems."

40. M. Eugene Boring, "The Gospel of Matthew," in *The New Interpreter's Bible,* vol. 8 (Nashville, Tenn.: Abingdon, 1995), 372.

41. Luke 5:1–11; Matt 14:13–21//Mark 6:30–44//Luke 9:10–17//John 6:1–15; Matt 15:32–39//Mark 8:4–12; John 21:1–14.

42. I owe this provocative interpretation of "paying the tax to Rome as subversive praxis" in Matt 17:24–27 to Warren Carter, *Matthew and Empire: Initial*

Explorations (Harrisburg, Pa.: Trinity Press International, 2001), 130–44.

43. Compare Sir 29:21, "The necessities of life are water, bread, and clothing, and also a house to assure privacy." See John J. Pilch, *The Cultural Dictionary of the Bible* (Collegeville, Minn.: Liturgical Press, 1999), 14–20.

44. Matt 6:28–30//Luke 6:26–28; cf. Gen 3:21.

45. Matt 3:4//Mark 1:6. Wearing makeshift garments from animal skins rather than manufactured clothing demarcates John as a marginalized, ascetic figure. Compare Jerome H. Neyrey, "Clothing," in *Biblical Social Values and Their Meanings* (ed. John J. Pilch and Bruce J. Malina; Peabody, Mass.: Hendrickson, 1993), 22.

46. Matt 3:11//Mark 1:7//Luke 3:16//John 1:27.

47. Thus biblical law stipulated that a cloak given as collateral for a debt must be returned to its owner each night. See Exod 22:26–27; Deut 24:10–13; Pilch, *Cultural Dictionary*, 16.

48. See Num 15:37–41; Deut 22:12.

49. See Exod 13:9, 16; Deut 6:8; 11:18.

50. Matt 27:27–31//Mark 15:16–20; cf. Luke 23:11; John 19:1–5.

51. Compare Matt 27:35//Mark 15:24//Luke 23:34.

52. Compare Neyrey, "Clothing," 20: "Clothing of any sort was valuable, hence, executioners competed for the garments of a crucified man (Mark 15:24); thieves took the clothing of the man they robbed (Luke 10:30)."

53. See the website www.whatwouldjesusdrive.org/action/pledge.php and the fall 2002 issue of *Creation Care,* a quarterly journal sponsored by the Evangelical Environmental Network, ed. Jim Ball (also available on-line at www.creationcare.org).

54. See Bauer, Arndt, Gingrich, and Danker, *Greek-English Lexicon,* 673; Rousseau and Arav, *Jesus and His World,* 25–30.

55. Mark also reports, as an aside, that "other boats were with him." Does this suggest a fleet of available vessels, or perhaps that portions of the crowd are still trying to tag along? In any event, the storm story that ensues focuses exclusively on the single boat containing Jesus and his disciples (4:37–41).

56. "And when he got into the boat, his disciples followed him" (Matt 8:23); "One day he got into a boat with his disciples" (Luke 8:22).

57. Mark 5:2, 21; 6:45, 47, 51, 53; 8:10, 13, 14.

58. Matthew 21:2–7//John 12:14–15. Matthew actually depicts two animals, a donkey (*onos*) and her colt (*pōlos*), apparently motivated by the Zechariah prophecy. This text, however, while using both terms, equates the two as the same animal—that is, a young donkey.

59. "Look, your king is coming to you" (Zech 9:9), reminiscent of Solomon's royal procession as David's successor on David's "own mule" (see 1 Kgs 1:33–35).

60. Various Jewish priestly rituals required "pure" animals who had never been yoked or employed in labor; see Num 19:2; Deut 21:3; 1 Sam 6:7.

61. See Harrington, *Gospel of Matthew,* 293.

62. Whereas in Mark 11:3 "the Lord" is both the one who "needs" the animal and who will "send" it back, Matt 21:3 implies a shift in subject from "the Lord needs them" to "and/but [*de*] he [i.e., the owner] will send them immediately." On this shift, see Robert H. Gundry, *Matthew: A Commentary on His Literary and Theological Art* (Grand Rapids, Mich.: Eerdmans, 1982), 408.

63. Matt 25:14–30; see Rousseau and Arav, *Jesus and His World,* 55–61.

64. Summarizing the model of social stratification in agrarian societies developed by Gerhard Lenski, Jerome Neyrey notes the position of the artisan class at the bottom of the scale between landed peasants and various marginal outcasts. Artisans were frequently drawn from landless or dispossessed peasants, who had no choice but to ply some trade in an urban marketplace. Depending on their skill and particular product, artisans could become fairly well-off but could just as easily struggle to make ends meet ("Luke's Social Location of Paul: Cultural Anthropology and Status of Paul in Acts," in *History, Literature, and Society in the Book of Acts* (ed. Ben Witherington, III; Cambridge, U.K.; Cambridge University Press, 1996), 251–79.

65. An adaptation of the suffering Job's classic formulation in Job 1:21.

6

Work Ethic

At the heart of the "American dream," deeply entrenched in this country's political rhetoric and popular myth, is the notion that hard work pays off. Opportunity knocks for anyone, regardless of background or inherited status, to climb the ladder of success if he or she simply has enough drive and dedication (grit and gumption) to make it happen. While there's no "free lunch," there's plenty of "free enterprise" to go around—at least for those who are industrious and "enterprising" enough to "work the system." This perspective is sometimes identified as the "Protestant/Puritan work ethic," although there is nothing peculiarly Protestant, or Christian, or even religious about it. The Jewish Scriptures, especially in the wisdom tradition, extol the virtue and value of diligent, disciplined labor over against the pitfalls of slack, slothful leisure.[1] And quite apart from pietistic concerns, in our athletics-absorbed society, competitors are routinely evaluated not just on their skill level, but on their work ethic—that is, how hard they train to maximize the abilities they possess. Winning has as much to do with what happens in the training room as on the playing field. But this is scarcely a new idea, as Paul's picture of the dedicated Olympic-style athlete, "exercising self-control in all things" to garner the prize, attests (1 Cor 9:24–27).

So almost anyone, ancient or modern, might subscribe to a strong work ethic: the harder you work, the more you win; the more effort expended, the more benefits achieved. Our concern, however, is not with just anyone but with Jesus in particular: does he adhere to such a vocational philosophy in the gospels? A number of his parables provide moral instruction from common agricultural scenarios of sowing and reaping, but the final lesson is rarely as straightforward as "you reap what you sow"—in other words, prepare the ground, plant the seed, pull the weeds, work the land by the sweat of your brow, and you will be guaranteed a bumper crop. The primordial Adamic "curse" acknowledged that the earth was not that compliant; farming was not that convenient (Gen 3:17–24). Jesus' classic parable of the sower recalls the sober reality of birds who swoop down and snatch loose seed as well as rocks and stones, thorns and thistles, which inevitably choke a portion of the harvest and thwart the farmer's best efforts (Matt 13:1–9//Mark 4:1–9//Luke 8:4–8). For day laborers dispossessed from their land and subject to employers' capricious wage scales, the possibility looms of callous exploitation, on the one hand, or whimsical generosity, on the other hand, as featured in Jesus' parable of the vineyard workers.[2] Either way, it is not a simple equation of getting what you deserve.

In the divine economy this is ultimately good news, since none of us can work hard enough to merit God's favor, and fortunately, God's blessing flows from God's boundless grace, not some kind of cosmic payroll account meting out wages for services rendered. So, as Jesus announces in the common sayings tradition in Matthew and Luke, God is quite happy to provide for the birds of the air and lilies of the field just because they are God's creation, not because they "sow and reap" or "toil and spin"—which, of course, they don't do! (Matt 6:28–30//Luke 12:27–28). And in his many dealings with the destitute and disadvantaged in the gospels, Jesus never hints for a second that their misfortune derives from their own indolence or incompetence. Jesus doles out a fair bit of blame in the gospels, but it is never directed to victims of poverty and oppression. They hurt enough without the added burden of guilt and shame. Instead of regarding them as blameworthy, Jesus esteems the poor as bless-worthy: "Blessed are you who are poor, for yours is the kingdom of God" (Luke 6:20; cf. Matt 5:3).

Obviously, then, Jesus' teaching raises as many questions as it answers concerning his work ethic. But what about his own personal conduct? How do we rate Jesus as a "worker"? What would go into his "annual evaluation" file? First, we face the problem of determining the focus of the evaluation. What "job" does Jesus hold? It would be nice to have some reports of Jesus' work as a carpenter, but the canonical gospels do not discuss this aspect of Jesus' life. In fact, they don't even agree exactly that Jesus was a carpenter by trade. In a single, unelaborated comment, placed on the lips of astonished townsfolk in Nazareth, Mark identifies Jesus as "the carpenter." But in parallel passages, Matthews calls Jesus "the carpenter's son," while Luke reads simply, "Joseph's son," without ever alluding to Joseph's profession.[3] The apocryphal *Infancy Gospel of Thomas* presents the charming woodshop tale in which the boy Jesus bales Joseph out of a jam. In constructing a bed frame ordered by a wealthy client, Joseph inadvertently cuts one crossbeam shorter than the other and doesn't know what to do to remedy the error. But not to fear: the young Jesus steps in and miraculously lengthens the shorter plank to match the other. Apart from stretching the truth (as well as the plank), this story offers little guidance for contemporary vocational ethics, since we cannot simply zap away our mistakes on the job. (Oddly enough, a few years back I had several slats cut that turned out to be too short to support the box springs and mattress in my bedroom. No amount of pulling, praying, or hocus-pocus corrected the problem: I had to replace them.)

Whatever his woodworking experience or whatever other "jobs" Jesus might have had, the only vocation that matters in the gospels is, to quote his own job description in John, "to work the works of him [God] who sent me" (9:4). No surprise here: Jesus is an evangelist, a prophet, a religious teacher, and as such may offer important guidance in "ministerial ethics" for professional clerics but otherwise provide scant help to the vast majority of persons engaged in so-called "secular work." But such a perspective is too narrow and naïve for at least four reasons. First, while utterly devoted to serving God, Jesus does not appear in the gospels as part of the religious establishment; in fact, he often clashes with the official clergy because of his pedestrian (non-priestly) pedigree and eccentric behavior. Second, the modern dichotomy between "spiritual" and "secular" pursuits is alien to Jesus' Jewish worldview. While priests serving in the temple had special duties and obligations that set them apart from the common people, all Israelites labored as stewards of God's gracious bounty. All worked, so to speak, for God, especially in cultivating the sacred land of divine promise. Third, if we still insist on pressing a distinction between mundane or menial labor and religious or ritual service, Jesus personally blurs such boundaries in his own activity. As he preaches and teaches, he feeds and heals; each endeavor complements the other. His service to God involves serving God's people at a common table or along a dusty road more than at a holy altar or behind a formal pulpit. And, finally, since Jesus indeed works long and hard at a variety of tasks befitting his vocation—he is no lordly prima donna demanding that others wait upon him hand and foot, nor does he exploit his considerable power to snap his fingers and put everything in order (Mary Poppins style)—he displays a rigorous, robust work ethic of potential relevance to all kinds of laborers.

We turn now in particular to explore the type of work Jesus tackles, the time he spends on the "job," and the ways and means he employs in accomplishing his business.

Lord and Labor

While some gospel uses of the title "lord" (*kyrios*) with reference to Jesus may reflect simple respect or politeness ("sir," "mister"), most imply a good bit more authority—"Lord," "Master" (notice the capitals)—even bordering on the divine (as in "Lord God"). One of the earliest Christian confessions of faith—"Jesus is Lord" (1 Cor 12:3)—finds ample foundation in numerous references to Jesus as Lord throughout the four gospels. Jesus calls and the disciples heed; Jesus leads and they follow; Jesus teaches and they learn; Jesus acts and they emulate. The hierarchy is clear: Jesus is Lord of God's kingdom; his disciples are loyal subjects and servants.

But for all his sovereign authority as Lord, Jesus routinely exercises his royal prerogative against the status quo. Simply put, Lord Jesus Christos does not always act very lordly, certainly not according to the standards of Lord Caesar Augustus or King Herod Antipas. As we have seen, Jesus settles in no palace, controls no property, and amasses no possessions. While popular with hordes of admirers, he does not court their favor. His call to "take up the cross and follow me" does not play well in the polls. Among those who do take up the challenge of discipleship, their primary duty is to help carry out Jesus' mission, not to attend to his personal needs. In Luke's gospel, Martha does cook for Jesus, but he is less interested in such service than in sharing his message with sister Mary—and presumably with Martha as well, if she weren't otherwise distracted (10:38–42). Mary Magdalene, Joanna, Susanna, and other women offer financial support to Jesus, but they also participate with Jesus in his mission ("The twelve were with him, as well as some women") and benefit personally from his healing ministry ("who had been cured of evil spirits and infirmities") (8:1–3). Patently, these women are not Jesus' maids or slaves. They, along with his other followers, do not so much work for Jesus as with him in advancing "the good news of the kingdom of God" (8:1).[4] More than that, Jesus works for them, not merely as gracious benefactor, but also as lowly servant. Here's the paradoxical shocker: Lord Jesus rules by serving; his authority shines through his humility. He not only announces but enacts the maxim, "[T]he greatest is least of all and servant of all."[5] Two characteristic activities particularly stand out in this regard: serving food and washing feet.

Serving Food

The hierarchical distinction between managerial/white collar professions, on the top, and manual/blue collar occupations, on the bottom, was as typical of the ancient world as of our own. The majority of folk who worked with their hands ranked lower on the social pyramid than the few privileged rulers who made laws and speeches and had others do the "dirty work" for them. The Jewish sage and teacher, Jesus Ben Sira, writing from Jerusalem in the second century B.C.E., offers a conventional contrast of the respective demands and significance of intellectual and physical labor. In the first case, the wise scribe or judge needs sufficient "leisure" to study, think, and render decisions; he (no equal opportunity here) cannot afford to get bogged down in mundane business pursuits. As a result of such devotion to wisdom, sages will be "sought out for the council of the people . . . attain eminence in the public assembly . . . [and] sit in the judge's seat," unlike the preponderance of workers—farmers, artisans, smiths, potters, and the like—who "rely on their hands" and "set their hearts" day and night on their tedious manufacturing projects. Ben Sira is not without appreciation for these skilled artisans; he acknowledges, "without them no city can be inhabited" and "they maintain the fabric of the world." But while their work is necessary, it is not primary. Manual laborers have neither time nor talent to rule: that is left to educated elites.

Moreover, although Ben Sira admires the community's artisans even as he ranks them below the sagacious rulers, he does not even mention the myriads of peasant farmers and domestic slaves, female and male, who also work with their hands—but not to fashion marketable commodities; they toil simply to eke out a meager subsistence and to cater to their masters' needs. The everyday tasks of serving food or waiting tables occupy this basement level. Notice the combination of field work and waiting tables as the standard duty of "worthless slaves" in Jesus' illustration:

> Who among you would say to your slave who has just come in from plowing or tending sheep in the field, "Come here at once and take your place at the table?" Would you not rather say to him, "Prepare supper for me, put on your apron and serve me while I eat and drink; later you may eat and drink?" Do you thank the slave for doing what was commanded? So you also, when you have done all that you were ordered to do, say, "We are *worthless slaves*; we have done only what we ought to have done!"(Luke 17:7–10)[6]

If a household was not prosperous enough to have male or female table-waiters, then wives and daughters typically fulfilled that function, reinforcing women's servant status in a patriarchal culture. Preparing and serving food was characteristically "women's work," as witnessed in Jesus' parable of the yeast and in the narrated activities of Simon's mother-in-law ("she began to serve them") and Martha of Bethany ("she was distracted by her many tasks [much serving]," Matt 13:33//Luke 13:20–21; Matt 8:14–15//Mark 1:29–31//Luke 4:38–39; Luke 10:38–42).

Perhaps these scenarios help explain why the twelve apostles in Acts 6 bristle so over the prospect of becoming personally involved in distributing food to needy widows: "It is not right that we should neglect the word of God to wait on tables" (6:2). Like Ben Sira, they view their chief duty as one of meditating and mediating divine wisdom commensurate with their honored place of leadership in the early church: "We, for our part, will devote ourselves to prayer and the ministry of the word" (6:4). Interpreters commonly assess this vocational commitment on the apostles' part as exemplary in every way, particularly since they also arrange for the effective management of the food crisis through an appointed committee of seven table servants—all "men of good standing" in the fellowship. Women's (widows') dietary needs are thus taken care of by male waiters. This surely reflects significant social progress in the Christian community.

To some extent the apostles get it right, but in one important respect, clearly established in Luke's first volume, they don't go far enough. They still have a lot to learn when it comes to modeling their master Jesus' vocational priorities. For the Lukan Jesus never passes the buck of service, including food service, to a kitchen or benevolence committee, nor does he juxtapose serving food and serving the word as mutually exclusive or hierarchically differentiated activities. Indeed, in Jesus' teaching and practice, these are thoroughly complementary forms of religious *diakonia* ("ministry/service"). The disciples are as slow to grasp this radical work ethic in Luke's gospel as they are in Acts 6. Notice two key gospel incidents involving Jesus, the Twelve, and table service: (1) feeding the multitude at Bethsaida along the northern Galilean seashore; and (2) sharing a final Passover meal in a borrowed second-story apartment in Jerusalem. We will keep our main focus trained on Luke's narratives but will bring in comparative material from other gospels as warranted.

Feeding the Multitude

After a period of following Jesus and witnessing his dynamic ministry, the Twelve are dispatched by Jesus to conduct their own campaign of proclaiming the good news of God's kingdom and performing miraculous acts of exorcism and healing. Jesus instructs them to travel light and to depend on the hospitality of grateful respondents. Thus, the apostles are fed and catered to as "payment" for their powerful words and deeds (9:1–6; cf. 10:7, "the laborer deserves to be paid"). Given this arrangement, they might well assume that it is not their business to feed or wait on others. But they soon learn—or at least Jesus tries to teach them—that their job description is more diverse and inclusive than they think.

When the Twelve return to Jesus, brimming with excitement about "all they had done," a crowd quickly encroaches on their private time with Jesus in a "deserted place" (9:10–12). Jesus gladly "welcomes" the intrusion, however, and proceeds to inform the throng about God's kingdom and to provide healing to the infirm—precisely the same tasks which the Twelve had recently been assigned (in Mark 6:34, Jesus teaches the crowd; in Matt 14:14 and John 6:2, he works miraculous signs; only in Luke 9:11 does he do both). But there's more work to do, namely, attending to the multitude's nutritional needs. The disciples are slow to grasp this responsibility, however. As the day wears on, they insist on dismissing the mob to fend for themselves. Jesus promptly counters by commanding: "You give them something to eat." The Twelve then further object that, even if they wanted to feed the crowd (which they don't), they haven't the means to do so. They pose the plan of going into town to "buy food for all these people" as a thoroughly ludicrous idea, not as a serious consideration. But Jesus is not deterred; feeding the hungry is as integral to his vocation as preaching the gospel and healing the sick. So he takes in his hands the available provisions and distributes them "to the disciples to set before the crowd" (9:13–16). Yes, a mathematical miracle occurs as Jesus stretches five loaves and two fishes to feed five thousand men (not counting their families). But Luke and the other Synoptic Gospels make little of the wonder itself (only the fourth gospel reports the crowd's amazement).[7] For Luke it's the act, not the arithmetic, of feeding/serving that counts here. It can be no accident that Jesus employs the reluctant Twelve as waiters and even as busboys. As it happens, exactly "twelve baskets of broken [leftover] pieces" need to be gathered after dinner (9:17)—one for each of the apostles!

Sharing the Passover

Although shifting from a public, outdoor picnic (dinner on the grounds) to a private, inside Passover feast, issues of eating and serving remain very much on the table. For all of its evident sacramental significance, this last Jewish Passover and first Messianic Eucharist Jesus shares with his disciples is a full-fledged meal with bread, wine, lamb, and herbs (although the latter two items are not mentioned)—not, as is typical in many modern American churches, a token "appetizer" of wafer and juice before rushing home or out to a restaurant for the proverbial "Sunday dinner."[8] Accordingly, Jesus is instructing the apostles about service as well as sacrifice, bread and wine as well as body and blood, work ethic as well as redemptive faith. He begins in Luke's account with the cup, taking it in his hands, blessing it, and passing it on to his twelve companions to "divide . . . among yourselves." Unlike the simple "he gave it to them" in Matthew and Mark, the Lukan Jesus purposefully involves the apostles in the act of serving (Matt 26:27//Mark 14:23// Luke 22:17). Although celebrating the feast in guest quarters, there is no hint of hired servants or attending waiters. Jesus and his disciples wait on each other; more specifically, Jesus serves the Twelve so that they may serve each other. Everyone around the table both serves and receives. Humble mutuality defines the etiquette of this repast.

As clear as Jesus' lesson has been, however, the Twelve once more prove to be incredibly obtuse. Once the meal is concluded, instead of singing a hymn and departing for the Mount of Olives, as we find in Matthew and Mark, the disciples in Luke cap off their master's poignant illustration of sacrificial service with another of their tedious disputes about which of them is the greatest. It's hard to imagine a more jarring non sequitur (Luke 22:24).[9] Jesus sets the stage for a moving scene of compassion and self-denial, and the Twelve completely miss their cue by bursting on stage primed for battle. So Jesus tries once more to correct their misguided ambition. Conventional manifestations of authority in Jesus' day took the twin forms of domination and benefaction. While the latter expression may appear charitable, helping the less fortunate with generous gifts, it ran the risk of merely reinforcing the oppressive domination system. Benefactors, Jesus reminds the apostles, love not so much being benefactors as being "called benefactors" (22:25). They give in order to boost their own honor, to see their noble names inscribed in monuments and to hear them heralded in speeches. Patronage can easily become patronizing and self-serving. "But not so with you," Jesus demands. And not so with himself: "I am among you as one who serves (*diakonōn*)"—not only one who serves God as prophet, priest, or apostle, but as one who serves others at table, the common meal of bread and wine. "Who is greater," Jesus asks his companions, "the one who is at the table or the one who serves? Is it not the one at the table?" (22:26–27). It is indeed, if Jesus is truly Lord.

Washing Feet

Although the fourth gospel dramatically portrays Jesus as the "bread of life" who offers his "flesh and blood" as life-giving nourishment (6:48–58), it has no precise counterpart to the Synoptic Gospels' account of Jesus' Last Supper. It does, however, feature a farewell dinner that Jesus shares with his disciples "before the festival of the Passover" (not the Passover meal itself; 13:1). Like the Synoptics' final supper scene, John's displays rich symbolic overtones with a particular spotlight on Jesus' act of table service. Here, however, the primary serving gesture is not table waiting but foot washing, another menial hospitality chore usually performed by the guests themselves (with water and towel provided by the host) or by household servants in preparation for dining (washing up before supper). We may recall previous gospel incidents in which Jesus was the recipient of such attention: one, in Luke 7:36–50, at the hands of a lowly, intrusive "sinner-woman" who provided the water and towel from her own body (since Simon the host had shamefully provided nothing); and another, set "six days before the Passover" in the previous chapter in John, at the hands of Mary of Bethany. In this latter story, while no servants or outsiders are involved, sister Mary washes Jesus' feet while sister Martha serves the meal to Jesus, brother Lazarus, Judas, and the other male disciples seated at table in "the home of Lazarus," as it is called—a thoroughly conventional domestic scene displaying a gender-coded division of labor (12:1–8).

But in John 13, convention goes out the window. No women or servants are present, as far as we know. This is a private moment between Jesus and the disciples. Then who's to do the waiting and washing, the preparing and refreshing? John reports very little about the dinner arrangements, but one brief scene stands out featuring Jesus' dipping a morsel of bread in sauce and distributing it to Judas, of all people, the one Jesus knows is about to betray him (13:21–28). Again we see Jesus cast in the role of table servant. But this remarkable token of sacrificial

love pales in shock value and moral and spiritual significance to Jesus'
preceding act of washing the feet of all the disciples (Judas again
included) as they recline around the table. Sometime during the course
of the meal (not before as was customary), Jesus "got up from the table,
took off his outer robe, and tied a towel around himself. Then he poured
water into a basin and began to wash the disciples' feet and to wipe them
with the towel that was tied around him" (13:4–5). Jesus plays his servant part to the hilt: he dons the appropriate costume and does the work
of fetching water and washing feet entirely by himself, with his own
hands.

How do the disciples react to their Lord's unusual act of service? As in
the Synoptic Gospels, once more Jesus catches them off guard. Peter, in
particular, is stunned by Jesus' behavior and adamant in refusing to be a
part of it: "[Lord] you will never wash my feet" (13:8). Notice that Peter
doesn't offer to help Jesus or to take over the foot-washing duty ("Here,
Lord, give me the towel, I'll do it!"). Peter is not thinking about service at
all. And that's part of Jesus' purpose here: to change Peter and the other
disciples' perspectives on ministry. Whatever the deeper symbolic import
of Jesus' foot-washing service—to portend his imminent sacrificial death
for his people (stripped of clothing, pouring out his "water and blood"),
to invite his followers into intimate, life-giving communion with him
("Unless I wash you, you have no share with me"),[10] or to illustrate a ritual act of cleansing (a kind of "baptism")[11]—it still constitutes on its
most basic level a menial yet meaningful gesture of hospitality performed
by Jesus the Lord on the dusty feet of his disciples. The action may convey more than it appears, but not less. And if there be any doubt as to
whether Jesus intends a literal application of his work ethic, notice his
follow-up remarks, after he had re-dressed and "returned to the table":

Do you know what I have done to you? You call me Teacher and
Lord—and you are right, for that is what I am. So if I, your Lord
and Teacher, have washed your feet, you ought also to wash one
another's feet. For I have set you an example, that you also should
do as I have done to you. Very truly, I tell you, servants are not
greater than their master, nor are messengers greater than the one
who sent them. (13:13–16)

Here Jesus cleverly uses his hierarchical relationship with his disciples to subvert their common perception of hierarchical privilege. To paraphrase: "Since I am your Teacher, Lord, and Master, you must do what I say and do what I do. And what I say you must do is what I've just shown you to do, which is to act as each other's servants." In this arrangement, the master joins the ranks of the servants not to free them from their duty, but to "set an example" for their conduct. The emphasis is close to the synoptic principle, "the greatest among you is servant of all," with the exception that the Johannine vision of mutual service seems more limited in scope to the community of believers ("wash one another's feet") than to the world at large ("I have chosen you out of the world").[12] For the Synoptic Gospels, table service is primarily an expression of evangelistic outreach, whereas in John it demonstrates pastoral care.

Nights and Weekends

To a great extent our culture measures work in terms of time. The adage "Time is money" reflects a fundamental conviction that productivity is directly related to how much time an employee invests in a task or project and how wisely one uses that time: the longer one works (putting in overtime) and the harder one works (making the most of every moment), the better. Our professional lives are preoccupied with schedules, calendars, and appointments. At work, we're "on the clock," perhaps literally punching a timecard to monitor our efforts. The flip side is an equally absorbing counter-obsession with time off from work. "All work and no play" is a travesty in our leisure-loving society. And so we negotiate our work schedules to maximize weekly respites (the day off or weekend), annual leaves (holidays and vacations), extended periodic hiatuses (sabbaticals), and ultimately permanent release (retirement).

Of course, conceptions of time and work in our Western industrial and technological environment will differ from those governing the ancient Near Eastern agrarian and pastoral economy reflected in the Bible. For all the importance it attaches to forty temporal units—for example, forty days of flooding, fasting, or receiving the law on Mount

Sinai or forty years of wandering in the wilderness—the Bible knows nothing about a forty-hour work week; and for all the blessed events it thanks God for, Friday—as in "Thank God it's Friday" (T.G.I.F.)—is never singled out. Nonetheless, the Bible does present a fundamental weekly work rhythm rooted in primal narratives of creation and exodus as well as in core legal material.

Creation

And on the seventh day God finished the work that he had done, and he rested on the seventh day from all the work that he had done. So God blessed the seventh day and hallowed it, because on it God rested from all the work that he had done in creation. (Gen 2:2–3)

Creation/Decalogue

Remember the sabbath day, and keep it holy. Six days you shall labor and do all your work. But the seventh day is a sabbath to the LORD your God, you shall not do any work—you, your son or your daughter, your male or female slave, your livestock, or the alien resident in your towns. For in six days the LORD made heaven and earth, the sea, and all that is in them, but rested the seventh day; therefore the LORD blessed the sabbath day and consecrated it. (Exod 20:8–11)

Exodus/Decalogue

Observe the sabbath day and keep it holy, as the LORD your God commanded you. Six days you shall labor and do all your work. But the seventh day is a sabbath to the LORD your God; you shall not do any work. . . . Remember that you were a slave in the land of Egypt, and the LORD your God brought you out from there with a mighty hand and an outstretched arm; therefore the LORD your God commanded you to keep the sabbath day. (Deut 5:12–15)

As both an affirmation of God's created order and a repudiation of tyrannical slavery, the Israelites were commanded to work for six days and to rest the entire population—human and animal, slave and free—on the hallowed seventh day. Not a forty-hour workweek followed by a two-day weekend, but it's not that far off.

Turning to Jesus' activity in the gospels, we discover that he repeatedly appears to push the limits of the Bible's sacred weekly schedule in two ways: (1) by working through the night (not just six days), and (2) working on the Sabbath. That doesn't mean, however, that we can simply dub Jesus a workaholic or lawbreaker. Apart from the basic observation that Jesus works nights and Sabbaths, we need to explore exactly what he's doing on these occasions and why he's doing it.

Burning the Midnight Oil

In one of his lesser-known parables, reported only in Luke, Jesus tells a tale set at midnight, in which one neighbor needing bread (to serve a late-arriving guest) knocks at the door of another neighbor whose family is already asleep (11:5–8). The story assumes a conventional diurnal cycle: daytime is for work and productivity, nighttime for rest and recuperation. In the middle of the night, especially, one would expect a man and his children to be in bed and to be both jolted and irritated by a rapping door (or ringing telephone today). Not surprisingly, the awakened "friend" rebuffs his neighbor's plea with a curt reply: "Do not bother me"—that is, "Don't bother me at this ungodly hour, for goodness' sake!" But the neighbor persists in knocking and eventually nags his friend into getting up and meeting his request. Jesus tells this parable not to encourage midnight raids on neighbors' pantries, but to instruct his disciples in their practice of praying. This story of rash behavior at an ungodly hour in fact has a godly point. In petitioning God for "daily bread" and other needs (cf. 11:3), Jesus spurs his followers to pray with "persistence," to "ask—and keep on asking—and it will be given you" (Luke 11:9),[13] to not let go of God, so to speak, until God blesses.[14] It's not that God has to be dragged out of slumber ("He who keeps Israel will neither slumber nor sleep," Ps 121:4); rather, in contrast to the parable, if an awakened earthly father will eventually respond to a neighbor's

inconvenient demand, how much more will the heavenly Father attend
to his children's fervent supplications? Still, even with God's receptivity
at all hours of the day or night, the need for importunity in prayer
remains. In a precarious world of scarce resources and hostile forces,
God's children must be vigilant in soliciting God's help: they should
"pray always and not . . . lose heart" (18:1). Therefore, like the pesky
neighbor in the parable, Jesus and the disciples must rise to the occasion,
whatever the hour, seeking communion with God and bread for the
needy. The work of praying and serving—so basic to Jesus' ministry—
has no time limits.

This commitment on Jesus' part to round-the-clock vigilance is demonstrated in several gospel incidents. Staying with Luke for the
moment, we notice that Jesus previously spends an entire evening on a
mountain praying to God and preparing to appoint his twelve disciples
the next day (6:12–16). Before that, early in his ministry, he establishes a
pattern of nocturnal ministry to the sick and demon-possessed from sun-
set to daybreak, after a busy Sabbath day in Capernaum teaching in the
synagogue, silencing a disruptive evil spirit, and healing Simon's feverish
mother-in-law (4:16–41). At dawn, Jesus understandably seeks some
much-needed solace in "a deserted place" but is denied this respite by an
irrepressible crowd clamoring for his attention. This time Jesus declines
to offer further aid to the citizens of Capernaum—but not because they
interrupt his retreat; rather, he announces that it is time to convey the
good news of God's kingdom "to the other cities also" (4:42–44). Rest
can wait; the work must go on and expand.

This seemingly perpetual motion of Jesus day and night is consistent
with the scenario sketched in the previous chapter that "the Son of Man
has no place to lay his head." We should perhaps underscore again that
this breakneck, whirlwind evangelist tour is part of Jesus' eschatological
urgency. There is much to do in preparing for the imminent coming of
God's kingdom and precious little time to do it. Thus Jesus brooks no
personal encumbrances—no family to tie him down, no property to
maintain, no appointments to keep other than those arranged by God.
Needless to say, this is not "normal," everyday life. Jesus is not in it for
the long haul. Accordingly, believers in the modern world who expect to
raise families and to live a productive life for seventy-plus years must

apply his obsessive work ethic judiciously. On the other hand, the challenge remains to make the most of whatever years, months, days, and
nights we are given and to be open to extraordinary opportunities for
service at inconvenient hours. At the very least, emulating Jesus' work
ethic includes a willingness to break routine, to get out of bed occasionally in the middle of the night to help a neighbor in need.

Beyond Jesus' personal nocturnal work habits in conjunction with
his special eschatological mission, it is interesting to notice in Luke
other "night shift" workers, in more mundane occupations, closely
linked with Jesus. Two groups especially stand out: shepherds, who
"keep watch over their flocks by night" (2:8), and fishermen, who troll
the waters "all night long" to make a catch (or not make a catch, as the
case may be, on a frustrating night, 5:5). The first group is distinguished as the first witnesses of the Christ-child ("to you is born this
day . . . a Savior, who is the Messiah, the Lord," 2:11), and becomes
a model of Jesus' vocation to seek and save those who have "lost" their
way (15:1–7). Jesus draws his three leading disciples (Peter, James,
and John) from the second group of night workers, along with a key
analogy for his mission of outreach ("from now on you will be catching
people," 5:10). In several studies, American sociologist Murray Melbin
reveals that those who ply their trade in the dark, those who venture
into the shadowy "night frontier"—such as criminals ("thief in the
night") or prostitutes ("ladies of the night"), most blatantly, but also
factory workers or custodial staff on the "graveyard" shift—suffer a
common social stigma: they are regarded as suspicious characters, off-
beat and out of step with mainstream day-ly life.[15] Thus, by virtue of
their nocturnal professions, shepherds and fishermen in Jesus' world
were situated on the margins of respectable society, subject to scorn for
their shady reputations.[16]

Interestingly, however, the Lukan Jesus identifies with and reaches
out to marginalized persons on "the edge of night": not only to shepherds and fishermen but also to criminals, such as the so-called "thief
on the cross," whom Jesus ushers to paradise at the final hour when,
notably, "darkness came over the whole land" in the middle of the afternoon (23:39–44). Moreover, while we cannot know whether the "sinful
woman" embraced by Jesus in Luke 7 was a "lady of the evening" (see

chapter 3), the sympathies of Jesus' parable of the prodigal son lie with the younger brother, welcomed to the family table even after he has "devoured [his father's] property with prostitutes," rather than with the prejudicial elder brother, who has worked faithfully for his father and wants nothing to do with celebrating his profligate sibling's return (15:25–32).

Expanding our scope to the other gospels, we recall that Matthew more directly identifies prostitutes as those whom both Jesus and John the Baptist welcome into the kingdom of God (22:31–32). In the fourth gospel, as we have previously discussed, Jesus makes a spiritual connection with a working woman of marginal ethnic and marital status: a Samaritan water hauler separated from five husbands for unknown reasons (widowed? divorced?—again, not necessarily a prostitute). The timing of this suspicious encounter, "about noon," again fits the occasion (4:6). While seemingly the diametric opposite of midnight, the noon hour in ancient Palestine was equally out of sync with normal activity. As the hottest part of the day in an arid land, midday was a time for shaded repose and refreshment, not a time to be out and about drawing water or doing work of any kind.[17] But here Jesus is with the unfortunate woman, using her work as a model for his life-giving ministry ("The water that I will give will become in them a spring of water gushing up to eternal life," 4:14).

A previous story in John features Jesus' conference with a man named Nicodemus. On the surface, this liaison appears antithetical to Jesus' meeting with the Samaritan woman: Nicodemus is a well-respected male "leader of the Jews" who approaches Jesus "by night" (3:2). But the elements of controversy and marginality still emerge. Nicodemus is not the stigmatized worker in this case, but he evidently thinks that Jesus' reputation is suspicious enough among his fellow Pharisees to warrant a secret rendezvous under the cover of darkness.[18] Or perhaps Nicodemus's visit illustrates that Jesus works overtime late into the night as well as the standard "twelve hours of daylight" (11:9), pressing to fulfill his divine mission in the brief time allotted before the onset of an eternal "night . . . when no one can work" (9:4). By receiving Nicodemus at night, Jesus endeavors to help this perplexed teacher "come to the light" (3:19–21).

Bending the Sabbath Law

While we have suggested that the stories portraying Jesus as something of
a night owl reveal an eccentric dimension of his work habits, outside the
typical cycle of daily living, in fact, the gospels report no explicit objection to Jesus' nocturnal activities by his opponents. Pointed criticism of
Jesus' work routine focuses not so much on what he does "after hours" as
on what he does on that most sacred day of the week, the Sabbath. Here
the issue is not simply one of convention and propriety, but of law and
order—divine law and order, no less, woven into the fabric of the universe since creation. In the Jewish religious and ethical environment that
Jesus inhabits, what one should do or not do on the holy Sabbath day of
rest is governed wholly by God's will, not by human whim. The Sabbath
is serious business indeed, and Jesus is taken to task several times by religious experts for not taking it seriously enough.

Before examining the specific Sabbath conflicts presented in the
gospels and what they disclose about Jesus' work ethic, it is useful to set
these scenes within a wider history of struggle over proper Sabbath conduct. In both ancient and modern contexts, well-intentioned Jews and
Christians have debated and disagreed with each other over the correct
interpretation of Sabbath law. Starting closer to home, the majority of
contemporary Christians regard the first day of the week (Sunday) as the
hallowed "Sabbath" or "Lord's Day" of rest and worship, without always
acknowledging, however, that this represents a shift from the traditional
Jewish (including Jesus') observance of the Sabbath on the seventh day
(Saturday). The change derives from the eventual parting of the ways
between Judaism and Christianity and the watershed importance of
Jesus' Sunday resurrection for Christian faith and practice. But whatever
the day on the calendar, the biblical mandate to "remember the Sabbath"
still holds for the Christian church.

But what does this mean exactly for Christian conduct? It is generally
expected that faithful Christians will cease from their labors long enough
to "go to church" on Sunday, but beyond that, opinions and habits differ.
In addition to a variety of "blue laws" across the country prohibiting the
sale of certain items before certain hours on Sunday, a handful of successful American corporations have distinguished themselves by refusing to
conduct business altogether on Sunday due to their owners' avowed

Christian convictions. In the highly competitive retail food industry, for example, where most companies cater to a weekend clientele (people want to shop and eat out when they are off work), at least two businesses—the national restaurant chain Chick-fil-A®, founded by Truett A. Cathey, and a major regional supermarket enterprise established by the Ukrop family in Richmond, Virginia—remain closed all day every Sunday in an effort to support their employees' and customers' involvement in communities of faith and worship.

Not all Christians, however, take their convictions that far. A huge cultural phenomenon absorbing the attention of millions of Americans in the autumn and winter months swirls around the playing of professional football games in colossal sports arenas on Sunday afternoons. What does this have to do with a Christian work ethic? As it happens, through organizations like the Fellowship of Christian Athletes (FCA), numerous players trumpet their faith and see no contradiction with plying their very public trade (for which they are handsomely paid) on the Lord's Day. Indeed, it is not uncommon to see an athlete kneel and pray in the end zone after scoring a touchdown. The stadium thus becomes a kind of sanctuary where faithful football fans and Christians alike may assemble on Sunday afternoons. And myriads more participate vicariously by way of television. I never attended a professional football game while growing up in my home state of Texas, but that did not dampen my devotion. My youth happened to coincide with the heyday of the Dallas Cowboys' popularity as "America's Team" (apologies to Pittsburgh and Washington fans, among others) under the leadership of Coach Tom Landry and quarterback Roger Staubach—both of whom were well-known, dedicated Christians who managed to worship regularly and still work on Sunday. After faithfully attending Sunday school and worship in the morning, my family and I would rush home for Sunday dinner around the TV set to cheer the Cowboys to victory (God forbid the preacher should drone on past noon and make us miss the kickoff). We would then make it back to church for Sunday evening services, where invariably the pastor would work a football illustration into his sermon (we all knew what he was doing on Sunday afternoon).

After Sunday night worship, it was customary for church youth groups and others to go out to eat at a local coffee shop—where, of course, someone would have to be working on Sunday in order to serve us! I'll never forget being seated at a table with my pastor one Sunday evening when he began to "witness" to our waitress, specifically asking if she had been to church that day. With more than a little disdain in her voice, she replied something to the effect that worship did not fit into her schedule because she had to work on Sunday to feed her family and wait on the likes of us. Although this response didn't seem to faze my pastor, it floored me, even at a young age. Weren't we being a little hypo-critical here? And wasn't hypocrisy at the heart of Jesus' Sabbath conflicts with the religious leaders of his day?

On that note we turn to consider Jesus' situation more fully. It is often thought that the scribes, Pharisees, and other Jewish scholars quib-bled with Jesus (and each other) over nothing but trifling matters of Sab-bath observance, focusing on minute issues such as how far one could carry something on the Sabbath, precisely what kind of help one might offer an afflicted neighbor, and how food should be gathered and pre-pared for Sabbath consumption (sort of like, can we legitimately go out for Sunday supper?). As the story goes, Jesus was concerned with sub-stantive issues of utmost (eternal) significance, while the Pharisees were bogged down in pettifogging legalism. Such judgment, however, is cari-cature, not characterization. While rabbinic Judaism reflected in the Mishnah and other writings from the second century (and later) dis-cussed the fine points of Sabbath observance, we cannot confidently retroject specific debates into the first-century setting of Jesus and the gospels. More importantly, we must appreciate that, given the Sabbath's critical function in Jewish life as a foundational marker of ethnic and religious identity, it was scarcely possible to be too careful about proper Sabbath behavior. What might appear to be nitpicking or hypersensitive distinctions to outsiders might actually represent a vigorous commit-ment on the part of Pharisees and other devout Jews to applying God's law to every aspect of daily life, especially life on the week's most holy day.

Events surrounding a major national crisis, occurring a couple of cen-turies before Jesus' era, dramatically illustrate both the diversity of inter-pretation and the intensity of devotion to Sabbath observance among pious Jews in antiquity.[19] In the first quarter of the second century B.C.E., the Greco-Syrian ruler, Antiochus IV Epiphanes (as he was known), began to impose an aggressive program of Hellenization upon the Jews in Palestine, threatening the very survival of Jewish faith and culture. In promoting a superior Greek way of life, as he saw it, Antiochus built a gymnasium in Jerusalem, burned books of Jewish law, burgled the temple treasury, and banned—on pain of death—core practices of Israel's sacred covenant with Yahweh such as circumcision, kosher dietary practices, and keeping the Sabbath. Tragically and diabolically, according to the author of 1 Maccabees, some local Jewish leaders became traitorous "renegades," jumping on Antiochus's anti-Judaic bandwagon and abandoning the covenant of their ancestors. Many others, however, bravely stood their ground, opting "to die rather than . . . to profane the holy covenant" (1 Macc 1:63).

Among these resistors, two groups stand out—equally committed to maintaining the law (including the Sabbath), but disagreeing on the manner of expressing this loyalty. One group "seeking righteousness and justice" retreated to the Judean wilderness to live out their faith and possibly await God's apocalyptic vengeance against the wicked Hellenistic invaders and their "renegade" collaborators. Antiochus's forces pressed in on this rebel desert community and put them to the test by deliberately attacking on the Sabbath, when it would be unlawful for pious Jews to fight. What to do? Keep the law and die as martyrs or break the law temporarily in order to preserve their way of life? Not an easy decision. Ultimately, this wilderness sect opted for martyrdom—losing a thousand lives on that fateful Sabbath. But another protest group, led by Mattathias and sons (known as the Maccabeans or Hasmoneans) and based in the Judean hills, chose a different course of action. While equally "zealous for the law and covenant," these rebels decided to fight for their faith—even on the Sabbath: "Let us fight against anyone who comes to attack us on the Sabbath day; let us not all die as our kindred died in their hiding places" (1 Macc 2:41). And fight they did! These Maccabeans achieved a measure of independence from foreign control and thus upheld their right and duty to observe the Sabbath.

Obviously one group (the desert pacifists) was more "legalistic" and the other (the mountain freedom fighters) more "flexible" in interpreting Sabbath law in the heat of battle. But neither can fairly be accused of hypocrisy or complacency. Here was a serious controversy about a serious matter—literally, a matter of life and death.

The Maccabean crisis helps us gain a balanced perspective on the Sabbath conflicts between Jesus and the Pharisees reported in the gospels. For one thing, in the gospel narratives there is no hint of outside pressure from Roman overlords to ban the Jewish Sabbath or of any Jewish party playing the part of compromising "renegade." Both Jesus and the Pharisees are Sabbath devotees. The latter accuse Jesus of violating certain aspects of Sabbath law but not of ignoring the Sabbath altogether. How could they? Most of the conflicts take place in the synagogue, where Jesus consistently gathers with fellow Jews for worship and study of the Scriptures. Jesus is no Sabbath gadabout, doing whatever he pleases on the holy day of rest, irrespective of biblical traditions. Furthermore, the specific disputes that surface between Jesus and the Pharisees, while significant, do not approach the ultimate life-and-death decisions facing the Antiochene resistors. The gospel Sabbath incidents focus on issues of harvesting, healing, and hauling—worthy matters of legal debate, but hardly on the level of killing and being killed.

The evidence centers around three pairs of stories—one set from the synoptic tradition, the other two from Luke and John, respectively.

Synoptics: Plucking Grain and Curing Disease on the Sabbath

In each of the first three gospels, the Pharisees object to the disciples' gleaning in the grain field and to Jesus' restoring a man's dysfunctional hand on the Sabbath (Matt 12:1–14//Mark 2:23–3:6//Luke 6:1–11). Although Luke suggests that the second incident occurs on "another Sabbath," Matthew and Mark imply that both events happen on the same day. In the grain-field episode, the Pharisees legitimately raise the question of gathering or harvesting on the Sabbath, which was a prohibited act of labor according to biblical legislation.[20] Even before receiving the codified law at Mount Sinai, the wandering Israelites were instructed to gather a double portion of "manna" (God's daily provision of bread) the day before the Sabbath (Exod 16:22–30). In a shocking scene later in the wilderness journey, the entire Israelite assembly stoned a man to death simply for picking up sticks on the Sabbath day (Num 15:32–36; a terrible twist on the ditty, "Sticks and stones may break my bones).[21] The Sabbath was for resting, not for reaping. Although Jesus himself does not participate in the disciples' Sabbath gleaning, he defends their actions. Most significantly, his case also rests on scriptural evidence: this is an inner-Jewish, inner-biblical debate. Jesus' chief appeal is to the precedent in 1 Samuel where David and his men, on the run from Saul and in need of food, entered the holy sanctuary and ate the holy bread reserved exclusively for the priests' consumption on the Sabbath.[22] Matthew's Jesus adds the further point that, since the temple priests work on the Sabbath without penalty (offering sacrifices and such), why shouldn't Jesus and his disciples (12:5)? Of course they are not priests, and the cornfield is no sanctuary. Still, in a bold move Jesus assumes priestly prerogatives for himself and his men, just as David and his companions did.

But before we rush out in Jesus' name and shop and work as much as we please on the Lord's Day, two points bear consideration. First, both Jesus and David authorize Sabbath "harvesting" under extraordinary circumstances. These are men on the move with an urgent mission, without land, home, or resources to call their own. They are not harvesting on the Sabbath for sale or trade or even to stock their own cupboards; they gather what they can on the fly to meet the day's hunger. Second, while there is biblical warrant according priestly status to all of God's people ("you shall be for me a priestly kingdom and a holy nation," Exod 19:6), Jesus' claim to authority goes well beyond that. In Matthew he essentially claims to be "greater than the temple" (not just a servant in the temple, 12:6), and in all three Synoptics he proceeds to announce that he (as "Son of Man") is nothing less than "lord of the Sabbath." This assumes the closest of links with the divine Creator of the Sabbath. As God controls the Sabbath, so does Jesus. It's his day to do as he pleases and to allow what he pleases. But this is not a privilege Jesus fully shares with his followers. Although identifying with human beings as "Son of Man," he stands above them as God's viceroy on earth. This is a case where Jesus' unique authority overshadows his universal appeal. While permitting his itinerant disciples to glean on the Sabbath, Jesus in no way grants them or any of his followers carte blanche to do as they wish on this holy day.

In this authoritative mode, Jesus proceeds into the synagogue[23] where he encounters "a man with a withered hand" among the assembly. Only Luke specifies that the disfigured appendage is the man's "right hand" (6:6), that is, the primary symbol of human strength and the capacity to work. A later tradition, from the so-called *Gospel of the Nazarenes,* elaborates that the man especially pleads with Jesus for healing because he "was a mason, earning a living with my hands." Whichever hand is affected and whatever his particular profession, it is likely that the man's disability severely curtailed his ability to work. Thus, he presents a special anomaly to the standard weekly cycle: there is little work he can do for six days to rest up from on the Sabbath. In a sense, every day is an enforced Sabbath for this man, neutralizing, so to speak, the seventh day's unique sanctity in his experience.

So why shouldn't Jesus restore this man to health and productivity on the day set aside to celebrate the goodness of God's creation? It's not as if Jesus intends for this man to begin working immediately, before the Sabbath is concluded. One assumes that the man would now have all the more reason to remain in the synagogue praising God before commencing work the next day. It's not at all clear, then, what legal and moral concerns the Pharisees have in this situation. As Jesus emphasizes and as any devout Jew would endorse, there is no scriptural law against "doing good" on the Sabbath. How could there be when the primordial Sabbath established in Genesis 1 constituted the crown of God's "very good" creation? Later opinions registered by some Jewish scholars, that Sabbath healing was only valid in cases of life-threatening illness, may be relevant to the present incident, but the gospels do not frame the issue in these terms.

At the end of the day, this Sabbath conflict between Jesus and the Pharisees seems more personal than legal. In an earlier scene reported in Mark and Luke, Jesus cured a man possessed by an unclean spirit while teaching, once again, in the synagogue on the Sabbath (Mark 1:21–28// Luke 4:31–37). Here the local authorities do not challenge the legality of Jesus' healing activity, but they do take note of his remarkable exercise of authority and mounting fame throughout the region. When Jesus continues, in dealing with the man with the shriveled hand, to display his lordly power on the Sabbath and to outshine the Pharisees on their own turf, they become angry, I suggest, more at their own spiraling loss of status than at Jesus' violation of Sabbath law. In Mark's account, Jesus in turn reacts "with anger" against the stubborn Pharisees (3:5). Matthew and Luke conveniently omit this bit of information, probably because it casts Jesus as too emotionally involved. But the emotional factor cannot be ignored, intertwined as it is with an intense struggle for religious authority. In any case, in terms of work ethic, the story does not open loopholes in Sabbath regulation, permitting traditionally forbidden forms of labor. Jesus and the Pharisees alike affirm the Sabbath as the Lord's Day; they just disagree about who properly represents the Lord to be honored on this day.

Luke: Healing a Woman and a Man on the Sabbath

Following Luke's penchant for pairing stories involving male and female characters, the third gospel presents two closely related incidents of Sabbath healing—the first, featuring Jesus' liberation of a crippled woman bound by a debilitating spirit for eighteen years (13:10–17); the second, his curing of a man afflicted with dropsy (a serious condition of fluid retention) (14:1–6). The first story is set once more against the backdrop of Jesus' teaching in the synagogue, confirming he is no Sabbath renegade. After he frees the disfigured woman from her ailment, the "leader of the synagogue" vehemently objects that such curative work "ought" to have been done on one of the other six days of the week, not on the Sabbath. This is the closest we get in the gospels to a Jewish legal perspective that medical aid should be restricted on the Sabbath to emergency cases. But note well: such an opinion is voiced here by a particular leader in "one of the synagogues" where Jesus ministers (13:10). This does not reflect universal Jewish sentiment in Luke. As noted above, in response to an earlier Sabbath exorcism by Jesus in the synagogue at Capernaum, the audience was overwhelmed by Jesus' display of authority but suggested nothing about breaking Sabbath law. In the current case, Jesus flat out accuses the local synagogue president and his supporters of being "hypocrites." Since, Jesus reminds them, they routinely untie oxen and donkeys and lead them to water on the Sabbath, how dare they object to his releasing a "daughter of Abraham" from her bondage and bringing her to health. The "entire crowd" exults over "all the wonderful things" Jesus accomplishes on this Sabbath, proving that the critical synagogue leader does not even speak for the majority of Jews in his congregation (13:15–17).

The second story also involves a prominent religious figure, this time "a leader of the Pharisees" (14:1). The setting, however, is not the synagogue, but the leader's home where lawyers, Pharisees, and Jesus have gathered for a Sabbath meal. Also present "in front of" Jesus is a man suffering from dropsy. On this occasion, Jesus drops the gauntlet, asking, "Is it lawful to cure people on the Sabbath, or not?" (14:3). Obviously Jesus is aware that this is a sticking point with some scholars, but in fact in the present scene no one but Jesus brings the matter up. His audience remains "silent," whereupon he proceeds to heal the man and send him on his way (14:4). Then Jesus himself breaks the silence with an observation, similar to the one he made recently in the synagogue, that any decent person would scarcely think twice about rescuing an endangered child or ox on the Sabbath. Again, the host and guests have nothing to say in return ("they could not reply to this," 14:6). The utter silence and lack of anger on the part of the Pharisees and lawyers imply basic concurrence with Jesus' words and actions. While some tension simmers beneath the surface (they do not rejoice at Jesus' conduct), there is no overt conflict. The point is clear. Of course it's acceptable to "do good" and cure disease on the Sabbath; who could argue with that?

John: Healing Two Disabled Men on the Sabbath

The fourth gospel continues the theme of Jesus' disputed healing activity on the Sabbath but sets it in a different key. The first incident takes place, not on an ordinary Sabbath in a Galilean synagogue, but on a major "festival of the Jews" near the temple in Jerusalem (5:1). Specifically, Jesus encounters a lame man stationed at the pool of Beth-zatha (by the Sheep Gate entrance to the temple compound) who is hoping that some benevolent stranger might help him into the water. Doing better than that, Jesus announces to the man, "Stand up, take up your mat, and walk," which he proceeds to do (5:8–9). As we have come to expect, certain Jewish critics observe this action and register their protest. Only now the thrust of their complaint is not healing but hauling on the Sabbath: "It is the Sabbath: it is not lawful for you to carry your mat" (5:10). Standing and walking—resulting from Jesus' cure—are acceptable, but conveying goods is not.

This issue has solid grounding in biblical precept, but with a different purpose than that reflected in the situation here. The prophet Jeremiah exhorted the people of Jerusalem in his day: "For the sake of your lives, take care that you do not bear a burden on the Sabbath day or do any work, but keep the Sabbath day holy" (Jer 17:21; cf. 17:19–27). But it is doubtful that Jeremiah would classify carrying one's cot as a burden. In a later, postexilic context, the Judean governor Nehemiah puts the matter into perspective:

> In these days I saw in Judah people treading wine presses on the Sabbath, and bringing in heaps of grain and loading them on donkeys; and also wine, grapes, figs, and all kinds of burdens, which they brought into Jerusalem on the Sabbath day; and I warned them at that time against selling food. . . . Then I remonstrated with the nobles of Judah and said to them, "What is this evil thing that you are doing, profaning the Sabbath day?" (Neh 13:15–17)

The problem with bearing burdens on the Sabbath has to do with trade and commerce. If you're hauling in donkey-loads of foodstuffs for sale on the Sabbath, that is a patent violation of labor-prohibiting legislation. But the man who takes up his mat after thirty-eight years as an invalid is not buying or selling anything (likewise, the disciples plucking grain for themselves in the synoptic vignette).

In this case, the Jewish watchdogs for Sabbath purity do seem to be making a mountain of a molehill or, rather, a burden out of a bedroll. They again appear to have a more personal than legal axe to grind against Jesus. They are looking for something to object to, and as it happens, Jesus gives them more than they bargain for. Instead of arguing, as we have just done, that carrying a mat is not merchandising, Jesus takes the matter to the highest level possible. Whether teaching, healing, or whatever, Jesus claims the right, even the necessity, to work on the Sabbath, just as "my Father is still working" (5:17). Simply put, although God took the first Sabbath off, so to speak, God has worked every Sabbath since, sustaining the universe. As God neither slumbers nor sleeps, God takes no vacations. God is always at work and so is God's Son, Jesus, the divine Word made flesh who "was in the beginning with God" and through whom "all things came into being" (1:1–3). Again, the Sabbath question boils down to Jesus' unique authority. By "making himself equal to God" (5:18), as his opponents put it, Jesus claims special Sabbath prerogatives reserved for the Creator alone. One can accept or reject this exalted character of Jesus, but one cannot emulate it. Here we find ourselves wholly in the realm of Christology, not ethics.

The second Sabbath episode features Jesus' opening the eyes of a man who was born blind (9:1–41). Interestingly, this story also involves a pool of water in Jerusalem (Siloam), but in a different way. Whereas Jesus did not make use of the pool of Beth-zatha in healing the lame man, here he does tell the blind man to wash in the pool of Siloam as an act of faith. But in either case, Jesus unmistakably generates a miraculous cure on the Sabbath. And once again there is opposition from Jewish leaders, but it is not unanimous. "Some of the Pharisees said, 'This man is not from God, for he does not observe the Sabbath.' But others said, 'How can a man who is a sinner perform such signs?' And they were divided" (9:16). Even those who summarily object to Jesus' Sabbath conduct do not make specific charges against him (presumably it has something to do with his healing mission, but the offended Pharisees do not say so explicitly).

The crisis eventually focuses not so much on the Sabbath setting of the man's recovery of sight as on his persistent confession of faith in Jesus as an honorable healer sent from God. In the eyes of the Jewish synagogue leaders, this belief is tantamount to confessing Jesus as the Messiah, the anointed one of God. For this blasphemy, as they regard it, they expel the man from their assembly (9:34). Jesus meets the man again, outside the synagogue, and confirms his loyal devotion to Jesus as both Lord and Son of Man (9:35–37). Messiah, Lord, Son of Man: all of these titles converge in this story to stress Jesus' supreme authority. This is the fourth gospel's way of presenting Jesus as "Lord of the Sabbath," except that, unlike the Synoptics, Jesus and his followers are positioned outside rather than within the synagogue community. As numerous scholars have suggested, this marginal social location vis-à-vis the Jewish assembly may reflect the later history of the Johannine believers toward the end of the first century—after a formal split with the synagogue.[24] This more separatist perspective must be balanced by the Synoptics' presentation of Jesus' continuing commitment, amid conflict, to teach and worship in the synagogue on the Sabbath.

We may draw two key conclusions concerning Jesus' work ethic on the Sabbath:

1. While some (not all) Jewish legal scholars question certain of Jesus' Sabbath practices, they never prove their case by scriptural standards. Jesus may bend some disputed Sabbath traditions, but he does not break clear Sabbath laws. He does not practice or advocate commercial harvesting or hauling on the Sabbath, and his healing activity is consistent with the Sabbath's celebration of the goodness and wholeness of God's creation.

2. While Jesus' followers can emulate his fundamental commitment to worshiping God and "doing good" on the Sabbath, they cannot properly claim his absolute freedom to do as he pleases as Son of God and Lord of the Sabbath. In Christian practice, the Lord's Day is just that—the Lord Jesus' day, by virtue of his unique life, death, and resurrection. Still, during his life, while affirming his lordship over the Sabbath he also affirms his basic loyalty to Sabbath rhythms. Except for the fourth gospel with its heightened sense of division between church and synagogue, when it's Sabbath time (seventh day) in the gospels, Jesus is typically found teaching, worshiping, and ministering in the local synagogue. Quite simply, this "was his custom," as Luke puts it (4:16), as it was all for all pious Jews of the day.

Inspiration and Perspiration

All human achievement results in some measure from certain innate talents and abilities combined with expended effort and energy. One must both possess and practice a particular skill to accomplish something. As an educator, I have found the best students to be those blessed with raw intelligence and insight and those committed to working hard to make the most of their gifts. In religious terms, such a work ethic entails being a faithful steward of God's benevolence through diligent cultivation and utilization of one's God-given abilities. Although referring primarily to financial allotments, Jesus' parables of the prudent manager and the "talents" encapsulate this vocational perspective: "From everyone to whom much has been given much will be required; and from the one to whom much as been entrusted, even more will be demanded" (Luke 12:48). The inverse is also true: "From those who have nothing, even what they have will be taken away"—which is to say, "use it or lose it" (Matt 25:29).

While a biblical work ethic involves some blend of grace and grit, talent and toil, inspiration and perspiration, these elements are often unevenly mixed. Inevitably, one component outweighs the other, as illustrated, for example, in Elihu's contrast between prophetic and sapiental modes of operation in the last quarter of the book of Job. After hearing Job and his three friends drone on futilely about Job's miserable plight, Elihu, though younger and less experienced than the others, dares to interject his opinion on the following grounds:

> I am young in years, and you are aged; therefore I was timid and afraid to declare my opinion to you. I said, "Let days speak, and may years teach wisdom." But truly it is the spirit in a mortal, the breath of the Almighty, that makes for understanding. It is not the old that are wise, nor the aged that understand what is right. Therefore I say, "Listen to me; let me also declare my opinion." . . . For I am full of words; the spirit within me constrains me. (Job 32:6–10, 18)

Here Elihu bucks a venerable tradition that wisdom comes through long, hard years of study, inquiry, labor, and experience, with the bold prophetic claim, likewise rooted in Scripture, that God reveals understanding to whomever (young or old) through the inspiration of God's sovereign Spirit. Dynamic energy and insight come from God's breath more than human sweat. The apostle Paul, though rigorously trained from youth in the study of Jewish law and tradition, makes a similar point in his Corinthian correspondence:

> But we speak God's wisdom, secret and hidden, which God decreed before the ages for our glory. . . . These things God has revealed to us through the Spirit, for the Spirit searches everything, even the

depths of God . . . no one comprehends what is truly God's except the Spirit of God. Now we have received not the spirit of the world, but the Spirit that is from God, so that we may understand the gifts bestowed upon us by God. (1 Cor 2:7–12)

Obviously, Elihu and Paul put more stock in what results from the prophetic-charismatic gifts channeled by God's Spirit than that produced by human effort and ingenuity. Elsewhere, Paul also talks about discipline and "not growing weary in doing what is right" (Gal 6:9), but the accent falls more on grace than on works. Yes, you must "work out your own salvation with fear and trembling," but ultimately, "it is God who is at work in you, enabling you both to will and to work for his good pleasure" (Phil 2:12–13).

How does Jesus' work experience fit into this picture? We will analyze, in turn, the supernatural (Spirit-inspired) and natural (sweat-induced) forces propelling Jesus' endeavors in order to discern which exerts the most influence in his life.

Flowing Spirit

All four gospels cohere in characterizing Jesus as a charismatic "Spirit-person"[25] endowed with special divine energy to do extraordinary work. The birth narratives in Matthew and Luke announce Jesus' vital nexus with God's Spirit from the very beginning of life: the Holy Spirit "comes upon" the Virgin Mary to conceive the Christ-child (Matt 1:18–23; Luke 1:35). Before commencing his public ministry, Jesus is baptized by John in the Jordan River; on this momentous occasion, according to the Synoptics, the Spirit of God "comes upon" Jesus again (like a dove), equipping him with renewed supernatural power to fulfill his vocation (Matt 3:13–17//Mark 1:9–11//Luke 3:21–22). The fourth gospel does not describe the baptism scene itself but does recount John's witness of Jesus' anointing: "I saw the Spirit descending from heaven like a dove, and it remained on him" (1:32). This picture of the "remaining" or abiding Spirit suggests that everything Jesus accomplishes in his ministry derives from the Spirit's impetus and implementation. And while the depth and degree of Jesus' invigoration by the Spirit may be unique, he never intends for his relationship with the Spirit to be exclusive. All four gospels testify that Jesus "will baptize with the Holy Spirit" (Matt 3:11//Mark 1:8//Luke 3:16//John 1:33), that is, he will impart his spiritual energy to his followers. If they are to carry on his work, they must be imbued with the same driving force. Imitation of Jesus' actions is impossible apart from inspiration by Jesus' Spirit.[26]

John's gospel presents a particularly vivid image of the Spirit's activity within the lives of Jesus and his followers as a process of creative, dynamic flow: "'Out of his heart [or belly] shall flow rivers of living water.' Now he said this about the Spirit" (7:37–39). Interestingly, a body of current psychological research, spearheaded by Professor Mihaly Csikszentmihalyi and colleagues at the University of Chicago, focuses on the phenomenon of "flow" as a key component of optimal productivity and happiness in work. Here "flow" is understood as one's experience of total absorption in a task, oblivious to constraints of place and time. Whether a little child devoting all her attention to coloring a picture, or a songwriter lost in the creative flood of composition, or a factory worker, even, consumed with the job at hand for which he is skilled— when the task flows, time flies.[27] The project takes over the worker and almost "does itself." The worker is caught in the flow of productive energy and thereby achieves maximal results and realizes optimal joy.

While the gospels hint only sparingly at Jesus' psychological state, a passage later in the fourth gospel extends the idea of productive flow in a different idiom and associates it with Jesus' experience of joy. In this case, Jesus depicts the bond with his followers as an intimate, vine-branch conjunction through which the dynamic sap (of God's Spirit) flows and produces "much fruit" (15:1–11). The key response to such an arrangement is simply "abiding"—going with the flow, we might say. "Abide in me as I abide in you. Just as the branch by itself cannot bear fruit unless it abides in the vine, neither can you unless you abide in me. I am the vine, you are the branches. Those who abide in me and I in them bear much fruit" (15:4). And the key result is not only a fruitful harvest but also abundant joy coursing through vine and branch, Jesus and disciples, alike: "I have said these things to you so that my joy may be in you, and that your joy may be complete" (15:11).

Sweating Blood

While the gospels clearly stress the dynamic-charismatic dimension of Jesus' work, what about the tedious-laborious side? Does Jesus study hard, train hard, work hard to fulfill his mission? In previous chapters, we have discovered that Jesus adopts a rather Spartan, bare-bones lifestyle, roaming from place to place, ministering on the move, with no permanent residence and scant material resources. However, while working long hours under rough conditions, Jesus is not portrayed as a full-blown ascetic. He feasts when the opportunity presents itself, accepts others' hospitality, and does not deliberately engage in bodily discipline as a means of self-improvement. He bravely endures the agony of crucifixion, but not until he is certain that it is God's final and irrevocable plan for his life. If possible, he would prefer to bypass the cup of martyrdom. In short, Jesus does not seek pain and suffering as paths to building character.

But personal development and vocational achievement, while connected, are not coterminous. There is still the question of Jesus' training for specific tasks that he performs. Apart from being a willing channel of God's creative Spirit, what effort does Jesus expend, for example, in preparing to teach or to work miracles? As a professional teacher, I am very aware of the many years of study it took to qualify for the job and the ongoing pressures of further study to keep up with my field. The gospels, however, disclose nothing about Jesus' educational resume. He clearly evinces a thorough knowledge, both deep and wide, of the Jewish Scriptures, but exactly how he came by this knowledge, we do not know. Is Jesus' biblical "literacy" part of his divinely inspired genius or the product of intense study—or a combination of both? Complementing the fourth gospel's exalted portrait of Jesus the Son as possessor and mediator of the full knowledge and glory of God the Father who sent him, the common material in Matthew and Luke also highlights Jesus' role as the direct recipient of the Father's revelation by mysterious means distinct from normal channels of obtaining wisdom:

I thank you, Father [Jesus exults], Lord of heaven and earth, because you have *hidden these things from the wise and the intelligent* and have *revealed* them to infants; yes, Father, for such was your gracious will. *All things have been handed over to me by my Father; and no one knows who the Son is except the Father, or who the Father is except the Son and anyone to whom the Son chooses to reveal* him. (Matt 11:25–27//Luke 10:21–22; emphasis added)

Here revelation patently trumps education, consistent with the fact that nowhere in the gospels do we find Jesus poring over scriptural texts or commentaries in a library or private study. This may be how most biblical scholars (like myself) operate, but it is not Jesus' habit in the gospel narratives.

The only glimpse we get of Jesus' academic pursuits comes in that lone account of Jesus' adolescence in Luke 2. Bracketed by statements of Jesus' "growth in wisdom" (2:40, 52), the incident features Mary and Joseph's twelve-year-old son "in the temple, sitting among the teachers, listening to them and asking them questions" (2:46). But this is no indicator of Jesus' enrollment in, much less graduation from, a top rabbinic boarding school in Jerusalem, as perhaps was the case with the apostle Paul.[28] As we observed in chapter 2, the young Jesus slips in among the temple teachers without his parents' knowledge during a family visit to Jerusalem. He stays for only three days (most modern seminary degrees require three years), until his frantic parents find him and take him back to Nazareth. However, most notable for understanding Jesus' educational pedigree is the Lukan report that, for all his listening to and asking questions of the temple scholars, Jesus elicits the teachers' and congregants' amazement over "his understanding and his answers" (2:47). He teaches more than he's taught. So where does this precocious youth get all this knowledge and wisdom?[29] That's what the temple audience and Jesus' parents would like to know. The Lukan reader (and perhaps Mary, to some extent)[30] has an idea: this child conceived by the Holy Spirit has been instructed directly by the same Spirit to carry out "his [heavenly] Father's business" (2:49, KJV)

While Jesus' knowledge seems more inculcated by the Spirit than cultivated by effort, what about his power to perform wonders? Does he have to labor, in any sense, at working miracles? Granted that, by definition, working miracles entails a special linkage to supernatural power, is there still a developmental aspect of striving to harness and hone that power? Of course, Jesus no more goes to a "wizard school" (like Harry Potter) than he attends a biblical academy. But one synoptic healing incident does intimate that something is required of the healer beyond being a mechanical conduit of divine energy. Just after brilliantly manifesting his divine glory to Peter, James, and John in the famous "transfiguration" scene, Jesus descends the mountain to encounter his other disciples' inability to heal an epileptic boy controlled by an evil spirit (Matt 17:14–21//Mark 9:14–29//Luke 9:37–43). Jesus promptly steps in and cures the convulsive lad. But in Matthew and Mark, the embarrassed disciples push the matter further, privately inquiring of Jesus: "Why could we not cast it out?" Significantly, Jesus' explanation does not focus on their deficiency of power, but on their "little faith" (Matt 17:19–21) and lack of prayer and, in some manuscripts, fasting as well (Mark 9:28–29). Does such understanding come from Jesus' own experience, or is it another example of his supernatural insight? In any event, if Jesus' followers are successfully to perform mighty acts of healing and deliverance, they need more than access to spiritual power; they also need the discipline of faithful prayer (and fasting?) to put that power into effectual action.[31]

Although the gospels give little evidence of Jesus' obtaining superior wisdom or performing benevolent wonders by the sweat of his brow over the course of his life and ministry, we must still not forget the very real agony Jesus endures during his final days, culminating in brutal crucifixion. Although textually disputed and found only in Luke, the poignant image of Jesus on the Mount of Olives, "in anguish . . . [as he] prayed more earnestly, and his sweat became like great drops of blood falling to the ground" (22:24), illustrates Jesus' Herculean struggle—appropriate to an athletic contestant or military combatant—against the virulent forces of evil.[32] Except in the fourth gospel, where Jesus' arresting party rather than his agonizing perspiration "fall to the ground," Jesus frets, fights, and sweats in some measure throughout his passion ordeal in the gospels (18:6). That being said, however, Jesus is not without supernatural assistance, although he feels abandoned on the cross by God for a time in Matthew and Mark.[33] In the same passage from Luke describing Jesus' earnest praying and bloody perspiring, the narrator also stresses, "an angel from heaven appeared to him and gave him strength" (22:43).[34] For all their tendencies to cast Jesus in heroic terms, the gospels, John included, do not portray Jesus as self-sufficient, going it alone, doing the work all by himself. His dynamic fellowship with God the Father, the Holy Spirit, and attending angels is absolutely critical to his success and survival. As Jesus tells the disciples in John, "apart from me you can do nothing" (15:5), the gospels emphasize overall that "apart from God, Jesus can do nothing." Receptivity to God's wisdom, God's power, and God's will proves to be the primary key to Jesus' work ethic.

Conclusion

Although I doubt it is written down anywhere in such crass terms, anyone who has grown up in modern American or spent any significant amount of time here would recognize the following as a common national work ethic: "Work as long and hard as you can to become as successful and prosperous as you can in this unlimited land of opportunity. And may God (or 'the Force,' or whatever) be with you." We don't have to be taught this ethic; it's pretty much in the air we breathe. But it's not so much in the texts we read in the gospels, and it's not so much the work ethic Jesus displays.

In this country it is custom, if not law, to define work ethic in terms of material productivity and social advancement. If work leads to prosperity and prestige, without committing egregious crimes in the process, it is good and proper—in a word, ethical. The end motivates the means. Jesus' actions, as portrayed in the gospels, challenge this perspective in at least two respects. First, it is neither exaggerated nor pretentious to say that Jesus works not for gain, but for God. That's just the way it is. In the Lukan parable of the rich fool, Jesus exposes the ultimate futility of "those who store up treasures for themselves but are not rich toward God" (12:21). By all accounts, throughout the gospels Jesus models this philosophy. God's will drives his actions and, as we observed in the previous chapter, this will does not involve amassing a fortune or building a portfolio. Evidently believing his own stark alternative—"You cannot serve God and money"—Jesus opts to serve God. And what this service entails reveals Jesus' second challenge to the American work ethic. "Serving" is the operative word, not just in relation to God, but to others as well. While some may presume a posture of serving God through their acquisitive work habits—and, likewise, assume God's blessing on the bonanza that results—Jesus takes the vocation of service seriously and literally. Although Master and Lord of God's kingdom, he dons the apron and towel to feed and wash God's people and to demonstrate the type of work that rates in this new society.

Jesus' labor practices also follow significant time patterns. On the one hand, not so different from ambitious businessmen and entrepreneurs in the modern world, Jesus appears to be a workaholic. He works 'round the clock, deep into the night, ever "on call." But such eternal vigilance is truly about eternal matters pertaining to God's climactic reign of mercy and justice on earth. He is always "on call," not like an opportunistic merchant poised to make a deal, but more like a dedicated physician (without the exorbitant fees!) available to heal the sick. On the other hand, we must not miss the fact that, amid Jesus' busy itinerary, he faithfully takes regular "time off" to observe the Sabbath. Yes, he draws some fire for continuing to teach and heal on this holy day, and in the fourth gospel he astoundingly assumes divine prerogative to work when and how he pleases. But for all this freedom, Jesus still orders his life around the sacred rhythms of Sabbath worship rooted in synagogue and temple. His Sabbath labors of love aim not to profane this special day, but rather to restore wholeness to God's creation celebrated at the original Genesis Sabbath. And whatever his personal liberty as Lord of the Sabbath, except for allowing the occasional gleaning of grain (with scriptural justification), Jesus never encourages anything but devout Sabbath keeping among his followers. One suspects Jesus would be baffled today by the flurry of diverse activity on a typical Sabbath (whether Saturday or Sunday) in this "one nation under God."

Finally, when it comes to how Jesus works, we detect a somewhat different orientation from both the natural philosophy of the biblical wisdom tradition, extolling the virtues of indefatigable industry (modeled by the tiny ant),[35] or the "rugged individualism" of the American frontier, promoting unlimited opportunity for all determined to "pull themselves up by their own bootstraps." While scarcely indolent or complacent about doing God's work, Jesus does not rely on blood, sweat, and tears to get the job done as much as he depends upon the dynamic flow of God's Spirit. To be sure, Jesus "works" to appropriate the Spirit's presence and power through the diligent practice of spiritual disciplines such as Scripture meditation and prayer, which can be quite agonizing for him, especially when he is faced with the prospect of crucifixion. But rather than conjuring or manipulating the Spirit as if it were some magical potion[36] or mechanical robot, Jesus is controlled by the Spirit, filled with the Spirit, caught up in the Spirit graciously bestowed by God. The work of this thoroughly charismatic Jesus, this "Spirit-person," is driven more by inspiration than by industry, more by dynamics than by mechanics, and thus resists an easy fit within our increasingly callous and calculating techno-society.

NOTES

1. See, e.g., Prov 6:6–11; 10:4–5; 22:13; 24:30–34; 26:13–16; 31:13–27; Sir 22:1–2.

2. Matt 20:1–16; cf. Crossan and Reed, *Excavating Jesus*, 127–28.

3. Mark 6:3, Matt 13:55, Luke 4:22; cf. Crossan and Reed, *Excavating Jesus*, 39–41.

4. See Ben Witherington III, "On the Road with Mary Magdalene, Joanna, Susanna, and Other Disciples—Luke 8.1–3," in *A Feminist Companion to Luke* (ed. Amy-Jill Levine with Marianne Blickenstaff; London: Sheffield Academic Press, 2002), 133–39.

5. See Mark 9:35; 10:43–45; Luke 9:48; 22:24–27.

6. Jesus is not endorsing this social structure but simply describing the way things are in society and the way things ought to be for his apostles (cf. Luke 17:5) in their vocation as Jesus' emissaries in the kingdom of God. They must serve God and humanity in a variety of roles (as evangelists on the "mission field," as pastors tending the "flock," as ministers at the "Lord's table") without regard for praise or recognition—for that is their duty.

7. John 6:14, "When the people saw the sign that he had done, they began to say, 'This is indeed the prophet who is to come into the world.'"

8. Similarly, in an early Christian context, celebrating the "Lord's Supper" as a full communal dinner is implied in 1 Cor 11:17–34.

9. Right before this dispute, Luke also has Jesus predict his imminent betrayal by one whose "hand is on the table" (22:21–23).

10. See O'Day, "Gospel of John," 721–28.

11. See Moloney, *Gospel of John,* 373–79; Mark W. G. Stibbe, *John* (Readings: A New Biblical Commentary; Sheffield, U.K.: Sheffield Academic Press, 1993), 150.

12. Throughout Jesus' farewell discourse in John 13–17, we detect a tight focus on inner-community relations ("love one another"; "wash one another's feet") among believers in their struggle against a hostile, external world. See, e.g., 13:1–20, 31–35; 15:12–27; 17:20–26.

13. The present tense verb for "ask" (*aitete*) carries the notion of continuous, persistent petitioning.

14. As illustrated in Jacob's famous wrestling match with God in Gen 32:23–32, "I will not let you go unless you bless me" (32:26).

15. Murray Melbin, *Night as Frontier: Colonizing the World after Dark* (New York: Free Press,1987); "Night as Frontier," *American Sociological Review* 43 (1978): 3–22; "The Colonization of Time," in *Timing Space and Spacing Time,* vol. 2 of *Human Activity and Time Geography* (ed. T. Carlstein, D. Parkes, and N. Thrift; New York: John Wiley & Sons, 1978), 100–113; "Settling the Frontier of the Night," *Psychology Today* (June 1979): 40–52, 94–97.

16. Shepherds in the ancient world were typically associated with bandits, brigands, rebels, and other troublemakers. Compare Brent D. Shaw, "Bandits in the Roman Empire," *Past and Present* 105 (1984): 31: "Hence the equation 'shepherd equals bandit' comes close to being one that is true for all antiquity. Indeed, the very type of social organization that characterized highland shepherd communities enabled them to constitute the driving force behind three or four of the largest slave uprisings documented in ancient history." On the rebel-guerilla movement against Rome led by the Jewish shepherd Athronges in first-century Palestine, see Josephus, *Jewish War* 2.60–65; *Antiquities* 17.278–285.

17. See Sir 43:3, "At noon [the sun] parches the land, and who can withstand its burning heat?" Compare Gen 18:1–8; 43:16, 25; 2 Sam 4:5; Song 1:7; F. Scott Spencer, *Acts* (Readings: A New Biblical Commentary; Sheffield, U.K.: Sheffield Academic Press, 1997), 90.

18. Nicodemus appears again at the end of the fourth gospel, attending to Jesus' burial along with Joseph of Arimathea (19:38–42). He is identified as the one "who had first come to Jesus by night" and is associated with Joseph as a "secret one [disciple] because of his fear of the Jews." Although sympathetic to Jesus to some extent, Nicodemus evidently remains "in the dark" or at least in the shadows of full faith and discipleship.

19. See 1 Macc 1–2 for a concise description of this crisis.

20. See Exod 23:12; 34:21. The first reference even stipulates Sabbath relief for "your ox and your donkey," animals typically employed in farming duties; cf. Exod 20:8–10; Deut 5:12–14.

21. Presumably, the sticks would have been used to make a fire for warmth or cooking. See Exod 35:3: "You shall kindle no fire in your dwellings on the Sabbath day."

22. First Samuel 21:1–6; cf. Lev 24:5–9 on the priestly regulations for handling the "bread of the Presence" in the Lord's sanctuary on the Sabbath.

23. Matthew assumes heightened tension between Jesus and the Pharisees by placing the event in "their synagogue" (12:9). But Mark 3:1 and Luke 6:6 simply mention "the synagogue," the common Jewish gathering place for all Jews, including Jesus.

24. For a helpful discussion of the complex history of the Johannine community, see Brown, *Community of the Beloved Disciple: Introduction to the New Testament,* 373–76.

25. The identity of Jesus as "Spirit-person" or as a "Spirit-filled person in the charismatic stream of Judaism" has been especially emphasized by Marcus Borg in recent studies of the historical Jesus. See, e.g., Borg's *Jesus: A New Vision,* 22–75 (the citation is from p. 25); *Meeting Jesus Again for the First Time,* 31–36.

26. John 20:19–23 and Acts 2:1–4, 32–33 (from Luke's second volume) report the risen Jesus' imparting of the Holy Spirit to his followers.

27. See the key works by Csikszentmihalyi: *Flow: The Psychology of Optimal Experience* (New York: HarperPerennial, 1990). A particularly gripping illustration of a South Chicago welder named Joe Kramer, who managed to work with remarkable "flow," is presented on pp. 147–49; cf. the chapter "Work as Flow," 143–63. Also, *The Evolving Self: A Psychology for the Third Millennium* (New York: Harper/Collins, 1993), 175–278; *Finding Flow: The Psychology of Engagement with Everyday Life* (New York: Basic Books, 1997).

28. See Acts 22:3; 26:4–5; Gal 1:13–14; Phil 3:5–6.

29. In another context, surrounding the adult Jesus' teaching in his hometown synagogue, Mark reports a similar question among the audience: "Where did this man get all this? What is this wisdom that has been given to him?" (Mark 6:1–2; cf. Matt 13:54).

30. Luke 2:51 indicates, "his mother treasured all these things in her heart."

31. Compare James 5:15–16, "The prayer of faith will save the sick . . . pray for one another, so that you may be healed. The prayer of the righteous is powerful and effective."

32. Discussed briefly above in chapter 4. Compare Brown, *Death of the Messiah,* 1:189: "An athletic parallel offers an explanation for the profuse sweat that follows: The runner is tensed up to begin the trial, and sweat breaks out all over his body" (cf. pp. 189–90).

33. Jesus' "cry of dereliction" from the cross: "My God, my God, why have you forsaken me?" (Matt 27:46//Mark 15:34).

34. Also, Mark 1:13 reports "the angels waited on him" during Jesus' temptation ordeal in the wilderness.

35. "Go to the ant, you lazybones; consider its ways and be wise" (Prov 6:6; cf. 6:7–11).

36. As Simon Magus futilely attempts to do in Acts 8:9–24.

7

Honor Codes

Colleges and universities typically enforce institutional "honor codes" prohibiting cheating on exams, plagiarizing of papers, and various other misappropriations of the intellectual property of others. Further, if an "honorable" student becomes aware of an honor code violation, he or she is obligated to report it to school authorities. At the very least, honor means honesty—doing your own work, standing on your own two feet, telling the truth. In our cyber-age, where prepackaged papers are readily available on virtually every topic under the sun, the issue of honest educational achievement has become particularly acute.

Although specific standards might be different, the basic notion of honor as honesty was as valid for Jesus' world as for our own. "Thou shalt not steal" (taking what is not yours) and "Thou shalt not bear false witness" (telling what is not true) were fundamental prohibitions of the Jewish Decalogue and other "honor codes" governing ancient societies (Exod 20:15–16; Deut 5:19–20). Without honesty there can be no ordered society. To be sure, established norms regarding authentic authorship in first-century Mediterranean culture often strike modern students as "dishonest," given that it was acceptable for writers in that era to publish their work not as their own, but under the name of a famous hero. Many scholars believe that some of the New Testament letters attributed to Paul (e.g., Ephesians, 1–2 Timothy, Titus) were actually pseudonymous creations written in Paul's name by a Pauline enthusiast. Where we might view this as dishonorable, even fraudulent behavior, ancient writers and readers regarded pseudonymity as a high form of flattery—a means of honoring a prominent figure from the past and continuing his authoritative tradition. This was not plagiarism as such: pseudonymous authors were not passing off their hero's (or anyone else's) work as their own; rather, they were attributing their own work to another's inspiration.[1] While we must remain alert to these distinctive honor conventions, a shared appreciation for honesty transcends cultural horizons. The ethical guidelines set forth in one of the possible pseudo-Pauline works were commonplace in antiquity and still resonate with modern audiences: "So then, putting away falsehood, let all of us speak the truth to our neighbors, for we are members of one another. . . . Thieves must give up stealing; rather let them labor and work honestly with their own hands, so as to have something to share with the needy" (Eph 4:25, 28).

One of the soberest incidents in the New Testament features the sudden deaths of a married couple, Ananias and Sapphira, who dare to "lie to the Holy Spirit" and to the nascent Jerusalem church about their financial dealings (Acts 5:1–11). Bottom line: they claim to have given more to the community fund (from a sale of property) than they actually did (an ancient version of fiddling one's tax statement to exaggerate the amount of charitable contributions). It seems that the early church could forgive all manner of sin and weakness except dishonesty and hypocrisy. The survival of a nurturing community depends upon mutual trust and transparency. Without a strict, enforceable honor code, the community will die.

In Matthew's Sermon on the Mount, Jesus radically affirms the injunctions against falsehood and larceny. He pushes beyond the traditional emphasis on upholding sworn vows made to the Lord to stress the sanctity of any statement made to anyone under any circumstances, without the boost of a confirmatory oath. Simply, "let your word be 'Yes, Yes,' or 'No, No'" (5:33–37). Likewise, more than merely instructing his followers not to steal from others or to take more than is their due, Jesus encourages them in sacrificial giving, even to the point of allowing others to take advantage of them: "If anyone wants to sue you and take your coat, give your cloak as well. . . . Give to everyone who begs from you, and do not refuse anyone who wants to borrow from you" (5:40–42).

While the notion of honor starts with an individual commitment to personal honesty and integrity, it also has a public face associated with social popularity and responsibility. Self-presentation is only part of the honor calculus. It must be matched by societal recognition. An honorable person is not simply one who is true to his or her ideals, whatever those might be. The community has the final say as to who and what is honorable. Honor thus has everything to do with reputation, with self-worth or self-esteem mirrored in the evaluative eyes of the dominant culture. Personal identity becomes inextricably linked to public perception. And so Jesus queries at a critical juncture in the synoptic narratives: "Who do people say that I am? Who do you say that I am?" (Matt 16:13–15//Mark 8:27–29//Luke 9:18–20).[2] Scholars continue to debate the extent and distinctiveness of competition for public honor in Jesus' world,[3] but there is little doubt that ancient persons were no less preoccupied than modern folk with being praised by their peers and being well thought of in the community. To some in the United States today, money or "credit rating" may be more important than one's reputation or "honor rating" (if the bank validates your "worth," who cares what anyone else thinks?), but many wealthy persons still use their resources to gain public approval, either through philanthropy (we still name our buildings after generous benefactors) or politics (when was the last time a poor person was elected to national office in this country?).

Our primary concern is with the ethical pitfalls that surface along the path to public prominence. Cultural anthropologists typically distinguish between ascribed and achieved honor. The former refers to inherited status derived from one's genealogy and place of origin, and the latter with merited standing determined by one's activities, accomplishments, and conquests in public "honor contests." In patriarchal Mediterranean cultures, ancient and modern, such "contests" are typically zero-sum turf battles among male authorities: there is only so much (perceived) honor available, so every "duel" becomes a win-lose proposition (negotiation and compromise are not primary goals).[4] Within such an agonistic system, key ethical decisions cluster around self-promotion and self-protection. Simply put: How far is one willing to go to climb the honor ladder and to guard the "rung" one has reached? The arrogant, militant milieu of imperial Rome lauded and paraded the *miles gloriosus*—the mighty conquering hero, rapacious and relentless, "slaughterer of thousands."[5] In the modern age, the white-hot, honor-obsessed culture of American presidential politics routinely entices candidates to push ethical boundaries, including those related to honesty and integrity, to get elected and reelected (Richard Nixon being a notable, but by no means unique, example). Personal honor becomes a casualty to public acclaim.

In his teaching, Jesus seems to encourage his followers to opt out of such strife-ridden, glory-hungry honor games. Returning to Matthew's Sermon on the Mount, we note Jesus' insistence on doing honorable deeds—almsgiving, praying, and fasting—in secret, before God and no one else, content with private, divine approval at the expense of popular limelight (6:1–18). Also, the rather shocking advice about letting an adversary sue "the shirt off your back" (along with "turning the other cheek" and "going the second mile") suggests quite the opposite of fighting for one's honor and defending one's turf. Similarly, Jesus' instructions about table manners and settings, dripping with honor implications, tend to challenge conventional expectations:

> When you are invited by someone to a wedding banquet, do not sit down at the place of honor. . . . But when you are invited, go and sit down at the lowest place, so that when your host comes, he may say to you, "Friend, move up higher"; then you will be honored in the presence of all who sit at the table with you. For all who exalt themselves will be humbled, and those who humble themselves will be exalted.[6] (Luke 14:8–11)

Notice that Jesus is not opposed to honor as a goal. His challenge has to do with the means of attaining that honor.

In summary, Jesus' ethical ideals concerning the pursuit of honor focus on the twin virtues of honesty and humility. How does his conduct, as portrayed in the gospels, square with these commitments? Many a public figure talks a better honor game than he actually plays. What about Jesus? We will consider three facets of his honor performance: (1) his reputation for speaking and living the truth; (2) his record of trumpeting and boosting his own popularity; and (3) his response to attacks on his character and to challenges to his honor.

Keeping His True Word

The preface to Luke and the epilogue to John state explicitly what each gospel presumes about its story of Jesus, namely, that it is a true and faithful account of a true and faithful Lord and Messiah:

> I too decided, after investigating everything carefully from the very first, to write an orderly account . . . so that you may know the truth concerning the things about which you have been instructed. (Luke 1:3–4)

> This is the disciple who is testifying to these things and has written them, and we know that his testimony is true. (John 21:24)

Thus we would scarcely expect any intimation that Jesus is anything but fully honest and reliable in all his words and deeds. But the gospels acknowledge that not everyone agrees with this biased assessment of Jesus' character: not only foes, but followers as well, have difficulty from time to time believing his message and trusting his mission. In the context of these struggles regarding the truth about Jesus, we may sharpen our understanding of the gospels' five-star rating of Jesus' honor and integrity. We focus first on Jesus' speaking the truth in the Synoptics and then turn to probe his embodying the truth in the fourth gospel.

The Synoptic Gospels: "Truly I say unto you"

Throughout the Synoptic Gospels, Jesus' pronouncements are frequently punctuated with the introductory formula, "Truly I say unto you," or more literally, "Amen, I say unto you." The fourth gospel typically doubles the force with "Amen, amen" and "Verily, verily." While we are accustomed to putting the "Amen" at the end of homilies and petitions, Jesus puts it at the beginning, confident that everything he is about to utter is the "gospel truth." This is not an oath as such (he

doesn't say, "I swear"), but it is a signal of both the solemnity and reliability of the saying.

Many of Jesus' "Amen" statements are eschatological forecasts of final
judgment and heavenly reward, which by their very nature (futuristic,
otherworldly) remain unverifiable in this present age. For example,
Jesus' promises—"Truly/Amen I tell you, none of these [who welcome
prophets and 'little ones'] will lose their reward" (Matt 10:40–42//
Mark 9:41) and "Truly/Amen I tell you, today you [the criminal on the
cross] will be with me in Paradise" (Luke 23:43)—hold out marvelous
prospects of eternal bliss for their hearers after death, but cannot be
absolutely proven true by gospel readers this side of heaven. Other synoptic "Amen" predictions, however, have a more immediate target within
Jesus' generation:

> Truly/Amen I tell you, there are some standing here who will not
> taste death until they see the kingdom of God come with power.
> (Mark 9:1//Matt 16:28//Luke 9:27)

> Truly/Amen I tell you, this generation will not pass away until all
> these things have taken place. (Matt 24:34//Mark 13:30//Luke
> 21:32)

> Truly/Amen I tell you, not one stone [of the Jerusalem temple]
> will be left here upon another; all will be thrown down (Matt
> 24:2).[7]

These are notoriously difficult texts subject to a variety of interpretations. Most problematic for Jesus' honor as honesty is the apparent apocalyptic thrust of these statements, envisioning the imminent end of the
world and the climactic establishment of God's kingdom. By any historical reckoning, two thousand years and counting is not imminent
(although it has long been argued that, from the Lord's cosmic perspective,

"one day is like a thousand years").[8] But if we understand Jesus' apocalyptic vision in more world-shaking (changing) than world-shattering (ending) terms, a different picture emerges.[9] The disciples, according to the gospel accounts, in fact "do not taste death" until they witness the extraordinary unveiling of God's glory and power in Jesus' transfiguration and resurrection.[10] And a generation does not pass until catastrophic events, including the dismantling of the holy temple in Jerusalem, overtake Roman Palestine during the First Jewish Revolt of 66–70 C.E.[11] These occurrences may not fulfill the whole range of Jesus' apocalyptic agenda, but they constitute an impressive "down payment" on its final consummation.[12]

Specific conflicts concerning Jesus' truthfulness cluster in the synoptic reports of Jesus' final days in Jerusalem. Three episodes stand out. In one of a series of questions designed to "trap Jesus in what he said," the religious authorities attempt to exploit Jesus' reputation for honesty (Matt 22:15–22//Mark 12:13–17//Luke 20:20–26). The interrogators, whom Luke describes as priestly emissaries "who pretended to be honest," begin by affirming Jesus' integrity: "Teacher, we know that you are true (*alēthēs*), and teach the way of God in accordance with the truth (*alētheia*)" (20:21). Although insincere in this assertion and intent on exposing something untrue about Jesus, his opponents ironically offer a perfect confession of Jesus' honest character, from the prevailing viewpoint of the gospel narratives. And as the story ensues, Jesus only reinforces his honorable mien. When the inquisitors ask whether it is "lawful to pay taxes to the emperor, or not" (hoping he might prove himself traitorous to Jewish and/or Roman law), Jesus—perceiving their "malice" "hypocrisy" (Mark), and "craftiness" (Luke)—answers in such a way to maintain his integrity before God and the earthly powers that be and to render his interlocutors speechless: "Give to the emperor the things that are the emperor's, and to God the things that are God's." The thrust of the entire incident is to counterpoint Jesus' unshakeable honesty with his enemies' hypocrisy.

Second, we turn from the exchange with angry authorities in the temple compound to the encounter with the deluded disciples at the Mount of Olives. Jesus had previously celebrated the Passover meal with his followers in a borrowed room and jolted them with the announcement that one of their company would betray him. Now he drops another bomb-shell forecast, this time with direct reference to Peter: "Truly/Amen I tell you, this very night, before the cock crows, you will deny me three times" (Matt 26:34//Mark 14:30).[13] Despite Jesus' "Amen" assurance, Peter questions the veracity of Jesus' prophecy in no uncertain terms. Mark points out that Peter responds "vehemently," saying: "Even though I must die with you, I will not deny you" (14:31). Such rhetorical bravado, however, is not matched by real bravery. As surely as Judas betrays Jesus, Peter denies all knowledge of his Master under interroga-tion. Sadly, Peter adds his own perjury to other "false testimony" brought about Jesus at his trial. When the cock crows, Peter "remembers what Jesus had said" (Matt 26:75//Mark 14:72//Luke 22:61). Jesus' words prove painfully true for his leading apostle. Moreover, the few words Jesus speaks on his own behalf before his priestly prosecutors reveal an honorable truth that, ironically, leads to his death. When pointedly pressed (under oath in Matthew) as to whether he is the Messiah, Jesus implies that he is in Matthew and Luke and candidly confesses—"I am"—in Mark. Such a "blasphemous" claim, from the priests' perspec-tive, merits Jesus' execution (Matt 26:63–65//Mark 14:61–64//Luke 22:67–71). By contrast, from the evangelists' viewpoint, Jesus speaks the truth even under threat of death. Jesus will not lie to save his own neck.

A final test of Jesus' truthfulness focuses on his threefold, synoptic prediction to his disciples that "he will rise again on the third day" after his violent death. On the occasions when Jesus makes these announce-ments, the apostles completely ignore this promise of resurrection, since they cannot bring themselves to believe that Jesus will ever die, at least not in the ignominious manner he suggests.[14] When he in fact is cruci-fied, his followers are shell-shocked and scarcely entertain the slightest hope of Jesus' coming back to life. Mary Magdalene and other female supporters don't abandon the crucified Jesus, as his male followers had done, but they don't expect Jesus to rise from the dead, either. The women come to the tomb "on the first day of the week, at early dawn" (the "third day" after Jesus' death), as Luke puts it, to anoint Jesus' decaying body with spices (24:1). They are expecting no miracle and thus are utterly surprised (and "perplexed") when they find the stone rolled away from the tomb's entrance and Jesus' body missing. At first the distraught women receive little comfort when mysterious messengers proclaim, "He is not here, but has risen." But as the attendants jog their memories—"Remember how he told you"—the light dawns.[15] Jesus keeps his promises in the gospels, even the most incredible one—the one that the male apostles continue to dismiss even after (or perhaps because of) the women's testimony. Luke tells us that they treated the empty-tomb report as "an idle tale" spun by grieving and gullible (hysterical?) women (24:11). Of course, they are soon proven wrong as the living Jesus appears personally to them. In the face of the disciples' dullness and prejudice, Jesus' honor and truthfulness triumph.

The Fourth Gospel: "I am the Way and the Truth"

At a critical point in Jesus' capital trial before the Roman governor Pilate, Jesus exclaims in the Gospel of John: "For this I was born, and for this I came into the world, to testify to the truth. Everyone who belongs to the truth listens to my voice" (18:37). If this trial is about getting to the truth of the matter (as trials should be), then Jesus makes crystal clear what the verdict will be. Unfortunately, his judge in this case leaves much to be desired in his famous, fence-sitting response: "What is truth?" (*ti estin al theia,* 18:38). Pilate leaves himself maximum wiggle room to determine his own truth or to disregard it altogether. But in the complex, ironic world of the fourth gospel, naïve and nefarious Pilate asks the ultimate question which the entire narrative is designed to answer. Whereas here Jesus leaves Pilate's query hanging in the air, from the prologue on, the fourth gospel propounds what—and more crucially, who—truth is. And consistent with the breadth of Pilate's question, John's narrative presents a multifaceted philosophy of truth.[16]

As in the Synoptics, the fourth gospel underscores that Jesus speaks the truth in frequent "Truly/Amen" pronouncements; in fact, as noted above, John typically doubles the force of these statements: "Truly, truly, I say unto you. . . ." But Jesus' commitment to truth in John extends beyond reliable testimony.[17] It also involves knowing and revealing not merely truths, but *the* truth encompassing the cosmos, the essence of reality, the very truth of God.[18] In short, in Jesus the truth of God is fully shown and known:

We have seen his glory as of a father's only son, full of grace and truth . . . grace and truth came through Jesus Christ. No one has ever seen God. It is God the only Son, who is close to the Father's heart, who has made him known. (1:14, 17–18)

You will know the truth, and the truth will make you free. (8:32)

And this is eternal life, that they may know you, the only true God, and Jesus Christ whom you have sent. . . . I have made your name known to them whom you gave me from the world. . . . Now they know everything you have given me is from you; for the words that you gave to me I have given to them, and they have received them and know in truth that I came from you. (17:3, 6–8)

But pushing still further, the Johannine vision of truth inextricably linked to Jesus is not purely intellectual and philosophical, a concept to be grasped, but is also profoundly existential and ethical, a life to be lived. Truth is who Jesus is and what Jesus does. He is "the truth"—"the true light," "the true vine," the incarnation of the one "true God," of God's "word [which is] truth"—and as the world's true light he blazes the path for all "who do what is true" (3:21).[19] The Johannine Jesus shines as a model of active integrity, which he expects his followers to emulate.

Two encounters in the fourth gospel with inquiring disciples—Nathanael and Philip, respectively—reinforce this emphasis on embodied, enacted truth. Initially, Nathanael scoffs at Philip's introduction of Jesus as the fulfillment of Israel's scriptural hopes, objecting primarily to Jesus' place of origin: "Can anything good come out of Nazareth?" (1:46). This query reflects a common Judean bias against backwater villages like Nazareth and the wider region of Antipas's Galilee. Nathanael's snap judgment labels Galileans as dishonest, disreputable folk.[20] By contrast, Jesus' first words to Nathanael take the form of a compliment:

"Here is truly an Israelite in whom there is no deceit" (1:47). Being falsely branded as "no good," Jesus nonetheless highlights his critic's honest nature. He repays accusation with affirmation. More importantly, he signals his prime interest in and commitment to personal integrity. In turn, Nathanael is struck by Jesus' intimate knowledge of his character, even though they had never met. This amazement quickly blossoms into faith as Jesus further reports that he clairvoyantly "saw" Nathanael under a fig tree before their meeting (1:48–50). Jesus clearly knows the truth about people,[21] not as a cheap parlor trick, however, but as a sign that he has come to reveal in word and deed the truth about God and the cosmos. Nathanael is left, finally, with the breathtaking image of Jesus as the personal bridge or ladder linking heaven and earth, God and humanity: "Very truly I tell you, you will see heaven opened and the angels of God ascending and descending upon the Son of Man" (1:51). This scenario recalls the experience of the original "Israel," a.k.a. Jacob, who had a dream of angels moving up and down a ladder reaching the heavens. But one greater than Jacob is here. We may be reminded that Jacob's very name charted his history as "cheater" and "deceiver." Thus Jesus' description of Nathanael functions within the narrative as an ironic, counter-Jacob, self-portrait: Jesus himself proves to be "the true Israelite, in whom is no deceit."[22]

The same Philip who appears briefly as the liaison between Jesus and Nathanael surfaces later in the fourth gospel in a direct encounter of his own with Jesus. It follows sharp on the heels of Jesus' proclamation that he is "the way, the truth, and the life. . . . If you know me, you will know my Father also. From now on you do know him and have seen him" (14:6–7). As clear a statement as this is of Jesus' manifestation as the incarnate truth of God, Philip doesn't get it. With alarming naïveté, he dares to challenge Jesus: "Lord, show us the Father, and we will be satisfied" (14:8). With some irritation, Jesus reminds Philip that he has already been shown plenty of truth about God, not only through Jesus' words, but especially, unmistakably, through his works: "Believe me," Jesus exhorts Philip, "because of the works themselves" (14:11). Again Jesus seems to be conveying that divine truth is not simply a theoretical principle, but a practical reality exhibited in noble actions. Jesus has displayed honor by doing honest works and has set a pattern of ethical behavior for Philip and the other disciples: "Very truly I tell you, the one who believes in me will also do the works that I do" (14:12).

Blowing His Own Horn

In stressing the importance of performing pious acts for God's approval alone and not for human applause, Jesus blasts the counter-tendency of certain "hypocrites" to "sound a trumpet" in the streets and sanctuaries, announcing their charitable contributions (almsgiving) for public notice and adulation (Matt 6:1–4).[23] It is unlikely that even the most egocentric almsgivers carried around a literal trumpet with them or hired a brass band to extol their benevolence. Although the suggestion has been offered that Jesus envisages here the temple's horn-shaped collection "plates" in which deposited coins would noisily rattle around (or "resound"),[24] the more the louder, he probably exploits an exaggerated metaphor for effect: "Some of you religious types are so obsessed with promoting your piety that you act like[25] pompous kings requiring a fanfare publicizing everything they do." Anyone who has long been involved in religious institutions knows that plenty of folks fall into the trap of pride (it's the first of the "seven deadly sins," remember), showing off their spirituality for social advancement. I think this was at the root of poor Ananias and Sapphira's problem (alluded to earlier): padding the amount of their gift to the church sprang not so much from a cold-blooded, diabolical scheme (though Peter detects Satan's influence) as from a basic (and base) human desire to impress one's peers and "keep up with the Joneses"; Barnabas and others were selling land and handing over the entire proceeds to the apostles—we're as good as they are (Acts 4:32–5:11).

Since, as we have observed in previous chapters, Jesus accumulates no fortune to give away magnanimously and repeatedly enacts the part of the humble servant, he seems to be unconcerned with conventional notions of prestige and popularity. But he remains a quintessentially public figure, consumed with a mission to announce and advance a powerful kingdom—a realm within which he not only toils as Suffering Servant but also rules as Sovereign Lord. A new kind of king, to be sure—a truly sacrificial leader, not simply a "benevolent despot"—but a king, nonetheless, the King of kings, in fact, according to the gospels. The gospels are written in large measure to promote the supreme greatness of the Lord Jesus Christ (Messiah). Jesus is indeed the servant of all, but in his own words, we may recall, such a reputation qualifies him to be the greatest of all. Characters from John the Baptist to Pontius Pilate call on readers to "Behold the man."[26] Look at Jesus, consider him, believe in him, follow him: that's what the gospel narratives aim for above all. However, while the gospels are unashamedly all about promoting Jesus, the question still remains—with profound ethical repercussions for Jesus' followers then and now: to what extent does Jesus promote himself within the gospel reports? Does Jesus routinely "blow his own horn" or personally encourage others to advance his name? In modern media terms, what is Jesus' "publicity campaign?" How does he handle "public relations?"

Our probing of these questions may profitably start with the phenomenon in Mark's gospel often known as "the messianic secret," which encapsulates Jesus' frequent habit of "sternly ordering" various audiences to keep quiet about his identity and achievements, to not spread the good news. Various explanations for this "secret" have been floated, including the theory that it reflects a Markan cover-up for the historical Jesus' supposed disavowal that he was the Messiah. Jesus never claimed to be what Mark later believed he was, so Mark gets around this problem by "inventing" a reticent Jesus.[27] But our concern is with the effects of Jesus' quiescence on the narrative at hand, not on speculative editorial motives behind the text.

Quiescent Ministry

Mark's story commences with the dramatic baptism of Jesus at the hands of John the Baptist. John is cast as Jesus' "advance man," "preparing the way of the Lord"—the way of Jesus, that is, Israel's "mighty one." All the signs point to an explosive, eye-popping entrance of "Jesus Christ, the Son of God" on the public scene (1:1–11). But our expectations are frustrated, because "immediately" following Jesus baptism, "the Spirit drove him [Jesus] into the wilderness" for an isolated, forty-day testing period

(1:12–13). Then, "after John was arrested," Jesus finally begins his public mission—not around the Jordan, however, where the "whole Judean countryside and all the people of Jerusalem" had flocked to John, but in his native environment of rural Galilee. He actively promotes a new order, a new "kingdom" encompassing all who "repent and believe in the good news" (1:14–15). But, interestingly, while the opening statement of Mark's narrative heralds "the good news of Jesus Christ" himself, Jesus proclaims "the good news of God" (1:14). Jesus is not so much pushing his own agenda as he is advancing God's agenda. He is God's "advance man," as John was his. Jesus is not out to build his own empire but rather to bolster the reign of God.

But imbued with divine authority to teach and power to heal, Jesus naturally draws attention to himself: "At once his fame began to spread throughout the surrounding region of Galilee" (1:28). But it is not a fame that Jesus wholeheartedly solicits and savors. A tension surfaces early in his mission. While ministering to needy crowds deep into the night, he also craves time alone and apart (in "a deserted place") to pray and collect himself. When the throng continues to press in, he promptly moves on—partly to avoid becoming an established local hero, but also partly to "proclaim the message," to spread the word to other towns (1:35–39). Withdrawal from and witness to the crowds: both elements characterize Jesus' strategy in Mark. Moreover, early on he displays his tendency to silence others' witness about him, but with only limited effect. He forbids the demons he expels to speak about him, not simply because he aims to throttle their evil influence, but also "because they knew him" (1:34). Though opposed to Jesus' ways, the demons well knew the unlimited reach of Jesus' divine power—and it is this wonder-working reputation that Jesus seeks to mitigate. A similar pattern soon emerges with respect to those Jesus heals. Upon curing a pathetic leper, Jesus "sent him away at once" to the local priest for inspection, but only after "sternly warning him . . . [to] say nothing to anyone" about the circumstances of his healing. But the man cannot help himself and proceeds to "freely . . . spread the word, so that Jesus could no longer go into a town openly" (1:40–45). Doesn't Jesus know that this is the way of human nature? Is the "secret" that Jesus really thrives on this popularity, that he "doth protest too much" (and not very effectively), that fame is exactly what he wants? We must read on.

As his itinerant ministry ensues, Jesus continues his attempts to hush loud-mouthed demons (3:11–12), to find private solace ("he entered a house and did not want anyone to know he was there," 7:24), and to quash reports of his miracles (raising the dead, 5:43; opening deaf ears, loosening thick tongues, 7:36)—again, however, with limited success. The demons obey, but Jesus' solitude is once again broken by an intruder (at some annoyance to Jesus, 7:24–27), and witnesses to Jesus' miracles will not be muffled: "the more he [Jesus] ordered them [to tell no one], the more zealously they proclaimed it" (7:36). Is this a case of ironic, reverse psychology: the more an action is prohibited, the more desirable it becomes?

A curious exception emerges in Jesus' encounter with the so-called Gerasene demoniac, a deranged tomb dweller tormented by a "Legion" of unclean spirits. Jesus dispatches the demonic horde into a herd of swine, who then drown themselves in the sea (that takes care of any testimony the demons might offer!). The freed victim has now remarkably regained "his right mind" and desires to be with Jesus wherever he goes. But, strangely, faced with this enthusiastic new disciple, "Jesus refused" to allow him to follow, telling him instead: "Go home to your friends, and tell them how much the Lord has done for you." The former demoniac turns evangelist, "proclaim[ing] in the Decapolis [the ten-city, trans-Jordan region] how much Jesus had done for him" (5:19–20). What is this about? Suddenly Jesus encourages public notoriety such that "everyone was amazed" (5:20). Why the change in strategy? Part of the answer may lie in the Gerasenes' initial response to Jesus' wonderworking: they are not so much enamored with his deliverance of the demoniac as they are "afraid" of (and perhaps angered with) his strange, volatile power, which just cost them a couple thousand head of swine (5:13). This man is not exactly a boon to the local economy. Best to "beg Jesus to leave their neighborhood" (5:17). Since these folks are not Jesus' fans, perhaps Jesus reasons that the healed man's testimony is unlikely to spread and get out of hand (but, of course, this is precisely what happens). Notice that Jesus directs the man to "your friends." How many friends could this poor fellow have left? And who would have guessed that he would take his message on the road and evangelize the entire region? Even so, he reaches the environs of the Decapolis, a primarily Gentile area east of the Jordan, beyond Galilee, outside Jesus' primary constituency and "voting district." Once back on "the other side" of the Sea of Galilee (5:21), on home turf, Jesus returns to his quiescent way. After raising the local synagogue leader's daughter from her deathbed, for example, "he strictly ordered them that no one should know of this" (5:43).

So much for Jesus' dealings with demons and the diseased. What about his twelve disciples? Surely he wants them to broadcast the good news. Well, yes and no. On one occasion, Jesus dispatches the Twelve in six pairs to heal the sick and exhort the sinful (6:7–13). They thus mirror Jesus' own mission but do not actually proclaim Jesus himself as Messiah or anything else. Their message derives from Jesus but is not Jesus-centered at this point. And this is just the way Jesus wants it; in fact, "he sternly orders them not to tell anyone about him," apparently because their understanding of his messianic vocation is skewed by "satanic" visions of grandeur and conquest (8:29–33). If the disciples will not announce Jesus' identity as God's suffering, cross-bearing servant who saves others' lives by losing his own, he would rather they not announce anything at all (8:34–38). And so it stands to the end of the gospel. Descending the mountain after his dazzling private manifestation of glory (transfiguration) before Peter, James, and John, Jesus commands the befuddled disciples "to tell no one what they had seen, until after the Son of Man had risen from the dead" (9:9). But even after the resurrection, witness is restrained. Mary Magdalene and other women are instructed at the empty tomb to report their discovery to Peter and the male disciples. But as it happens, according to Mark's original ending, the women left and "said nothing to anyone, for they were afraid" (16:8). And that was that. The matter of trumpeting the good news of Jesus' vindication is left tantalizingly open.[28]

While in Mark Jesus is generally reticent to promote himself or to encourage others to publicize his name, he does invite those who are in dire need to call upon him for aid. For example, when a blind beggar named Bartimaeus vociferously implores Jesus' mercy on the outskirts of Jericho, it is the crowd around Jesus (including disciples)—not Jesus himself, this time—who "sternly ordered him [Bartimaeus] to be quiet" (10:48). Maybe the disciples think they are echoing Jesus' quiescent wishes, but once again they misread the situation. Here Jesus endorses the public plea; in fact, he purposefully halts his journey to heal the blind man who persists "even more loudly" to attract Jesus' notice. Of course, shouting to catch Jesus' attention and petition his personal ministry is different from shouting to push Jesus' reputation and create a public stir. But, as it turns out, Jesus is about to shift gears and assume a higher public profile. In the very next scene, Jesus makes a grand entrance into Jerusalem amid robust choruses of "Hosanna." These proclamations he does not hush. There is a time for silence and a time for shouting. Now it's time to shout. Why this sudden crescendo? How does Jesus' "triumphal entry" square with his humble roots and "secretive," retiring demeanor heretofore? We turn to consider such questions not only in Mark's story, but in the other gospels as well.

Triumphant Entry

All four evangelists converge in reporting this incident, albeit with distinctive features (Matt 21:1–11//Mark 11:1–10//Luke 19:28–40//John 12:12–19). We have previously discussed Jesus' special procurement of a colt as the means of transportation into Jerusalem. Each of the Synoptics underscores Jesus' sovereign right to commandeer such a vehicle: "The Lord needs it" is all that has to be said. And so Jesus clearly and self-consciously enters Jerusalem as Lord astride a beast of burden. It beats walking, but does this action constitute a dramatic entrance, a spectacular parade? Not yet, although Jesus' specification in Mark and Luke of "a colt that has never been ridden" suggests (as noted above) some kind of unique, consecrated ceremony. It is after Jesus rides into town that pomp and circumstance break out. Suddenly a sizeable crowd gathers, strewing outer garments and leafy branches along Jesus' path. They are rolling out the red carpet for Jesus, reminiscent of Jehu's coronation as the new king of Israel, ousting the corrupt house of Ahab,[29] and the Maccabeans' glorious entrance into the citadel and temple of Jerusalem, both reclaimed from the polluting clutches of the pagan Greco-Syrian ruler, Antiochus IV Epiphanes.[30] These gestures are punctuated by paeans of praise, loud Hosannas extolling this "blessed . . . one who comes in the name of the Lord." The lyrics stem from Psalm 118, one of the Hallel hymns (Psalms 113–118) sung at the Jewish Passover, recalling God's mighty deliverance of Israel from Egyptian bondage.

From colts to coats, from palms to psalms, this episode smacks of royal procession and political revolution. A new king has come to town: blessed is he! No more hiding for Jesus; no more hushing the crowds. The spotlight is on and the amplifier is turned up. The question is: To what extent does Jesus support this outburst? We have seen that, apart from arranging for the colt, neither Jesus nor his apostles initiate or orchestrate these proceedings. But how does Jesus respond when the enthusiastic demonstration erupts? And how do the evangelists interpret these events?

Mark reports no direct reaction from Jesus at all. He proceeds (along with his entourage?) to the temple compound and surveys the area, leading us to anticipate some dramatic action. But, in fact, since "it was already late," Jesus simply retires with the Twelve to his lodgings in Bethany on the outskirts of the city (11:11). After entering the stage in grand style, Jesus appears to exit quietly behind the curtain. But not for long. The next morning Jesus returns to the temple to offer the most theatrical and controversial exhibition of his career. Wholly on his own initiative, he begins to drive out the bodies and upend the tables of the temple cashiers and to excoriate the temple hierarchy for turning God's holy house of prayer into a despicable den of thieves. This is not the calm, quiet Jesus, meek and mild. He launches into a curt jeremiad, literally echoing the original Jeremiah's tirade against the corrupt temple system of his day (as he perceived it), punctuated by destructive symbolic action (smashing pots [Jeremiah]/upsetting tables [Jesus]).[31] Jesus intends to provoke; he aims to be noticed. But to what end? This is not the best strategy for winning a popularity contest. The crowds are still "spellbound" by his words and deeds, but they must also become wary of his eccentricity and potential for sparking violent reprisal. Indeed, the temple establishment begins "looking for a way to kill him" (11:18). He has threatened their authority and jeopardized their security in an already precarious state of Roman vassalage. He has to go. Jesus persists, however, in ensuing days to challenge the authorities, offering provocative commentary on the hottest political and religious issues of the day, from tax policy to moral law to personal eschatology.[32] He goes public to drive home his prophetic agenda of God's kingdom, but with little concern for its appeal. He is not currying favor, testing the waters, or angling for votes as much as he is simply announcing his message. If the crowds turn, if a cross awaits, then so be it.

Matthew's account of Jesus' final entry into Jerusalem adds an illuminating interpretation from the prophet Zechariah, which, ironically, stresses both the lowliness and loftiness of Jesus' action. He comes to Zion (Jerusalem) on the "humble" back of a donkey but still very much as "your king" worthy of homage (Zech 9:9//Matt 21:5). The crowds not only shout "Hosanna to the Son of David" but also affirm, "This is the prophet Jesus from Nazareth in Galilee" (21:9–11). This anointed prophet-king proceeds to the temple, but unlike in Mark, he does not postpone his action to the following day. He plunges ahead to "clean house" and to heal the infirm and decrepit, eliciting further cries of adulation—this time from noisy youngsters in the assembly. The authorities object to this raucous display, and Jesus promptly rebuts, with a psalm citation of his own, that God has ordained babes and infants to bellow forth just such praise (21:12–16). What Jesus doesn't state but no doubt implies from the full text in Psalm 8:2 is that God takes special pleasure in children's ebullient babble "to silence the enemy and the avenger." In this case, the "chief priests and scribes" play the unexpected and unenviable role of the "enemy" of God's purpose and people. After his retort, Jesus then retreats to Bethany for the night (21:17). Clearly, however, Matthew portrays a more aggressive Jesus than does Mark, more aggressive, that is, in promoting his cause, accepting praise, and resisting hostile judgments. But the result will be the same as in Mark. Matthew's Jesus will just as surely submit to death on a cross as the culmination of God's will for his life. Though fully authorized to summon twelve angelic legions to his immediate aid (a unique Matthean report), Jesus opts to forego this privilege and accept his destiny of suffering (26:53–56).

In Luke's gospel, while the adoring crowd of sympathizers hails Jesus as Israel's coming king, they also "praise God joyfully" for all they have witnessed. Jesus is accorded "glory in the highest heaven," but he ultimately remains God's servant and God's agent (19:37–38). Luke's account of the first Palm Sunday is further distinguished by the emergence of certain Pharisees in the audience who insist that Jesus command his followers to be quiet, to stop their boisterous display (19:39). The motivation behind these Pharisees' plea is unspecified. Perhaps they regard this praise of Jesus as blasphemous or traitorous in some measure or, maybe, just too extreme or too spontaneous. In any case, Jesus has no intention now of muffling anyone's testimony or damping anyone's enthusiasm. His strategy has shifted, not so much by choice as by necessity: "I tell you," he informs the Pharisees, "if these [people] were silent, the stones would shout out" (19:40). The glorious good news of God's reign in Jesus is too good to bottle up. By its very richness and vitality, it inevitably bursts the boundaries of anyone or anything that would dare to contain it. Its essence is explosive. Yet Jesus is not preoccupied with personal accolades. Far from basking in the glow of public honor and salivating over his prospects of royal ascendancy, Jesus weeps over a city ultimately unwilling, in his judgment, to welcome God's reign, and thus sadly destined to be crushed under foreign rule. With tragic, bitter irony, Jesus intimates that the city's mighty building stones—the same stones which would gladly declare God's glory if they could—will be dismantled "one stone upon another" (19:41–44). Jesus knows that popularity is fleeting. Today's shouts of praise can be tomorrow's cries for blood. Today's holy city can be tomorrow's filthy ruin. But rather than rejoice that fickle Jerusalem will receive her just desserts for spurning the "visitation" of God's Messiah, Jesus mourns the missed opportunity. No *Schadenfreude* here, only a broken heart—a heart overflowing until the end with grace and mercy, as witnessed in Jesus' dying prayer: "Father, forgive them, for they do not know what they are doing" (23:34).

Turning to the fourth gospel for the first time in this section on Jesus' habits of self-promotion, we observe a more mixed picture than is often appreciated. On the surface it appears that, quite unlike the reserved, quiescent figure of the Synoptics, the Johannine Jesus is consistently trumpeting who he is and what he came to accomplish. The famous catena of "I am" statements ("I am the bread of life"; "I am the light of the world," etc.) is sufficient to confirm the point. But to view Jesus in John's narrative as egotistical or narcissistic, wholly absorbed with calculated self-interest, is to miss another vital point. Along with being the incarnate Word of God, coexistent and coequal with the divine I AM, Jesus is repeatedly portrayed as the "sent one" in the fourth gospel, sent to do God's bidding and to fulfill God's mission.[33] In the face of slanderous accusations that he is ethnically inferior and demon-infested, Jesus responds, not with thunderous rebuke, but with humble appeal to his Father's higher authority: "I do not have a demon, but I honor my Father, and you dishonor me. Yet I do not seek my own glory; there is one who seeks it and he is the judge. . . . If I glorify myself, my glory is nothing. It is my Father who glorifies me . . ." (8:49–50, 54). Jesus honors God above all and acknowledges that the measure of his own honor is solely determined by God.

Moreover, while there is no "messianic secret" in John and no attempt to stifle true witness about Jesus (quite the contrary, testifying about Jesus "so that all might believe" is a major Johannine theme),[34] Jesus remains reluctant in the fourth gospel to fulfill the crowd's wishes for a new material-political ruler. For example, following his miraculous feeding of the Galilean multitude, "Jesus realized that they were about to come and take him by force to make him king"; instead of welcoming such advances, however, he promptly "withdrew again to the mountain by himself" (6:15). In the scene surrounding his final entry into Jerusalem, Jesus inspires and accepts the "Hosannas" of the crowd but does not initiate or accentuate them (12:12–19). The throng is still buzzing about Jesus' recent raising of Lazarus from the tomb and appears to have little understanding of Jesus' mission beyond that of a wonder-worker (12:17–18), confirming Jesus' long-standing frustration with the people: "Unless you see signs and wonders, you will not believe" (4:48). The disciples seem equally clueless about Jesus' destiny in Jerusalem and, according to John's narrative, only wise up "when Jesus was glorified," that is, in retrospect, after his death and resurrection (12:16).

So why has Jesus ventured into Jerusalem? Not to attract a crowd, although that is what happens. In fact, certain Pharisees kibitz among themselves with bewildered awe, "You see, you can do nothing. Look, the whole world has gone after him" (12:19). Well, maybe not the "whole world," but Jesus' fans do include Greek pilgrims to the Passover festival as well as Jews. In the very next scene, some of these Greek visitors to Jerusalem seek to obtain an audience with Jesus (12:20–22). Surprisingly, however, Jesus "answers" these inquirers not by welcoming them into his presence, but by announcing that he has a more pressing engagement. "The hour has come for the Son of Man to be glorified," Jesus says, but we soon learn that such "glorification" does not fit conventional expectations. Jesus will be glorified by death—by falling into the ground and dying like a grain of wheat, by "losing" and "hating" his own life, by being "lifted up" on a cross (12:23–35). Not the kind of "uplifting" experience his signs-seeking audience has in mind. And so, Jesus "departed and hid from them" (12:36). He spends the bulk of his final days before crucifixion not pleading his case in public squares or civic courts, but in preparing his disciples in private quarters for his departure (chs. 13–17). Although more self-assured about his identity and in control of his destiny than we find in the Synoptics (remember, there is no Gethsemane anguish in John), the Jesus of the fourth gospel is no more self-advancing or solipsistic and certainly no less service oriented (recall the unique Johannine foot-washing episode) and sacrificial. If anything, because this Jesus fully determines his own fate, his humbling death stands out as a deliberate moral choice on his part. No one coerces his submission: "No one takes [my life] from me, but I lay it down of my own accord" (10:18).

Guarding His Good Name

It is one thing not to boast about one's accomplishments or to boost one's reputation; we tend to admire such restraint in others (even if we don't practice it ourselves) as a noble and congenial virtue. It is another thing, however, not to delineate one's achievements when under inspection (as in a resume for a job interview) or to defend one's character when under attack. We tend to view this reluctance negatively as weakness or foolishness—not standing up for oneself, letting others walk all over you. But this is exactly what Jesus seems to advocate in his Sermon on the Mount/Plain, even daring to call passive and pacifist responses to persecutors "blessed":

> Blessed are you when people revile you and persecute you and utter all kinds of evil against you falsely on my account. . . . Love your enemies, and pray for those who persecute you. (Matt 5:11, 44)

Love your enemies, do good to those who hate you, bless those who curse you, pray for those who abuse you. (Luke 6:27–28)

Loving, blessing, praying for, doing good to attackers: that's hard enough to do, utterly against our natural instincts.[35] But can we at least set the record straight in the process and clear our good name? Jesus does not explicitly address this matter, leaving open the possibility of self-vindication if not accompanied by hostile retaliation. How does Jesus himself respond to personal affronts in the gospel narratives? We explore reactions to two types of attacks associated with principal stages of Jesus' career: (1) incidental, verbal assaults on his reputation during his public ministry; and (2) capital, physical threats to his very existence, culminating in arrest, trial, and execution.

Rhetorical Duels: Challenge and Riposte[36]

Even a cursory reading of the Synoptic Gospels will demonstrate that Jesus does not let critiques of his ministry go by without comment. He engages in no extensive debates and offers no lengthy defensive speeches, but he does succinctly make his point, often in vivid and witty fashion. A broad sample of Jesus' various rhetorical responses (ripostes) to personal attacks (challenges) may be gleaned from two synoptic clusters of conflict incidents in Jesus' ministry: one earlier, in and around the seaside village of Capernaum in Galilee, and the other toward the end of Jesus' life, in the holy city of Jerusalem in Judea. We will focus our attention on the first of these units.[37]

In Mark 2–3 and parallels, various critics confront Jesus on five main issues. Our concern is not so much with what Jesus says or where he stands on these issues as with how he defends himself and his position.

A Question of Blasphemy

While teaching to a packed house in a private residence in Capernaum, Jesus is unexpectedly faced with a paralyzed man who has been lowered through the roof, aboard his cot, by enterprising friends (Matt 9:1–8// Mark 2:1–12//Luke 5:17–26).[38] Impressed by this bold expression of faith, Jesus turns his full attention to the bedridden cripple, announcing,

"Son, your sins are forgiven." This statement incites some local religious scholars (scribes) to levy charges of blasphemy against Jesus, because, as any good Torah teacher knows, "God alone" has the authority to forgive sin. Actually, according to the synoptic accounts, these accusations are not made publicly, but rather amongst themselves and "in their hearts." But no matter—Jesus "perceives" the challenge to both his power and piety and fights back with two counter-questions designed to set his critics back on their heels: "Why do you raise such questions in your hearts?" and "Which is easier to say to the paralytic, 'Your sins are forgiven'; or ... 'stand up ... and walk'?" The second query functions effectively to double the impact of Jesus' authority. Healing or forgiving—either is possible; both are within Jesus' jurisdiction. And to prove his point he moves from word to deed, enabling the lame man to walk away, bedroll in hand. Far from shrinking from conflict, Jesus cleverly uses it to his advantage.

A Question of Table Fellowship

Shifting to another home in the region, owned by Levi/Matthew the toll agent, Jesus provokes another stir among the religious experts by eating with an assembly of Levi's business associates and other assorted "sinners" (Matt 9:9–13//Mark 2:13–17//Luke 5:27–32). This time Jesus' opponents explicitly voice their disapproval in the form of a "why" question, posed, however, not to Jesus directly, but to his disciples: "Why does your teacher eat with tax collectors and sinners?"[39] Still, it is Jesus himself who responds, not his disciples (defending his reputation is not something Jesus is willing to delegate). On this occasion, however, he comes back not with a probing question, but with a prosaic observation and a personal application: "Those who are well have no need of a physician, but those who are sick [observation]; I have come to call not the righteous, but sinners [application]." Jesus naturally accepts sinful persons as a doctor accepts sick patients. Who can object to that? The problem, of course, is accepting sinners as they are, irrespective of their intention to reform. Lest there be any confusion on this point, Luke stresses that Jesus calls "sinners to repentance" (5:32). Matthew and Mark's Jesus, however, leaves the matter open (Matt 9:13//Mark 2:17).

Whether or not "sinners" clean themselves up before coming to the table or somehow become renewed during the meal, Jesus eats with them as an act of mercy and compassion. His "Hippocratic" oath binds him to care for those infected by sin.

A Question of Fasting

The next challenge exposes negligence in the duty of fasting. Though the interrogators vary in each of the synoptic accounts, they concur on the basic problem: "Why do John's disciples and the disciples of the Pharisees fast, but your disciples do not fast?"[40] While the charge may appear to be directed at the disciples and not at Jesus himself, it in fact targets Jesus quite personally. By definition, "disciple" denotes a student or follower whose actions reflect positively or negatively on the character of the master or teacher. John made sure his adherents fasted, as did the rabbis among the Pharisees. Why, then, is Jesus so lax with his followers about this important discipline? Why is he such an irresponsible teacher? We have discussed Jesus' eating habits in a previous chapter; here, we are concerned with his defense strategy. In this instance, he offers no simple illustration and pithy punch line, as in the preceding episode. Rather he sketches three more developed images for consideration pertaining to marrying, sewing, and bottling. How these pictures relate to each other and to the issue at hand is not immediately transparent, although they all loosely cohere around the scenario of a wedding celebration (bridegroom, tailored garments, decanted wine) and the theme of joyous newness (new relationship, new clothes, new wine). The dietary point seems to be that, since Jesus is mediating a new age of God's grace—a fresh "update" of God's covenant with Israel—this is a time of feasting, not of fasting; a time of revitalizing the present, not of reinforcing the past; a time of hopeful expectation, not of mournful regret. However, while Jesus makes the point, he doesn't hammer it home as if scoring points in a debating tournament. He operates in allusive (and elusive) parabolic mode, leaving his inquirers thinking—and no doubt discussing further offstage—what Jesus means.

A Question of Sabbath Observance

Given our prior investigation of these Sabbath controversies (grain pick-ing in the field; hand healing in the synagogue) in considering Jesus' work ethic, we need not linger here, except to underscore Jesus' riposte tactics. Again the issue initially concerns the disciples' behavior (harvest-ing), not Jesus', but again Jesus takes it personally (as it is intended) and mounts a defense. Once in Mark and Luke and twice in Matthew, Jesus sarcastically goads his critics, "Have you not read . . . ?"[41] With this query focused on biblical literacy, Jesus raises the stakes of the argument, even as he turns up the temperature of the rhetoric. He appeals here not merely to mundane, natural observation, but to higher scriptural author-ity,[42] and he dares to suggest that his Pharisaic inquisitors have not done their homework. Or if they have, they've forgotten what they learned. "Have you not read?" Of course, they have read, but Jesus insinuates that they have not understood. In the next scene, centered around restoring the man's withered hand on the Sabbath, Jesus pushes the envelope fur-ther. In Mark and Luke, he poses another Catch-22 question to his accusers, based on biblical law—"Is it lawful to do good or to do harm on the Sabbath, to save life or to kill?"—which they do not answer (Mark says "they were silent," Mark 3:4//Luke 6:9). In Matthew, the Pharisees ask essentially the same question of Jesus, which he flatly answers (with the aid of a pastoral illustration): "It is lawful to do good on the Sabbath" (Matt 12:10–12).[43] In any case, after this verbal exchange, Jesus proceeds to heal the disabled man in the assembly (the initiative is all Jesus' here; the man has said or done nothing to seek a cure) and thus provokes a furious reaction from the Pharisees. Embar-rassed and embittered one time too many, they now "conspire against [Jesus], how to destroy him." If this appears to be a classic case of over-reaction, of emotions careening out of control, we must not ignore Mark's report that Jesus "looked around at [his critics] with anger; he was grieved at their hardness of heart" (3:5). This is more emotion than Matthew and Luke can handle. Matthew drops the statement altogether, and Luke only retains Jesus' "looking around at all of them." But in Mark's view, nothing short of disgust and disappointment spur Jesus' healing action on this occasion. The Pharisees are not the only ones hot under the collar.

A Question of Demonization

Up to this point, Jesus' opponents have quibbled over the propriety of particular practices. Now, they up the ante and strike at the core of Jesus' identity and inspiration. Who does he think he is, and what drives him? His critics submit he is none other than Beelzebul's minion, fuelled by Satanic energy. The conflict has escalated from legal debate to visceral slander. No one can deny that casting out demons is a good thing—unless such power flows, for some strange reason, from a demonic source. Jesus cannot allow such defamation of character to stand, so he launches into a more extended response than we have seen heretofore, proceeding rhetorically from (1) logical observation, to (2) supporting illustrations, to (3) implicit accusation, and, finally, in Matthew's account, to (4) explicit vilification (Matt 12:12–37//Mark 3:19–30//Luke 11:14–23).

Jesus' first point exposes his attackers' logical fallacy: "How can Satan cast out Satan? If Satan has risen up against himself and is divided, he cannot stand." The statement is clear enough, but Jesus buttresses it with illustrations highlighting the vulnerability of divided kingdoms and houses and the necessity of binding and disarming a powerful ruler (like Satan) before divesting him of his possessions. With point delivered and buttressed, however, Jesus presses on to make some serious accusations of his own. The first is implied across the synoptic tradition, as Jesus announces that God can tolerate anything except blaspheming God's Spirit, which in the present situation seems to entail heinously misrepresenting the work of the divine Spirit as that of its polar opposite, the diabolical Satan. Jesus stops short of directly branding his interlocutors as irredeemable blasphemers, but he comes close. In Matthew, but in Matthew only, the implicit becomes explicit; the general "whoever" becomes a pointed "you": "You brood of vipers! How can you speak good things, when you are evil?" (12:34). This is blatant name-calling, pure and simple, and it is intended to cut deeply. The Pharisees are not just ignorant and misguided; they are corrupt and toxic—evil vipers full of poison. Such harsh, deviant labeling is more characteristic of Matthew's Jesus than of Mark or Luke's.[44] Another classic example is Jesus' unique invective in Matt 23: "Woe to you, scribes and Pharisees, hypocrites! For you cross sea and land to make a single convert, and you make the new convert twice as much a child of hell as yourselves" (23:15). Strong stuff, even shocking—but perhaps we should recall that Jesus is not beyond denouncing even Peter, his leading disciple, as "satanic" (*satanas*) and "scandalous" (*skandalon*), if the occasion warrants.[45]

We must not forget to include the fourth gospel in the mix of Jesus' responses to personal challenges. Here we find barbed retorts replete with name-calling similar to that encountered in Matthew. To select one egregious example, in John 8 Jesus blatantly questions the sincerity of "the Jews who had [supposedly] believed in him," going so far as to impugn not merely their devotion to him but their inclusion in the family of God. Instead of being people descended from father Abraham, they are, according to Jesus' stark judgment, nothing but violent and devious children of "your father the devil . . . a murderer from the beginning and . . . a liar and the father of lies" (8:31–44). Name-calling, from playgrounds to courtrooms, often comes around to insulting someone's parentage or ethnicity. "The Jews" respond in kind, maliciously labeling Jesus a demon-possessed "Samaritan" (8:48). But here, it must be underscored, they are responding to Jesus' initial slur against them. Fortunately, this is not the only way Jesus makes his case in the fourth gospel. He also takes the high road in defending his reputation by appealing to the higher authorities of Father God and holy Scripture, as well as the corroborative word of faithful witnesses such as John the Baptist and the hard evidence of his own dynamic works.[46]

Moreover, many scholars are quick to note that Jesus' extremely harsh language against his own people ("the Jews") in both the first and fourth gospels is reminiscent of prophetic attacks against rebellious Israelites (especially leaders) in the Jewish Scriptures and may reflect escalating hostility between Jewish believers (in Jesus Christ) and nonbelievers in Matthew and John's communities as much as (or more than) Jesus' own historical situation. If you are being increasingly ostracized (even expelled?) from your native religious community (the synagogue) because of your faith in Jesus the Messiah, a tragic scenario which both Matthew and John intimate, you might well resort to bitter recriminations against your attackers.[47] Nevertheless, whatever peculiar social and political circumstances may have shaped the gospels' presentations, as contemporary Christians we still confront canonical texts that place acrimonious invective on Jesus' lips. But we must also recall that such language constitutes but one option among a range of rhetorical strategies that Jesus employs in countering his opponents. More than direct accusation, Jesus opts for probing questions, mundane observations, and suggestive illustrations to protect his position and reputation.

But what about when his life is on the line, when the cross looms close on the horizon? We turn now to explore Jesus' conduct as a defendant in capital trials.

Capital Trials: Interrogation and Vindication

In tracking Jesus' responses to lethal-judicial threats against his life and work, we consider a triple complex of events in all four gospels proceeding inexorably from Jesus' arrest to trial(s) to execution.

Arrest

Judas arrives with a posse of the high priest's armed servants and, in Matthew (26:47–49) and Mark (14:43–45), identifies the suspect Jesus with a kiss, a bitterly ironic token of affection (Luke has Jesus pull away before the kiss ["Judas, is it with a kiss that you are betraying the Son of Man?"], and John eliminates the gesture altogether (Luke 22:47–48// John 18:1–5). Thus mocked and marked for seizure, Mark's Jesus says nothing, while Matthew's responds with alarming congeniality, laced, however, with a pinch (or is it a pound?) of sarcasm: "Friend" ("Comrade," "Companion")[48]—some friend—"do what you are here to do" (26:50). In any case, Jesus offers no physical resistance and for the most part submits quietly to his captors.

In the fourth gospel, however, a unique surge of power accompanies Jesus' surrender. When he offers himself for arrest with the simple, "I am [he] (*egōeimi*)," he conveys much more than "I'm the one you're looking for." The Johannine reader knows that "I am" means "I AM"—as in "Before Abraham was, I AM" (8:58)—and thus it comes as no surprise in the present scene when Jesus' utterance mysteriously compels the arresting party to pull back and fall to the ground (18:6). This reaction does not imply a retaliatory strike on Jesus' part. He neither pushes nor curses his captors (all he says is "I am"), and they are not injured in the process—at least, not physically. But certainly their pride has been hurt, and they have been put in their place. Jesus remains fully in charge in John's gospel, and the only way the arrest succeeds is because Jesus voluntarily acquiesces. Matthew makes a similar point with a distinctive twist. Here Jesus makes clear that, while he could easily summon an angelic S.W.A.T. team (72,000 strong!) to clear up this mess, he gives himself up "so that the scriptures of the prophets might be fulfilled" (26:53–54).

Although Jesus refrains from violent resistance, one of his companions is not so pacific. In all four accounts, he unsheathes his sword and slices off the ear (the right ear, according to Luke and John) of the high priest's slave (Matt 26:51//Mark 14:47//Luke 22:50//John 18:10). Since it is most unlikely that this soldier, or any of his companions, will "turn the other ear," we expect a bloody brawl to erupt. But Jesus promptly intervenes to stanch the flow of violence, although each gospel describes the situation somewhat differently. Mark's account is the briefest and most obscure. It identifies the assailant ambiguously as "one of those who stood near" (14:47). We may assume (from the preceding context) that he is a disciple, one of the Twelve, but he is not so designated. Could he be "a certain young man" who we soon discover is also on the scene (14:51)? Whoever he is, Jesus completely ignores this swashbuckling hothead, neither condoning nor condemning his attack. Instead, Jesus turns to those who have come to seize him and, by way of a provocative question and statement, subtly mocks their efforts: "Have you come out with swords and clubs to arrest me as though I were a bandit?" (14:48). The upshot of this query seems to be: "Look, you've sparked an impulsive sword strike by bringing swords against me as if I were a common thug, when in fact, as you can plainly see, I carry no weapon at all and give no orders to fight." In his follow-up statement, Jesus explains that, far from being a thief, he is a teacher who daily expounds God's word in the temple (14:49)—a vocation that may cause controversy but scarcely constitutes a criminal act meriting police arrest.

While appreciating that Mark's Jesus does not encourage or endorse his companion's ear-lopping assault against the high priest's servant, we might expect more explicit denunciation of such violence from the peace-making Jesus (unless this is one of those strange situations where Jesus comes "not to bring peace . . . but a sword").[49] As it happens, the other gospels expect more from Jesus as well—and provide it. In Matthew, as the identity of the attacker is sharpened—pinpointing a disciple, "one of those with Jesus" (26:51)—so is Jesus' response. As noted New Testament scholar Raymond Brown discerns: "Since Matthew makes it clear (contrast Mark) that it was one of Jesus' followers who cut off the ear of the high priest's servant, it is morally important that Jesus comment unfavorably on such force."[50] More than a comment, Jesus issues a command to his disciple: "Put your sword back into its place; for all who take up the sword will perish by the sword" (26:52).

In John, the profiles of both perpetrator and victim become even more specific, to the point of name identification. It is Simon Peter, we discover, who severs the ear of the high priest's slave, Malchus (19:10). Such personalizing adds significant pathos to the scene. We too casually dismiss news reports of victimized "John Does" and unfortunate statistical groups (we regularly hear that "thousands of children across the globe starve to death every day"—so what?). The faceless and nameless, homeless and helpless, are often lost in the shuffle. But not on this occasion in John. We know precisely who harms and who gets hurt, not only in the present setting, but again later in the narrative, as Peter is challenged at a critical moment by another "slave of the high priest, a relative of the man whose ear Peter had cut off," asking, "Did I not see you [Peter] in the garden with him?" (18:26). Peter's victim (as do all victims) has a name, a face, and a family—someone who cares about him. And Jesus cares, too, at least enough to stem the tide of Peter's violence ("Put your sword back into its sheath," 18:11).

The most salient sign, however, of Jesus' compassion toward his ailing enemy comes in Luke. After a strong objection to his associate's aggression ("No more of this!"), Jesus moves to touch the injured servant and heal him (22:51). Here, the radical notion of loving one's enemies translates from ideal to reality, from attitude to action. However, Jesus' followers—and Luke's readers—may be forgiven for some confusion about Jesus' response. Earlier that same evening, the Lukan Jesus altered his marching orders to his disciples. Whereas before he had sent them forth "without a purse, bag, or sandals," now he instructs them, in light of imminent persecution, to take purse, bag, and sword—selling one's clothes, if need be, to buy the weapon! (22:35–36). Is Jesus suddenly, at the eleventh hour, planning to fight or at least to defend his cause? Doubtless, the disciples have been waiting for their master to become more aggressive, and thus they seize the moment: "Lord, look, here are two swords" (22:38). Their enthusiasm is scarcely matched by their resources (two swords does not an armory make), but they seem eager for some action and willing to obtain more swords. But then Jesus rather cryptically replies: "It is enough" (22:38). What is enough? The disciples' militant zeal ("Enough of this impetuous saber rattling—that's not what I'm talking about!") or the pair of swords (two will do the job)? If the latter, Jesus is either being incredibly naïve or intentionally sardonic: two swords are obviously not enough against the Roman legions, temple police, or any serious threat. Of course, two thousand swords wouldn't be enough either in the hands of a ragtag band of twelve captains, one of whom is about to betray Jesus, another to deny him, and the rest nowhere to be found. Perhaps, then, Jesus' advice to "get a sword" (an eerie ancient equivalent to "get a gun") is not a literal call to arms or self-defense but rather a symbolic indicator of the hostile environment increasingly engulfing the Jesus movement. Jesus—and by association, his followers—will soon be (falsely) "counted among the lawless" criminals facing capital punishment (22:37). If not the sword of Damocles, then definitely the sword of Caesar (and his clients) hangs heavy over their heads. But while they may well die by the sword in a sword-dominated world, they are not to live by the sword as a primary course of action. They are to respond initially like emergency rescue workers ("first responders") at accident sites, bringing healing and relief to afflicted victims, as Jesus does to the wounded member of the arrest team. Concern for personal safety and honor is secondary.

Trials

Following his arrest, Jesus is quickly shuttled through a series of interrogations (not exactly formal trials) by Jewish and Roman officials. The gospels diverge on a variety of details relative to these proceedings but agree that Jesus' fate lies in the collusive hands of the Jewish chief priests, Caiaphas and cohorts, and the Roman prefect, Pontius Pilate (Luke also includes a session before the Galilean tetrarch, Herod Antipas [23:6–16]). When he says anything at all, Jesus' responses to the criminal charges and threats of execution are remarkably frank and terse considering what is at stake, but not without bite. He appears resigned to his violent destiny but does not go altogether gently into that dark night.

In the trial before the Jewish council, Matthew and Mark both stress the fraudulent nature of the testimony brought against Jesus (encouraged by the chief priests!), with Mark also underscoring (twice) that the witnesses "did not agree" with one another even on their trumped-up charges (Matt 26:59–60//Mark 14:55–59). If legal convention required corroborative testimony from at least two or three witnesses, there is clearly no case here.[51] Still, one issue is singled out—Jesus' supposed, outrageous claim that he will personally raze and rebuild the temple—which the high priest presses Jesus to explain (Matt 26:61//Mark 14:58).[52] On this matter, Jesus remains silent. But when the high priest shifts to a direct question of identity, "Are you the Messiah, the Son of God?" punctuated in Matthew by an official placement of Jesus "under oath before the living God," Jesus musters a succinct, two-pronged response. First, he replies with a straightforward "I am" confession in Mark, adjusted to a somewhat more oblique and insolent, "You have said so," in Matthew. Second, he makes a shocking announcement to his priestly interrogators: "you will see the Son of Man seated at the right hand of Power and coming on the clouds of heaven" (Matt 26:62–64//Mark 14:60–61). We cannot be sure of all that Jesus means by this statement, but the coming Son of Man was a well-known agent of apocalyptic judgment in early Jewish thought, and "Son of Man" is Jesus' favorite self-designation in the gospels, although not always in an apocalyptic context.[53] In the present setting, Jesus seems to suggest that, whatever the council's decision, he is destined to be vindicated by God ("the Power") and fully vested with divine authority. Thus, he does not resort to defensive arguments or actions against his accusers; rather, he rests his case in the righteous and powerful hands of God (the "right hand of Power"). Luke links up with Matthew and Mark at this point, but also adds Jesus' snide assessment of his prosecutors that whatever he tells them, "you will not believe" (22:67–69). It is futile to debate and reason with such callous judges; the only language they understand is power, and Jesus waits for God's just power to triumph. In the meantime, the council mounts its own show of force, spitting in his face, slapping him around, and mocking his messianic pretensions. And in return, at this vulnerable moment, Jesus turns the other cheek (Matt 26:65–68// Mark 14:63–65//Luke 22:63–65, 70–71).

In the fourth gospel, Jesus predictably exudes a calm self-assurance before the high priest's tribunal, effectively turning the tables on his inquisitors by asking them two "why" questions. First: "Why do you ask me [to explain myself, since throughout my career] I have spoken openly to the world . . . I have said nothing in secret?" (18:20–21). No quiescent Jesus here. This Jesus has provided full disclosure from the beginning. Thus the present examination is an unnecessary and illegitimate charade. Secondly, instead of ignoring the bailiff's striking his face, Jesus responds with the rhetorical query—"Why do you strike me?"—after challenging his accusers to supply hard evidence against him to match their hostile emotions (18:22–23). The unflappable Johannine Jesus lacks the fiery temper of Paul in a similar situation in Acts ("God will strike you, you whitewashed wall," Acts 23:1–5),[54] but his protest is lodged just as surely. If anyone needs to explain his conduct, it is the capricious high priest and his cronies, not Jesus.

As the scene moves to Pilate's court, the focus likewise shifts to Jesus' royal claims. "Are you the king of the Jews?" the Roman magistrate asks in all four gospels (Matt 27:11//Mark 15:2//Luke 23:3//John 18:33). Jesus responds in the synoptic accounts with an abrupt and dispassionate, "You say [so]" (*su legeis*). When Pilate (in Matthew and Mark) and Herod (in Luke) attempt to push Jesus further, he does not budge. He offers "no further reply," "no answer, not even to a single charge" (Matt 27:12–14//Mark 15:3–5//Luke 23:4–9). Jesus' defense, if one can call it that, rests. So say the first three gospels. But the Gospel of John once again takes a different direction. Here Jesus first engages Pilate in polite, professional dialogue, first determining the source of Pilate's concerns ("Do you ask this on your own, or did others tell you about me?") and then allaying Pilate's fears of a violent political revolution: "My kingdom is not from this world. If my kingdom were from this world, my followers would be fighting to keep me from being handed over to the Jews. But, as it is, my kingdom is not from here" (18:34–36). The prefect remains unclear about the precise contours of this "kingdom" Jesus promotes and the "truth" he propounds, but if Jesus doesn't directly threaten Roman military rule, that's good enough for Pilate (18:37–38).

As the mob's rowdy demands for Jesus' execution persist, however, Pilate is forced to question Jesus again and suddenly finds him not so congenial. At first, Jesus stonewalls Pilate, just as in the Synoptics: "Jesus gave him no answer" (19:9). This offends Pilate, and now his encounter with Jesus modulates from philosophical discussion to power struggle (honor contest). Pilate wants Jesus to know who wears the pants in this relationship: "Do you not know that I have power to release you, and power to crucify you?" Jesus, in turn, concedes the battle but not the war: "You would have no power over me unless it had been given you from above" (18:10–11). And thus Jesus scores a forceful victory without lifting a finger or even raising his voice, as far as we know. Jesus doesn't need to fight because ultimate triumph is already assured. All power is God's and Jesus is God's Son, wholly aligned with God's purpose. While that purpose happens to include death on a cross, it inherently transforms such a destiny from execution to exaltation, from tragedy to triumph. This is God's drama—not Pilate's, not Caiaphas's, not any other so-called "power's."

We continue to be impressed by the spectrum of Jesus' responses to both verbal and physical attacks, ranging from silence to sarcasm, from tender gestures of comforting his enemies to trenchant criticism of their ignorance and impotence. He authorizes no violent reprisals, but neither does he simply "take" his punishment with bland equanimity. In his own way, he resists; he protests. But what about at the very end, in those final gruesome hours he hangs on the cross? The gospels do not rush to the resurrection. They linger at Golgotha to demonstrate not only what Jesus suffers and who inflicts the pain, but also how Jesus reacts to this climactic assault on his dignity.

Execution

Again, Matthew and Mark provide closely parallel accounts of Jesus' execution, emphasizing a common pattern of maltreatment by the authorities: they strip Jesus naked, dress him up as a mock-king, crown him with thorns, strike him with a reed, spit upon him, and gamble for his clothes. Throughout this horrific ordeal, Jesus offers no physical resistance and no verbal remonstrations against his torturers. Indeed, the only words he utters from the cross in the first two gospels are directed to God. To be sure, these are chilling words of protest, but they focus wholly on God's troubling activity (or lack thereof), not his persecutors': "My God, my God, why have you forsaken me?" (Matt 27:46//Mark 15:34). Jesus echoes here the scriptural lament language of Psalm 22:1 and may well have in mind the entire hymn. If so, the anguish of God's perceived absence is balanced by a deep abiding trust in God's ultimate faithfulness and deliverance. For as clearly as the psalmist bemoans his God-forsaken condition in which evildoers appear to have free reign, he also expresses his firm conviction that "dominion [still] belongs to the Lord," who will by no means "despise or abhor the affliction of the afflicted" (22:24–28). In short, God's good purposes will triumph, not the vile machinations of the psalmist's or Jesus' enemies. But—and this is a vital caveat—from the perspective of Psalm 22, divine rescue from innocent suffering involves frustrating the enemies' plans but not annihilating the enemies themselves. Vindication for God's righteous servant, yes; retribution against the wicked persecutors, no. In fact, the psalmist appears to envisage the final transformation of his torturers. While mincing no words concerning the vicious "dogs," "lions," and "strong bulls of Bashan" who "mock at me . . . make mouths at me . . . and divide my clothes among themselves, and for my clothing they cast lots" (again, it is obvious why the dying Jesus would gravitate to this text), the poet concludes with the eschatological hope that "all the ends of the earth shall remember and turn to the LORD; and all the families of the nations shall worship before him" (22:27). I would like to think that, even in the midst of his terrible pain, Jesus maintains such a restorative vision for his enemies. The remarkable confession of the attending Roman centurion just after

Jesus expires ("Truly this was God's Son!" Matt 27:54//Mark 15:39) points in this direction.

The gospel of Luke stresses the gracious demeanor of the dying Jesus in more explicit terms. The different tone of the Lukan Jesus' final utterances from the cross is immediately evident in his addressing God twice as "Father," in contrast to the double-desperate "My God, My God" in Matthew and Mark. He also demonstrates breathtaking compassion toward others in the midst of his personal anguish, praying, "Father, forgive them"—that is, his executioners—"for they do not know what they are doing" (23:34). While textual critics doubt that this intercession was part of Luke's original text (it is missing from the earliest available manuscripts), eminent Greek scholar Bruce Metzger presents the consensus view that it "bears self-evident tokens of its dominical origin" and was added "relatively early in the transmission of the Third Gospel"[55] (most modern English translations retain the verse but place it in brackets). It certainly fits the modus operandi of one who reached out to heal, rather than harm, one of his captors (recall that only Luke portrays Jesus' repairing the slave's ear). Although not directed to one of his persecutors, Jesus' next statement from the cross continues his redemptive response to death, as he assures one of the criminals hanging at his side of future fellowship and blessing: "Today, you will be with me in paradise." (23:43). Finally, as he takes his last breath, Jesus cries out not so much in torment as in confidence: "Father, into your hands I commend my spirit" (23:46). Jesus' destiny rests wholly is God's loving hands. Presumably, if any judgment is to be meted out against Jesus' attackers (and such is not assumed here), that is in God's hands too.

Likewise, in the Gospel of John, Jesus' three unique sayings from the cross do not betray any perceptible tones of vengeance or despair. The first exclusively targets Jesus' mother and the beloved disciple, tenderly committing them to each other's care in view of Jesus' imminent departure (19:26–27).[56] The last speaks a confident word (literally one word in Greek, *tetelestai*) of mission accomplished: "It is finished" (19:30). The middle statement, "I am thirsty" (also a single word in Greek, *dipsō*), is the one most pertinent to those superintending Jesus' crucifixion, eliciting their provision of a sponge full of wine attached to a hyssop branch just before Jesus expires (19:28–29). While the narrator notes parenthetically that Jesus' admission of thirst serves "to fulfill the scripture," the larger story of the fourth gospel also suggests a more relational, less mechanical purpose. Jesus' request for drink recalls his earlier encounter with the Samaritan woman at the well, which amounted to an engaging invitation for her to receive living water from him. Jesus asks for water not to quench his physical thirst, but to make a connection, to establish a channel for himself as "Savior of the world" to satisfy this foreign woman and her people's spiritual thirst. Similarly, we may imagine, by revealing his thirst at the cross, Jesus prompts the attending Roman guards to reach up to him, to his mouth in particular, from which flow "words of eternal life." Moreover, as the hyssop branch extends to Jesus' mouth, the soldier's spear pierces his side, producing an outpouring of "blood and water," which, in Johannine terms, is not merely a natural concomitant of physical death, but also a symbolic sign of spiritual life flooding a parched and anemic world.[57]

The Seven Sayings of Jesus from the Cross

Matthew and Mark
1. My God, my God, why have you forsaken me? (Matt 27:46//Mark 15:34).

Luke
2. Father, forgive them; for they do not know what they are doing (23:34).
3. Truly I tell you, today you will be with me in Paradise (23:43).
4. Father, into your hands I commend my spirit (23:46).

John
5. Woman, here is your son. . . . Here is your mother (19:26–27).
6. I am thirsty (19:28).
7. It is finished (19:30).

Conclusion

The fact that the gospels portray Jesus as a man of honor comes as no surprise, but certain dimensions of this noble profile stand out as somewhat unconventional, either by secular or by spiritual standards. In the United States, as in many other countries, honor is often most closely associated with military duty and bravery. The coveted Congressional Medal of Honor, as it is called, is awarded to intrepid wartime heroes. By such a measure, Jesus ranks quite poorly. He never takes up arms or retaliates violently against even his mortal enemies, preferring rather (in Luke) to heal their bloody wounds, impetuously inflicted by one his followers, and to pray for their forgiveness as he dies unjustly as a shameful criminal. Shifting from the military to the religious front (although too often these lines converge, as in "holy war," with lethal results), honor is typically calibrated in proportion to the supreme majesty and splendor of Almighty God. While John in particular, but all the gospels in some measure, accord Jesus the highest honor as God's Son and depict him as a direct channel of God's power, they do not deny or disguise his vulnerable humanity culminating in crucifixion—the very antithesis, it would seem, of divine eminence. What, for honor's sake, is God's Son doing on a cross?

In more positive terms, Jesus' honorable activity in the gospels may be encapsulated in three words: honesty, humility, and dignity. The Synoptics consistently stress that Jesus tells the truth, even when it is not in his best interest to do so and even when interrogators are aiming to entrap him in their web of deceit. Such fundamental honesty is expected of honorable persons; those whose word is suspect will likewise find their reputation damaged. Beyond basic truth telling, however, the fourth gospel remarkably links Jesus' integrity with his doing and being the truth. Honor thus pervades his faithful actions and trustworthy character. He is the truth.

Part and parcel of his commitment to benevolent service as the greatest good, Jesus exemplifies humility as the path to true honor. Far from using patronage as a calculated means to curry public favor or garner political support, Jesus lives as if humble service is itself the honorable goal. In the synoptic narratives, the quiescent Jesus repeatedly shies away from popular adulation, albeit with only limited success. And even in the fourth gospel, where he is much more self-revealing as the exalted "I am," Jesus still acknowledges in no uncertain terms that all glory belongs to God and derives from God and that he does nothing without God's initiative and approval.

While Jesus does not aggressively push himself forward in the public eye and shows little concern for worldly acclaim, he does not wholly allow himself to be pushed aside by detractors or sit by idly as his reputation is dragged through the mud. In Jesus, humility does not equate with humiliation, but rather retains an important element of dignity. Although not retaliating with martial force or physical violence and finally submitting to crucifixion as part of God's will for his life, Jesus repeatedly defends his good name through an impressive array of rhetorical strategies, ranging from silent mystique to strident critique in all four gospels. Honor is too vital a part of Jesus' identity to leave in others' hands, certainly the hands of opponents who aim to shame him, but also those of supporters who may or may not (more often) stick up for him (witness Peter's fickle loyalty right up to the end). Ultimately, from the gospels' point of view, the God of all glory unequivocally vindicates Jesus by raising him from the dead. But Jesus is not simply content to let God clear his name posthumously. Before his death and resurrection, Jesus mounts his own defense and clears the way for his climactic exaltation.

NOTES

1. On the issue of pseudonymous writing in the New Testament and biblical world, see the judicious assessment of James D. G. Dunn, "Pseudepigraphy," in *Dictionary of the Later New Testament and Its Developments* (ed. Ralph P. Martin and Peter H. Davids; Downers Grove, Ill.: InterVarsity, 1997), 977–84; David G. Meade, *Pseudonymity and Canon* (Wissenschaftliche Untersuchungen zum Neuen Testament 39; Tübingen: J.C.B. Mohr, 1986).

2. These questions come in the middle of Jesus' career in the Synoptic Gospels, as his thoughts begin to turn toward his ultimate rejection and death. At this critical turning point, it is important for Jesus to gauge public opinion, to track his standing in the polls, so to speak.

3. In numerous illuminating studies, Bruce J. Malina and Jerome H. Neyrey have pioneered a fruitful exploration of honor and shame as "pivotal values" in the biblical world. See, e.g., Malina, *New Testament World,* 27–57; Malina and Neyrey, "Honor and Shame in Luke-Acts: Pivotal Values of the Mediterranean World," in *The Social World of Luke-Acts,* 25–65; Neyrey, *Honor and Shame in the Gospel of Matthew* (Louisville, Ky.: Westminster/John Knox, 1998). Note the brief summary in Carolyn Osiek, *What Are They Saying about the Social Setting of the New Testament?* (New York: Paulist Press, 1992), 26–27. Critiques concerning (1) the pervasiveness and uniformity of honor-shame values in first-century Mediterranean society, (2) the validity of applying selected modern anthropological case studies to antiquity, and (3) the appropriateness of certain gender-based distinctions (males compete for honor; females guard their shame) may be found in F. Gerald Downing, "'Honor' Among Exegetes," *Catholic Biblical Quarterly* 61 (1999): 53–73; Marianne Sawicki, *Seeing the Lord: Resurrection and Early Christian Practices* (Minneapolis, Minn.: Fortress, 1994), 246–50; *Crossing Galilee,* 61–80.

4. See Malina, *New Testament World,* 27–57. The rigid, ruthless honor system prevailing within and among Mafia "families" (headed by "Godfathers") represents an extreme, high-profile example. But it is symptomatic of a wider, albeit tamer, competitive struggle for male honor throughout Mediterranean (and other) societies. It reared its head in every sandlot I ever played in as a boy and surfaces frequently in most committee and business meetings (even in church!) I attend to this day.

5. In a popular musical farce by Stephen Sondheim, Burt Shevelove, and Larry Gelbart, *A Funny Thing Happened on the Way to the Forum* (based on the comedies of ancient Roman playwright Plautus and first performed on Broadway, 8 May 1962), the Roman general named "Miles Gloriosus" trumpets the "virtues" of the imperial conqueror in hyperbolic, but, nonetheless, typical terms:

> I am my ideal! I, Miles Gloriosus, I slaughterer of thousands
> I, oppressor of the meek, subduer of the weak,
> Degrader of the Greek, destroyer of the Turk,
> Must hurry back to work!
> I, Miles Gloriosus . . . I, paragon of virtues . . .
> I, in war most admired, in wit most inspired, in love the most desired,
> In dress the best displayed, I am a parade!

6. Compare S. Scott Bartchy, "The Historical Jesus and Honor Reversal at the Table," in *The Social Setting of Jesus and the Gospels* (ed. Wolfgang Stegemann, Bruce J. Malina, and Gerd Theissen; Minneapolis, Minn.: Fortress, 2002), 175–83.

7. Mark 13:2 and Luke 21:6 contain the same prediction, but without the prefatory "Amen."

8. This argument is advanced in 2 Pet 3:8–9 as an assurance of the Lord's faithfulness to his promises and a sign of his patient outreach to sinful humanity: "But do not ignore this one fact, beloved, that with the Lord one day is like a thousand years, and a thousand years are like one day. *The Lord is not slack about his promise,* as some think of slowness, but is patient with you, not wanting any to perish, but all to come to repentance" (emphasis added).

9. The precise contours of Jesus' apocalyptic vision for the world are hotly debated among contemporary scholars; see, e.g., Robert J. Miller, ed., *The Apocalyptic Jesus: A Debate* (Santa Rosa, Calif.: Polebridge, 2001). In any case, the fundamental petition in the Lord's Prayer—"Your kingdom come, your will be done, on earth as it is in heaven"—clearly conveys that Jesus is not anticipating the literal end of the earth but rather, in some sense, its transformation, its restoration, its infusion with heavenly character. Compare Wright, *Jesus and the Victory of God,* 207–8: "In particular, we must stress that those among Jesus' Jewish contemporaries who were looking for a great event to happen in the immediate future were *not* expecting the end of the space-time universe" (p. 207). Wright summarizes his own view of Jesus' apocalyptic eschatology "as the climax of Israel's history, involving events for which end-of-the-world language is the only set of metaphors adequate to express the significance of what will happen, but resulting in a new and quite different phase *within* space-time history" (p. 208).

10. The mountaintop transfiguration scene, in which Jesus' clothes begin to shine "in dazzling white" before Peter, James, and John, occurs immediately after Jesus' prediction that the disciples will not taste death until they have glimpsed God's glorious kingdom (Matt 17:1–8//Mark 9:2–8//Luke 9:28–36) and clearly foreshadows their climactic vision of Jesus' glory after his resurrection.

11. Historical Jesus scholars debate whether Jesus actually predicted the temple's destruction forty years before it happened or whether the gospels, written post-70 C.E., place the prophecies on Jesus' lips after the fact (*vaticinium ex eventu*). Either way, Jesus' word proves reliable. Those who believe that the gospel writers are responsible for the predictions cannot prove that Jesus did not or could not have made them during his lifetime.

12. Paul utilizes language of "first installment," "guarantee," or "pledge" to describe the believer's partial experience of God's eschatological bounty now, in anticipation of full payment in the age to come: "But it is God who establishes us with you in Christ and has anointed us, by putting his seal on us and giving us his Spirit in our hearts as a first installment" (2 Cor 1:21–22; cf. 5:5; Eph 1:13–14).

13. Luke sets Jesus' prediction of Peter's denial before the excursion to the Mount of Olives (22:34).

14. First prediction, Matt 16:21–23//Mark 8:31–33//Luke 9:22; second prediction, Matt 17:22//Mark 9:31–32 (Luke 9:44 contains the forecast of Jesus' betrayal, but not his death and resurrection); third prediction, Matt 20:17–19//Mark 10:32–34//Luke 18:31–34.

15. Each of the Synoptics presents a distinctive announcement by different messengers at the empty tomb, but the effect is the same. In Matthew, an angel of the Lord says, "He is not here; for he has been raised, as he said" (28:2–6). In Mark, a young man dressed in a white robe says, "He has been raised; he is not here. . . . But go, tell his disciples and Peter that he is going ahead of you to Galilee; there you will see him, just as he told you" (16:5–7). And in Luke, two men in dazzling clothes proclaim, "He is not here, but has risen. Remember how he told you, while he was still in Galilee, that the Son of Man must be handed over to sinners, and be crucified, and on the third day rise again" (24:4–6).

16. On the rich concept of "truth" in John, see C. H. Dodd, *The Interpretation of the Fourth Gospel* (Cambridge, U.K.: Cambridge University Press, 1953), 170–78.

17. In John 5:31–39, Jesus appeals to four corroborative witnesses to the truth beyond his own word: (1) the testimony of God the Father, (2) the testimony of John the Baptist, (3) the testimony of Scripture, and (4) the works that Jesus does.

18. Compare Dodd, *Interpretation of the Fourth Gospel,* 177: "It is *the* Truth, the revelation of eternal reality, that Christ declares."

19. A similar ethical emphasis on "doing the truth" and "walking in the light" is found in the Johannine letters. See 1 John 1:6–10; 2:3–11; 3:18–24; 2 John 4–6; 3 John 11–12.

20. Compare the Pharisees' biased reply to Nicodemus when he suggests giving Jesus a fair hearing: "Surely you are not also from Galilee, are you? Search and you will see that no prophet is to arise from Galilee" (7:52).

21. Compare 2:24–25: "But Jesus . . . knew all people and needed no one to testify about anyone; for he himself knew what was in everyone."

22. Compare Rensberger, "The Gospel According to John," 2015. The relevant Jacob stories are found in Gen 27:18–36; 28:10–17; 32:22–28. The fourth gospel also develops the portrait of Jesus as "greater than Jacob" in 4:10–14.

23. Compare the entire section, Matt 6:1–18, which Garland, *Reading Matthew,* 77, entitles, "Acts of Devotion: For Applause or for God?"

24. Harrington, *Gospel of Matthew,* 94, attributes this interpretation to N. M McEleney, "Does the Trumpet Sound or Resound? An Interpretation of Matthew 6:2," *Zeitschrift für die neutestamentlichen Wissenschaft* 76 (1985): 43–46, and offers the apt critique that this reading "lessens the caricature and presupposes a setting in the Jerusalem temple." The scenario of making "loud" monetary deposits into the temple treasury better fits the story surrounding the widow and her two coins in Mark 12:41–44//Luke 21:1–4.

25. The Greek term *hypocritēs* "designated an actor who performed behind a mask" (Harrington, *Gospel of Matthew*, 77).

26. In John 1:29, John the Baptist declares with respect to Jesus, "Behold (*ide*) the Lamb of God who takes away the sin of the world." In John 19:5, 14, Pontius Pilate presents Jesus to the angry crowd: "Behold (*idou*) the man!" "Behold (*ide*) your king!"

27. See the concise summaries of modern critical analysis of Mark's "messianic secret" (beginning with German scholar William Wrede) in John R. Donahue and Daniel J. Harrington, *The Gospel of Mark* (Sacra Pagina 2; Collegeville, Minn.: Liturgical Press, 2002), 27–29; Ehrman, *New Testament,* 68; for a more detailed study, see the collection of seminal essays edited by Christopher M. Tuckett, *The Messianic Secret* (Philadelphia, Pa.: Fortress, 1983).

28. Modern English translations, like the NRSV, typically print, in brackets, a so-called "shorter ending" of Mark, extending v. 8, and a "longer ending," adding vv. 9–20. Both addenda include Jesus' commissioning of his disciples to spread the good news of salvation, in line with similar material at the end of the first and third gospels (Matt 28:16–20; Luke 24:44–47). But most textual critics argue that the best evidence points to the first half of 16:8 as the original ending of Mark. While the women at the empty tomb are instructed to report their findings, they in fact "said nothing to anyone, for they were afraid." See Bruce M. Metzger, *A Textual Commentary on the Greek New Testament* (2d ed.; Stuttgart: United Bible Societies, 1994), 102–6.

29. 2 Kgs 9:13, "Then hurriedly they all took their cloaks and spread them before him on the bare steps; and they blew the trumpet, and proclaimed, 'Jehu is king.'"

30. First Maccabees 13:49–53; 2 Macc 10:1–7, "Therefore, carrying ivy-wreathed wands and beautiful branches and also fronds of palm, they offered hymns of thanksgiving to him who had given success to the purifying of his own holy place" (10:7).

31. See Jer 7:1–15; 19:1–15; 26:1–15; cf. esp.: "Has this house, which is called by my name, become a den of robbers in your sight?" (Jer 7:11); "But you have made it [the Lord's house] a den of robbers" (Mark 11:17).

32. In rapid fire, the authorities challenge Jesus on five main issues: (1) his personal authority (11:27–33); (2) paying taxes (12:13–17); (3) resurrection and afterlife (12:18–27); (4) the greatest commandment (12:28–34); (5) David's messianic lineage (12:35–37).

33. See John 3:17, 31–36; 5:36–38; 6:29, 38; 8:12–19; 17:3–4, 20–26.

34. "He [John] came as a witness to testify to the light, so that all might believe through him" (1:7); "But these things are written so that you may come to believe that Jesus is the Messiah, the Son of God, and that through believing you may have life in his name" (20:31).

35. See Topel, *Children of a Compassionate God,* 131–48, 226–27.

36. On the pattern of challenge and riposte as fundamental to "a constant social tug of war, a game of social push and shove," see Malina and Neyrey, "Honor and Shame," 29–32.

37. The second cluster of conflict scenes, briefly alluded to above, appears in Mark 11:27–12:40 and parallels.

38. These synoptic accounts closely match each other, with only minor variations.

39. Matt 9:11; cf. Mark 2:16, "Why does he eat with tax collectors and sinners?"; Luke 5:30, "Why do you eat and drink with tax collectors and sinners?" Despite these variations, in each case a company of Pharisees addresses their concern about Jesus' behavior to his disciples.

40. In Matthew the interrogators are John's disciples, in Mark they are a less defined group of "people," and in Luke an even more nondescript "they." Otherwise the episodes are quite similar in Matt 9:14–17//Mark 2:18–22//Luke 5:33–39.

41. Matt 12:1–8//Mark 2:23–28//Luke 6:1–5. In addition to "Have you not read what David did . . .?" (12:3) and "Have you not read in the law . . .?" (12:5), Matthew's Jesus makes a third scriptural appeal to the prophet Hosea (12:7).

42. Malina and Neyrey, "Conflict in Luke-Acts: Labeling and Deviance Theory," in *The Social World of Luke-Acts,* 108–10, 117–20, discuss "appealing to higher loyalties" (such as sacred Scripture) as a key strategy in "interrupting the labeling/deviance process" and neutralizing false accusations in a forensic setting.

43. Jesus employs the pastoral illustration to good effect in Matthew 12:11–12: "Suppose one of you has only one sheep and it falls into a pit on the Sabbath; will you not lay hold of it and lift it out? How much more valuable is a human being than a sheep?"

44. Jesus is often the brunt of name-calling as well in Matthew. See Malina and Neyrey, *Calling Jesus Names.*

45. The Peter case demonstrates the occasional nature of Jesus' use of negative labels. He does not intend them to denote a permanent condition. Peter certainly rises above this deviant moment and eventually fulfills his destiny as "the rock" of the church (see Matt 16:16–23). By extension, the "hypocritical" Pharisees can also change.

46. As noted above, see especially John 5:31–47.

47. As pointed out in a previous chapter, see Brown, *Community of the Beloved Disciple,* for a balanced discussion of hypotheses related to the history of the Johannine community. On the struggles of the Matthean community in the Jewish family, see J. Andrew Overman, *Matthew's Gospel and Formative Judaism: The Social World of the Matthean Community* (Minneapolis, Minn.: Fortress, 1990), and his *Church and Community in Crisis: The Gospel According*

to Matthew (Valley Forge, Pa.: Trinity Press International, 1996); Anthony J. Saldarini, *Matthew's Christian-Jewish Community* (Chicago: University of Chicago Press, 1994). For sensitive treatments of the anti-Judaic overtones of Matthew's rhetoric in light of current pastoral and ecumenical concerns, see the following significant essays in *The Gospel of Matthew in Current Study: Studies in Memory of William J. Thompson, S. J.* (ed. David E. Aune; Grand Rapids, Mich.: Eerdmans, 2001): Amy-Jill Levine, "Matthew's Advice to a Divided Readership," 22–41; Daniel J. Harrington, "Matthew's Gospel: Pastoral Problems and Possibilities," 62–73; Anthony J. Saldarini, "Reading Matthew without Anti-Semitism," 166–84.

48. The Greek term is *hetairos.* See Max Zerwick and Mary Grosvenor, *A Grammatical Analysis of the Greek New Testament* (5th ed; Rome: Pontifical Biblical Institute, 1996), 89; and Barclay M. Newman, *A Concise Greek-English Dictionary of the New Testament* (Stuttgart: German Bible Society, 1993), 74.

49. Compare Matt 10:34–36//Luke 12:51–53. However, the application here is clearly metaphorical, referring to the division within families that Jesus provokes. Jesus does not come to wield a literal sword against Roman or any other armies.

50. Brown, *Introduction to the New Testament,* 200.

51. See Deut 19:15, "A single witness shall not suffice to convict a person of any crime or wrongdoing in connection with any offense that may be committed. Only on the evidence of two or three witnesses shall a charge be sustained." Compare Num 35:30; Deut 17:6.

52. In Matt 24:1–2//Mark 13:1–2, Jesus does predict the temple's dismantling but does not say that he will cause this disaster; in fact, he does not identify the agents of destruction at all.

53. Important background for the "Son of Man" image comes from the Book of Ezekiel (over 90 references applied to the prophet) and, in a patently apocalyptic setting, Dan 7:9–27 and 1 En 37–71. For a brief overview of this background and Jesus' varied usage of "Son of Man" in the gospels, see Stanton, *Gospels and Jesus,* 227–34; Harris, *Understanding the Bible,* 372–73. For fuller insights, see the major new study by Walter Wink, *The Human Being: Jesus and the Enigma of the Son of the Man* (Minneapolis, Minn.: Fortress, 2002).

54. When challenged about his brazen action ("Do you dare to insult God's high priest?"), Paul claims that he "did not realize . . . that he [Ananias] was the high priest." But this response may betray an underlying sarcasm: whatever Ananias's title, Paul doesn't think he is much of a high priest or faithful leader of God's people. See Richard J. Cassidy, *Society and Politics in the Acts of the Apostles* (Maryknoll, N.Y.: Orbis, 1987), 63–65; Spencer, *Acts,* 212.

55. Metzger, *Textual Commentary,* 154.

56. See chapter 2 for a discussion of this passage.

57. See John 4:7–42; 6:68; 19:34; and the splendid study exploring these various layers of Johannine imagery by Moore, *Poststructuralism and the New Testament*, 43–64.

8

Last Things First

I make no attempt in this closing chapter to rehash all the elements of Jesus' conduct sketched in the gospel narratives. I do try, however, to pull together a number of strands running through this study around the theme of "last things." Consider three variations on this theme: the first focuses on those things regarded as last in value (last = least), prone to be discounted and discarded, in conventional society; the second concerns those things associated with the critical last days (last = final) of individual life; and the third deals with those things surrounding the restoration of cosmic order in the last era of human history (last = climactic), the realization of God's dominion on earth. In brief, Jesus' ethical actions are strongly biased toward the *least,* supremely revealed in his *death,* and significantly determined by his urgent sense of the *end.*

The Flip of the Coin

In exploring Jesus' encounter with the religious authorities over the thorny issue of paying taxes to Caesar, we noticed that Jesus enacts a brief demonstration with provocative implications. Apparently having no money of his own or at least none that he cares to use in support of Caesar's cause, he asks to borrow a coin as a visual aid. After confirming the obvious fact that the coin bears Caesar's image and name, Jesus then announces that Caesar should be paid his due—but not at God's expense, since God must surely receive proper due as well. An innocent enough reply on the surface, but upon deeper reflection it begins to raise unsettling questions. What exactly does Jesus think Caesar has coming to him in comparison with God's divine glory? A measly coin that he had minted for himself in the first place? "Let him have it back," Jesus seems to be saying, "along with whatever else he deserves for how he has gained and used this money." Given how Jesus typically deals with the wealthy elites in Roman Palestine, we have a pretty good idea that he is not advocating paying homage to Caesar. Within the enigmatic cracks of Jesus' response lurks more than a hint of social and political protest. Although the gospels never report what Jesus does with the coin after his lesson, it's hard to imagine him pocketing it for personal use. It seems more apt that he flicks it back to its donor, as if to say, "Take back your badge of bondage to Caesar. I want nothing to do with it." In the absence of this radical gesture, we can still assume that in some sense Jesus metaphorically "flips the coin" on conventional values. If we shift the image and the setting to Jesus' table-toppling antics in the temple compound, we might say that he "turns the tables" on the status quo.

These disruptive actions are symptomatic of a wider counter-cultural, topsy-turvy pattern to Jesus' personal ethics, in which "the last will be first, and the first will be last" (Matt 20:16). Strangely, Jesus puts his natural family last and elevates anyone, no matter how lowly, who seeks God's will to an honored position as his beloved mother, brother, or sister in God's household. While the high-ranking, "first" men and women of society preoccupy themselves with obtaining and maintaining wealth and privilege, Jesus remains remarkably unconcerned with his own material possessions and popular ratings. And he seems quite content, even committed to, modeling the role of a servant—providing food, washing feet, healing diseases—as the measure of true greatness.

This tendency of Jesus' enacted ethics to clash with the social conventions of his own era certainly raises the prospect that Christians who want to do what Jesus did in our present day might well find themselves bucking cultural trends, questioning "accepted" values, and losing at the polls. Christian ethics modeled after Jesus' actions are more likely to serve minority and marginal interests than those of the powers that be, however "Christian" those powers may claim to be. But this perspective does not make for an easy transference from the gospel narratives to contemporary life, because what counted as counter-cultural then might be de rigueur now (and vice versa).

Raymond Brown poses an interesting example of what we might call "flipping the coin" on gospel ethics today. In a thoroughly religious Jewish milieu, where the vast majority esteemed prayer and fasting as necessary (daily/weekly) and noble practices, Jesus challenged the honor system of his day by warning against showing off such acts in the public arena. Praying and fasting "in secret" would suffice (Matt 6:5–18). In contemporary secular America, however, where most people, including devout Christians, blush at the notion of *public* prayer and fasting (except on "official" occasions—weddings, funerals, even sporting events—but here duly designated clerics voice the "invocation" with strict instructions from the organizers to keep it short and sweet), Jesus might well reverse his original opinion. Brown imagines that Jesus might say today: "When you pray, *pray publicly* to challenge those who never pray and see no sense in prayer; when you fast, *let others see it* so that their presuppositions about comfort may be challenged.[1]

Just as applying Jesus' teachings to contemporary life is no facile undertaking, so is applying his personal conduct difficult. Rigid rules regarding how to emulate Jesus' actions will likely prove wooden and worthless for those who seek to follow one who walked on the edge of his own society and found inestimable value in the last and least.

The Way of the Cross

It is no accident that the principal symbol for Christianity throughout the ages has been the cross. The scandal of the cross stands at the heart of Christian faith and, I would argue, at the heart of Christian ethics as well, at least that rooted in the gospels. In certain eras of Christian history, theologians have debated whether Jesus' death chiefly signifies the climactic judicial act of atonement for human sinfulness or the supreme moral example of conduct for human behavior. My experience has been that among contemporary American Christians, certainly among those in the thriving evangelical wing, the former judicial, or forensic approach to the cross, informed mainly by the teachings of the apostle Paul, predominates heavily over the latter moral or ethical viewpoint, reflected in the depictions of Jesus in the gospel narratives. While the gospels provide their own pronouncements that Jesus' death represents "a ransom for many" (Mark 10:45), a blood sacrifice "for the forgiveness of sins" (Matt 26:28), and a paschal offering that "takes away the sin of the world" (John 1:29), such statements are embedded within an extended passion story, not a theological treatise. Thus, Jesus' death in the gospels is much more a complex motion picture to be contemplated than a concrete juridical proposition to be affirmed. And compared with the fast-paced reporting of Jesus' life and mission, the passion narratives unfold in slow motion, inviting the reader to concentrate on every word and deed of Jesus during his final days on earth.

Modern Americans don't like to think much about death and dying, their own or anybody else's. We spend billions of dollars on beauty products, medical procedures, and entertaining diversions—all to cheat the inexorable course of aging and dying. Through incredible technological advances, we have managed to pad a few extra years on to three score and ten, but death still eventually comes to everyone as it always has, whether we like to think about it or not. In other societies (ancient and modern), more vulnerable to disease and disaster, thoughts of human mortality cannot be evaded. In fact, *ars moriendi,* the "art of dying," becomes an important obsession in such societies, not out of some ghoulish dementia, but out of a profound desire to discover the meaning of life, however short and tenuous it might be. How one dies reveals much about how one has lived or ought to have lived.

Time and again we observed the ethical significance of Jesus' actions amid the pressures of his imminent death. For example, while correcting misguided family and friends throughout his public ministry, his final days are marked by warm embrace of those closest to him. In the fourth gospel, he commends Mary for her prodigal perfuming of his body for burial, and, while hanging on the cross, he conjoins his mother and beloved disciple in a supportive family of faith and love. In Luke, even a feckless friend like Peter, whom Jesus had often rebuked, receives Jesus' final assurance of intercession and empowerment, neutralizing the shame of Peter's triple denial.

As for Jesus' approach to physical and material comfort during his agonizing last days—a time when he would surely be justified in seeking personal relief—he in fact eschews painkillers (except in John, where Jesus' anguish is muted) and dies naked and destitute, without as much as the shirt on his back. True to his teaching in the Sermon on the Mount, up to the very end he turns the other cheek and every other part of his body to his persecutors and gives everything he has to those who would beg, borrow, steal, or gamble (his last garment). He does not retaliate with acrimonious threats or acts of violence. He issues no battle cry or call to arms. And his focus remains on others' needs, as Luke so vividly illustrates, whether for healing (the injured slave in his arrest party), forgiveness (his executioners), or eternal salvation (the criminal hanging at his side). At the cross, "love your enemies" takes on breathtaking life.

In brief, Jesus' actions on the way to and upon the cross embody *self-denying, self-emptying service*. What does this mean for contemporary ethical reflection? However unique Jesus' death might be from a historical and theological perspective, ethically it sets the standard for all who would follow Jesus: "If any want to become my followers, let them deny themselves and take up *their cross* and follow me" (Mark 8:34). The gospels insist that their readers embody Jesus' self-denying, self-emptying service in their daily lives.

But two critical cautions are in order. First, the cruciform ethics of Jesus and the gospels must not be confused with body-hating asceticism. While he shows some signs of extreme self-denial during his life, largely regarding sex and money, these are not absolute (he welcomes erotic [not immoral] encounters with "sinful" and Samaritan women and receives the financial support of Galilean women). He accepts the final destiny of the cross without violent retribution, but he does not seek out such a fate as some sort of just penalty for having a body; in fact, he soberly but surely protests his death sentence before both God and his persecutors as an indefensible travesty of justice. With God, he pleads for a reprieve from drinking the cup of suffering and laments (in Matthew and Mark) God's mysterious absence in his hour of crisis. With his attackers, he repeatedly defends his honor in all four gospels through a panoply of rhetorical strategies. For all his reticence about promoting himself before adoring crowds, Jesus does not go quietly to the gallows. He surrenders to death, but not at the expense of his dignity and integrity.

Secondly, the cruciform ethics of Jesus and the gospels must not be confused with a numb tolerance of human suffering or blind acceptance of political oppression. As Richard Hays sagely warns:

The image of the cross should not be used by those who hold power in order to ensure the acquiescent suffering of the power-less. Instead, the New Testament insists that *the community as a whole* is called to follow in the way of Jesus' suffering. The New Testament writers consistently employ the pattern of the cross pre-cisely to call those who possess power and privilege to *surrender* it for the sake of the weak.[2]

By the same token, the weak should not regard the cross as yet another onerous burden to lug around, but rather as a glorious banner of liberating love and mercy mutually shared in the household of God.

The Beginning of the End

With apologies to Oscar Wilde, we might capture the ethos of Jesus' actions in the gospel narratives under the heading: *The Importance of Being* URGENT. Jesus is not always *earnest* in the sense of somber and serious (of course, neither are the characters in Wilde's satirical play); he loves paradox, hyperbole, and double entendre; he pushes the bound-aries of polite society to upset the balance of power. While not always earnest, however, Jesus is indefatigably *urgent.* He moves with purpose and determination under the pressure of God's imminent dominion over a revitalized community and cosmos. While still respecting the restful rhythm of the Sabbath, he does at times accelerate the beat: "My Father is still working, and I also am working" (John 5:17). There is no time to lose.

This sense of a climactic ending, of a seismic shift in the order of things, motivates, at least in part, some of Jesus' more eccentric patterns of behavior. His confirmed bachelorhood and celibate lifestyle (though, again, not void of erotic feeling) seem to stem in large measure from his urgent preoccupation with God's world-shattering kingdom—not a pro-pitious time for starting a family and settling down. He builds primary family ties with those who seek God's kingdom first (Matt 6:33). Like-wise, his itinerant mission, accompanied by no effort at gainful employ-ment and minimal concern for material comfort, fits with his intense anticipation of revolutionary change on the near horizon of human history.

What do we do with such an eschatologically charged Jesus two millennia later? How can we pretend to do what he did? How can we even look to him as a trustworthy model of conduct when the world patently did not end as he expected? Debates continue apace about such issues, but I throw my hat in with those who attempt to appreciate the whole gospel picture, rather than an isolated layer, and to accept a certain dynamic tension in Jesus' perspective between a just and gracious kingdom partially realized and yet not fully consummated. "Already/not yet" represents a common shorthand for this viewpoint. For me, this helps resolve the honor problem. I do not think that the gospels portray Jesus as dying in utter frustration over a failed mission. There is much yet to be done, yes, but Jesus has sown the vital seed of God's kingdom, hidden and dormant at various stages, but ready to explode at any moment (or any millennium) with an abundant harvest of renewal.[3] Jesus was not "wrong" about the inauguration of God's reign. His ministry of healing, feeding, liberating, and saving provide ample signs of miraculous restoration: "If it is by the Spirit/finger of God that I cast out demons, then the kingdom of God has come to you" (Matt 12:28//Luke 11:20). But a kingdom begun is not a kingdom completed. Jesus sparks the beginning of the end. Who knows when or if the ending of the end will come? For that matter, why should there ever be an absolute terminus for a world created by a loving, eternal God? Doesn't the resurrection of Jesus, with which all four gospels culminate, suggest that all apparent endings carry astounding potential for new beginnings?

However we negotiate the honor question surrounding Jesus' end-time expectation, as believers wanting to do what Jesus did, we must still grapple with what it means to emulate Jesus' radical, urgency-driven conduct pertaining to family, sexuality, employment, finances, and other personal matters. It is tempting both/either (1) to dismiss Jesus' behavior in these areas as part of his quaint, but quite impractical, eschatological mindset (if all of us quit mating and working, the world as we know it would come to an end!), and/or (2) to accentuate Jesus' more congenial, useful deeds of gentle, loving kindness—although these can be just as problematic to practice, either because of their supernatural means (exorcisms, resuscitations, etc.) or unnatural ends (washing feet, forgiving enemies, etc.). Both approaches, however, depend on a highly selective use of the gospel evidence, which this study has tried to resist. I offer no easy formulas for making all or most of Jesus' personal actions immediately "relevant" to contemporary living, but I enter a plea that anything worthy of being called Christian ethics must wrestle long and hard with the full force of Jesus' activity in the gospels until it hits us, shapes us, changes us for the better—even if we walk thereafter, as we inevitably will, with a marked limp.[4]

John Meier, author of the most exhaustive and arguably most persuasive and balanced study of the historical Jesus, grasps the nettle of Jesus' (im)practical value for modern consumption, particularly related to his extraordinary feats of eschatological renewal.

> All of this stands in stark contrast to one popular portrait of the historical Jesus often found in literature today: Jesus was a kind-hearted rabbi who preached gentleness and love. . . . The advantage and appeal of the domesticated Jesus is obvious: he is instantly relevant to and usable by contemporary ethics, homilies, political programs, and ideologies of various stripes. In contrast, a 1st-century Jew who presents himself as the eschatological prophet of the imminent arrival of God's kingdom . . . is not so instantly relevant and usable. Yet, for better or for worse, this strange marginal Jew, this eschatological prophet and miracle-worker, *is* the historical Jesus.[5]

"Not so instantly relevant and usable . . . this strange marginal Jew"—whether acting miraculously or otherwise as a "new age" (in his terms, not ours) prophet. Several times in this study we have explored the wondrous deeds of Jesus as part of his ethical conduct, emphasizing that, as a rule, he uses his power for beneficent, not selfish, ends. On this point, if we assume a broad meaning of "power," I think Jesus' behavior is in fact highly relevant (power in its myriad forms still corrupts as absolutely as it ever has). But honing in on some of Jesus' particular miracles can tie even the most dedicated Christian into ethical knots. Even if Jesus' power were available to us, I would not recommend fishing expeditions to pay one's taxes (at the rate of one coin per fish's mouth, it would take a tanker's haul to meet most modern tax bills) or violent transfers of our worst distresses to an unsuspecting pack of animals (although it's tempting to try this out on the incessantly yapping dog down the street). And neither would I recommend cursing barren trees (or under-stocked supermarkets) or knocking over public tables (bankers' desks, church pulpits)—which brings us full circle, to where we started in the preface.

"What Would Jesus Do?" is an exceedingly difficult question to answer in these perplexing days, very far removed from first-century Palestine. But the difficulty of the question does not nullify its value as a critical foundation for contemporary ethical reflection in the Christian community. A community claiming Jesus as Lord that doesn't seek to correlate its conduct with Jesus' in some fashion strikes me as a shallow community at best, a sham at worst. Nonetheless, the difficulty of bridging the gap between the gospel narratives and our own life stories does necessitate careful, thorough, and honest reading of the gospel reports. For believers committed to putting real flesh and blood on the "WWJD?" slogan (beyond wearing it emblazoned on T-shirts or dangling it from bracelets like a good-luck charm), the gospels must become much more than a repository of catch phrases and proof texts. They must be analyzed, agonized over, and absorbed in all their literary-cultural complexity and ethical-theological profundity. I am rarely certain what Jesus would have us do about the pressing issues of our day, but I'm pretty sure he would have us make the four canonical gospels principal partners in the discussion.

Notes

1. Brown, *Introduction to the New Testament,* 220 (emphasis added).

2. Hays, *Moral Vision of the New Testament,* 197.

3. This imagery is drawn partly from Jesus' Parable of the Growing Seed in Mark 4:26–29.

4. This imagery is drawn from the drama of Jacob's nocturnal wrestling match with a powerful and mysterious being in Gen 32:22–32 and is trenchantly applied to biblical interpretaton by Phyllis Trible in *Texts of Terror: Literary-Feminist Readings of Biblical Narratives* (Overtures to Biblical Theology; Philadelphia, Pa: Fortress, 1984), 4–5.

5. Meier, *A Marginal Jew,* 2:1045. Craig Hill cites Meier's comments and adds his own insightful discussion of "Jesus and the Things to Come" in *In God's Time,* 130–69. Although Meier's study of the historical Jesus extends over two thousand pages in three volumes, it is not yet complete. A fourth volume is currently in the works dealing with Jesus' teaching on the Law, his parables, his self-designations, and his death. For a preview, see Meier's "The Historical Jesus and the Historical Law," *Catholic Biblical Quarterly* 65 (2003): 52–79.

Recommended Reading

Allison, Dale C. *Jesus of Nazareth: A Millenarian Prophet.* Minneapolis, Minn.: Fortress, 1998.

Aune, David E., ed. *The Gospel of Matthew in Current Study: Studies in Memory of William J. Thompson, S.J.* Grand Rapids, Mich.: Eerdmans, 2001.

Barrett, C. K. *The New Testament Background: Selected Documents.* London: SPCK/ New York: Harper & Row, 1956.

Bauckham, Richard. *Gospel Women: Studies of the Named Women in the Gospels.* Grand Rapids, Mich.: Eerdmans, 2002.

Borg, Marcus J. *Conflict, Holiness, and Politics in the Teachings of Jesus.* New York: Mellen, 1984. Repr., Harrisburg, Pa.: Trinity Press International, 1998.

———. *Jesus, A New Vision: Spirit, Culture, and the Life of Discipleship.* San Francisco: Harper & Row, 1987.

———. *Meeting Jesus for the First Time: The Historical Jesus and the Heart of Contemporary Faith.* San Francisco: HarperSanFrancisco, 1994.

Boring, M. Eugene. "The Gospel of Matthew." In vol. 8 of *The New Interpreter's Bible.* Nashville, Tenn.: Abingdon, 1995.

Brown, Raymond E. *The Birth of the Messiah: A Commentary on the Infancy Narratives in Matthew and Luke.* London: Geoffrey Chapman, 1978.

———. *The Community of the Beloved Disciple: The Life, Loves, and Hates of an Individual Church in New Testament Times.* London: Geoffrey Chapman, 1979.

———. *The Death of the Messiah, from Gethsemane to the Grave: A Commentary on the Passion Narratives of the Four Gospels.* 2 vols. New York: Doubleday, 1994.

———. *An Introduction to the New Testament.* New York: Doubleday, 1997.

Cadbury, Henry J. *The Peril of Modernizing Jesus.* New York: Macmillan, 1937.

Carter, Warren. *Matthew and Empire: Initial Explorations.* Harrisburg, Pa.: Trinity Press International, 2001.

———. *Matthew and the Margins: A Sociopolitical and Religious Reading.* Maryknoll, N.Y.: Orbis, 2000.

Charlesworth, James H. *The Beloved Disciple.* Valley Forge, Pa.: Trinity Press International, 1995.

Chilton, Bruce. *Rabbi Jesus: An Intimate Biography.* New York: Doubleday, 2000.

Cosgrove, Charles H. *Appealing to Scripture in Moral Debate: Five Hermeneutical Rules.* Grand Rapids, Mich.: Eerdmans, 2002.

Crossan, John Dominic. *The Historical Jesus: The Life of a Mediterranean Jewish Peasant.* New York: HarperSanFrancisco, 1991.

———. *Jesus: A Revolutionary Biography.* New York: HarperSanFrancisco, 1994.

Crossan, John Dominic, and Jonathan L. Reed. *Excavating Jesus: Beneath the Stones, Behind the Texts.* New York: HarperSanFrancisco, 2001.

Csikszentmihaly, Mihalyi. *Flow: The Psychology of Optimal Experience.* New York: HarperPerennial, 1990.

Dodd, C. H. *The Interpretation of the Fourth Gospel.* Cambridge, U.K.: Cambridge University Press, 1953.

Donahue, John R., and Daniel J. Harrington. *The Gospel of Mark.* Sacra Pagina 2. Collegeville, Minn.: Liturgical Press, 2002.

Douglas, Mary. *Natural Symbols: Explorations in Cosmology.* New York: Pantheon, 1982.

———. *Purity and Danger: An Analysis of Concepts of Pollution and Taboo.* London: Routledge & Kegan Paul, 1966.

Dunn, James D. G. *Jesus and the Spirit.* Philadelphia, Pa.: Westminster, 1975.

Ehrman, Bart D. *Jesus: Apocalyptic Prophet of the New Millennium.* Oxford: Oxford University Press, 1999.

———. *The New Testament: An Historical Introduction to the Early Christian Writings.* 2nd ed. New York: Oxford University Press, 2000.

———. *The New Testament and Other Early Christian Writings: A Reader.* Oxford: Oxford University Press, 1998.

Esler, Philip F., ed. *Modeling Early Christianity: Social-Scientific Studies of the New Testament in Its Context.* New York: Routledge, 1995.

Fowl, Stephen E., and L. Gregory Jones. *Reading in Communion: Scripture and Ethics in Christian Life.* Grand Rapids, Mich.: Eerdmans, 1991.

Fredriksen, Paula. *From Jesus to Christ: The Origins of the New Testament Images of Christ.* 2nd ed. New Haven, Conn.: Yale University Press, 2000.

————. *Jesus of Nazareth, King of the Jews: A Jewish Life and the Emergence of Christianity.* New York: Knopf, 1999.

Funk, Robert W. *Honest to Jesus: Jesus for a New Millennium.* New York: HarperCollins, 1996.

Garland, David E. *Reading Matthew: A Literary and Theological Commentary on the First Gospel.* New York: Crossroad, 1993.

Green, Joel B. *The Gospel of Luke.* Grand Rapids, Mich.: Eerdmans, 1997.

Hanson, K. C., and Douglas E. Oakman. *Palestine in the Time of Jesus: Social Structures and Social Conflicts.* Minneapolis, Minn.: Fortress, 1998.

Harrington, Daniel J. *The Gospel of Matthew.* Sacra Pagina 1. Collegeville, Minn.: Liturgical Press, 1991.

Harrington, Daniel J., and James Keenan. *Jesus and Virtue Ethics: Building Bridges between New Testament Studies and Moral Theology.* Lanham, Md.: Sheed & Ward, 2002.

Harris, Stephen L. *Understanding the Bible.* 5th ed. Mountain View, Calif.: Mayfield, 2000.

Harvey, A. E. *Strenuous Commands: The Ethic of Jesus.* London: SCM/ Philadelphia, Pa: Trinity Press International, 1990.

Hays, Richard B. *The Moral Vision of the New Testament: Community, Cross, and New Creation. A Contemporary Introduction to New Testament Ethics.* New York: HarperCollins, 1996.

Hill, Craig C. *In God's Time: The Bible and the Future.* Grand Rapids, Mich.: Eerdmans, 2002.

Horsley, Richard A. *Jesus and Empire: The Kingdom of God and the New World Disorder.* Minneapolis, Minn.: Fortress, 2003.

————. *Jesus and the Spiral of Violence: Popular Jewish Resistance in Roman Palestine.* New York: Harper & Row, 1987.

Horsley, Richard A., and John S. Hanson. *Bandits, Prophets, and Messiahs: Popular Movements at the Time of Jesus.* San Francisco, Calif.: Harper & Row, 1985.

Horsley, Richard A., and Neil Asher Silberman. *The Message and the Kingdom: How Jesus and Paul Ignited a Revolution and Transformed the Ancient World.* Minneapolis, Minn.: Fortress, 2002.

Ilan, Tal. *Integrating Women into Second Temple History.* Peabody, Mass.: Hendrickson, 2001.

Johnson, Luke Timothy. *The Gospel of Luke.* Sacra Pagina 3. Collegeville, Minn.: Liturgical Press, 1991.

———. *Living Jesus: Learning the Heart of the Gospel.* New York: HarperCollins, 1999.

———. *The Real Jesus: The Misguided Quest for the Historical Jesus and the Truth of the Traditional Gospels.* New York: HarperCollins, 1996.

———. *The Writings of the New Testament.* Rev. ed. Minneapolis, Minn.: Fortress, 1999.

Keck, Leander E. *Who Is Jesus? History in the Perfect Tense.* Minneapolis, Minn.: Fortress, 2001.

Koester, Helmut. *Ancient Christian Gospels: Their History and Development.* Harrisburg, Pa: Trinity Press International, 1990.

Levine, Amy-Jill, ed. *A Feminist Companion to John.* London: Sheffield Academic Press, 2003.

———. *A Feminist Companion to Luke.* London: Sheffield Academic Press, 2002.

———. *A Feminist Companion to Mark.* Sheffield, U.K.: Sheffield Academic Press, 2001.

———. *A Feminist Companion to Matthew.* Sheffield, U.K.: Sheffield Academic Press, 2001.

Malbon, Elizabeth Struthers. *In the Company of Jesus: Characters in Mark's Gospel.* Louisville, Ky.: Westminster/John Knox, 2000.

Malherbe, Abraham J. *Moral Exhortation: A Greco-Roman Sourcebook.* Philadelphia, Pa.: Westminster, 1986.

Malina, Bruce J. *The New Testament World: Insights from Cultural Anthropology.* 3rd ed. Louisville, Ky.: Westminster/John Knox, 2001.

———. *The Social Gospel of Jesus: The Kingdom of God in Mediterranean Perspective.* Minneapolis, Minn.: Fortress, 2001.

————. *Windows on the World of Jesus: Time Travel to Ancient Judea.* Louisville, Ky.: Westminster/John Knox, 1993.

Malina, Bruce J., and Richard L. Rohrbaugh. *Social Science Commentary on the Gospel of John.* Minneapolis, Minn.: Fortress, 1998.

————. *Social Science Commentary on the Synoptic Gospels.* Minneapolis, Minn.: Fortress, 1992.

McKnight, Scot. *Turning to Jesus: The Sociology of Conversion in the Gospels.* Louisville, Ky.: Westminster/John Knox, 2002.

Meeks, Wayne A. *The Origins of Christian Morality: The First Two Centuries.* New Haven, Conn.: Yale University Press, 1993.

Meier, John P. *A Marginal Jew: Rethinking the Historical Jesus.* 3 vols. New York: Doubleday, 1991–2001.

Melbin, Murray. *Night as Frontier: Colonizing the World after Dark.* New York: Free Press/London: Collier Macmillan, 1987.

Metzger, Bruce M. *A Textual Commentary on the Greek New Testament.* 2nd ed. Stuttgart: United Bible Societies, 1994.

Miles, Jack. *Christ: A Crisis in the Life of God.* New York: Knopf, 2001.

Miller, John W. *Jesus at Thirty: A Psychological and Historical Portrait.* Minneapolis, Minn.: Fortress, 1997.

Miller, Robert J., ed. *The Apocalyptic Jesus: A Debate.* Santa Rosa, Calif.: Polebridge, 2001.

————. *The Complete Gospels: Annotated Scholars Version.* Sonoma, Calif.: Polebridge/San Francisco: HarperSanFrancisco, 1994.

Moloney, Francis J. *The Gospel of John.* Sacra Pagina 4. Collegeville, Minn.: Liturgical Press, 1998.

Moore, Stephen D. *Poststructuralism and the New Testament: Derrida and Foucault at the Foot the Cross.* Minneapolis, Minn.: Fortress, 1994.

Neyrey, Jerome H. *Honor and Shame in the Gospel of Matthew.* Louisville, Ky.: Westminster/John Knox, 1998.

Neyrey, Jerome H., ed. *The Social World of Luke-Acts: Models for Interpretation.* Peabody, Mass.: Hendrickson, 1991.

O'Day, Gail. "John." In *Woman's Bible Commentary.* Rev. ed. Edited by Carol A. Newsom and Sharon H. Ringe. Louisville, Ky.: Westminster/John Knox, 1998.

————. "The Gospel of John." In vol. 8 of *The New Interpreter's Bible.* Nashville, Tenn.: Abingdon, 1995.

Osiek, Carolyn. *What Are They Saying about the Social Setting of the New Testament?* New York: Paulist Press, 1992.

Overman, J. Andrew. *Church and Community in Crisis: The Gospel According to Matthew.* Valley Forge, Pa.: Trinity Press International, 1996.

Perkins, Pheme. "The Gospel of Mark." In vol. 7 of *The New Interpreter's Bible.* Nashville, Tenn.: Abingdon, 1995.

Pilch, John J. *The Cultural Dictionary of the Bible.* Collegeville, Minn.: Liturgical Press, 1999.

Pilch, John J., and Bruce M. Malina, eds. *Biblical Social Values and Their Meanings.* Peabody, Mass.: Hendrickson, 1993.

Powell, Mark Allan. *Fortress Introduction to the Gospels.* Minneapolis, Minn.: Fortress, 1998.

———. *Jesus as a Figure of History: How Modern Historians View the Man from Galilee.* Louisville, Ky.: Westminster/John Knox, 1998.

Reinhartz, Adele. *Befriending the Beloved Disciple: A Jewish Reading of the Gospel of John.* New York: Continuum, 2001.

———. "The Gospel of John." In *Searching the Scriptures: A Feminist Commentary.* Edited by Elisabeth Schüssler Fiorenza. New York: Crossroad, 1994.

Rohrbaugh, Richard L., ed. *The Social Sciences and New Testament Interpretation.* Peabody, Mass.: Hendrickson, 1996.

Rousseau, John J., and Rami Arav. *Jesus and His World: An Archaeological and Cultural Dictionary.* Minneapolis, Minn.: Fortress, 1995.

Saldarini, Anthony J. *Matthew's Christian-Jewish Community.* Chicago: University of Chicago Press, 1994.

Sanders, E. P. *The Historical Figure of Jesus.* London: Penguin, 1993.

———. *Jesus and Judaism.* London: SCM, 1985.

———. *Judaism: Practice and Belief: 63 BCE–66 CE.* London: SCM/Harrisburg, Pa.: Trinity Press International, 1992.

Sawicki, Marianne. *Crossing Galilee: Architectures of Contact in the Occupied Land of Jesus.* Harrisburg, Pa.: Trinity Press International, 2000.

———. *Seeing the Lord: Resurrection and Early Christian Practices.* Minneapolis, Minn.: Fortress, 1994.

Spencer, F. Scott. *Acts.* Readings: A New Biblical Commentary. Sheffield, U.K.: Sheffield Academic Press, 1997.

————. *The Portrait of Philip in Acts: A Study of Roles and Relations.* Sheffield, U.K.: Sheffield Academic Press, 1992.

Stanton, Graham N. *The Gospels and Jesus.* Oxford: Oxford University Press, 1989.

Stegemann, Wolfgang, Bruce J. Malina, and Gerd Theissen, eds. *The Social Setting of Jesus and the Gospels.* Minneapolis, Minn.: Fortress, 2002.

Taylor, Joan E. *The Immerser: John the Baptist within Second Temple Judaism.* Grand Rapids, Mich.: Eerdmans, 1997.

Theissen, Gerd. *The Shadow of the Galilean.* Philadelphia, Pa.: Fortress, 1989.

Topel, L. John. *Children of a Compassionate God: A Theological Exegesis of Luke 6:20–49.* Collegeville, Minn.: Liturgical Press, 2001.

Trible, Phyllis. *Texts of Terror: Literary-Feminist Readings of Biblical Narratives.* Philadelphia, Pa.: Fortress, 1984.

Tuckett, Christopher M. "Jesus and the Gospels." In vol. 8 of *The New Interpreter's Bible.* Nashville, Tenn.: Abingdon, 1995.

Vaage, Leif E., and Vincent L. Wimbush, eds. *Asceticism and the New Testament.* New York: Routledge, 1999.

Wink, Walter. *The Human Being: Jesus and the Enigma of the Son of the Man.* Minneapolis, Minn.: Fortress, 2002.

————. *When the Powers Fall: Reconciliation in the Healing of Nations.* Minneapolis, Minn.: Fortress, 1998.

Witherington, Ben III. *Jesus the Sage: The Pilgrimage of Wisdom.* Minneapolis, Minn.: Fortress, 1994.

Wright, N. T. *Jesus and the Victory of God.* Minneapolis, Minn.: Fortress, 2002.

Index

healing of blind man and, 188–89

healing of crippled woman in, 185–86

healing of man with withered hand in, 184, 228

Jairus, ruler of, 49n. 46, 85n. 30, 87n. 58, 154n. 9

in John, 230

in Matthew, 200n. 23, 230

in Nazareth, 5, 20n. 6, 31–32, 37, 114, 135, 175, 200n. 29

taxes, 139, 142–45, 209, 246n. 32, 251–52, 258

Jewish, 143–45

Roman, 142–43, 209, 246n. 32, 251–52

temple, the (in Jerusalem), 26, 92, 94, 121n. 7, 122n. 7, 163, 181, 183, 186, 197, 219

Jesus at age twelve in, 32–37, 43–44, 47n. 19, 54, 194

Jesus debating with authorities of, 58, 104, 208–9, 232, 235

Jesus tempted to jump off the pinnacle of, 123n. 28

Jesus upending tables in, ix–x, xiin. 1, 94, 104, 220–21, 252

taxes for the treasury of, 142–44

Ten Commandments (*See* Decalogue)

Thomas, the disciple, 75, 86n. 45, 126n. 68

Topel, L. John, 83n. 11, 246n. 35

Trible, Phyllis, 259n. 4

triumphal entry, *See* Jesus, major life events

What would Jesus do? (W.W.J.D.), x, 1–3, 6–7, 16, 23n. 27, 97, 105, 124n. 44, 148, 259

Wink, Walter, 157n. 35, 248n. 53

women, xi, 39–40, 41, 47n. 22, 48n. 33, 49n. 42, 54, 85n. 35, 90, 92, 106, 120, 122n. 18, 125n. 55, 125, 126n. 58, 252

crippled woman healed by Jesus, 185–86

hemorrhaging woman healed by Jesus, 137, 146

at Jesus' tomb, 49n. 51, 210–11, 218, 246n. 28

Samaritan woman at the well, 48n. 42, 110–12, 120, 177, 240, 255

Simon Peter's mother-in-law, 175

"sinful" woman in Luke, 90, 94–96, 107–10, 120, 125n. 53, 126n. 64, 170, 176–77, 255

supporters and followers of Jesus, 71, 137–38, 152, 155n. 21, 165

widows, 42, 45n. 11, 48n. 36, 87n. 58, 92, 112, 154n. 12, 166–67, 177, 245n. 24

See also Martha of Bethany, Mary of Bethany, Mary the mother of Jesus, Mary Magdalene